The
Vatican
Dictator

"People with hate in their hearts
may sound pleasant enough,
but don't believe them.
Though they pretend to be kind,
their hearts are full of all kinds of evil.
While their hatred may be concealed by trickery,
it will finally come to light for all to see."

Proverbs 26: 24 - 26

The
Vatican
Dictator

ALAN BAYER

ISBN: 979-8-89316-036-9 - paperback
ISBN: 979-8-89316-037-6 - ebook

To my wife, Melanie

PART I

Chapter 1

February 1, 2000
Tuesday
Rome, Italy

On that sorrowful morning, the Italian heavens were a canvas of brooding clouds as if the very sky was a mournful participant in the funeral procession below. Eight papal guardsmen, resplendent in their vibrant Renaissance-era uniforms, stood like statues at the rear of the hearse, awaiting their solemn duty to unload the casket. The towering clock, a sentinel of time, struck ten a.m. Its chimes reverberated through the air, stirring the eight men to life. With a reverence befitting the occasion, they carried the casket through the grand entrance of the historic Basilica of Santa Maria in Trastevere before disappearing inside its hallowed depths.

The church, a testament to the twelfth century with intricate mosaics and frescoes adorning its domed ceiling, echoed with the muffled weeping of mourners. The church pews, nestled between twenty-two imposing granite columns, were half-filled with a sea of grieving faces.

Sister Carlotta, a dear friend of the departed, wept openly as the eight guardsmen of the Vatican military solemnly carried the exquisite mahogany casket past her. "Ah, Giuseppe," she whispered, her voice choked with emotion, "you would have loved this."

Monsignor Giordano took his place at the altar and lit the incense burner, and its familiar scent wafted through the air. Carlotta managed a small smile through her tears, remembering her departed friend's peculiar quirks. *Here comes that smell you never liked,* she thought, recalling his aversion to the ever-present aroma one couldn't help but associate with the Church.

Upon reaching Monsignor Giordano, who stood like a beacon of faith in front of the altar, the eight papal guardsmen pivoted in perfect unison, moving to the front pew to take their seats. As the choir's ethereal melody faded into silence, Giordano swung the incense burner over the altar then turned to wave it over the casket.

Handing the incense burner to the altar boy, Giordano initiated the Mass with the traditional invocation.

"Peace be with you," he intoned, his voice resonating through the church.

"And also with you," the congregation echoed back.

As the Gospel reading and homily reached their conclusion, Monsignor Giordano positioned himself behind the casket to deliver his eulogy. "Dear brothers and sisters," he began, his voice heavy with sorrow, "we gather here today, our hearts burdened with grief, to bid our final farewell to our dear brother, Father Giuseppe Benedetti. A man of immense potential, his life tragically cut short at the pinnacle of his service."

Taking three measured steps forward, he stood beside the casket, his gaze falling on its polished mahogany. "I recall the day Giuseppe first set foot in our orphanage. He was a quiet child, brimming with life and wonder, often lost in his own world. I cannot say for certain if it was our shared moments together as I guided him towards the path of priesthood, but the joy I felt the day he expressed his desire to take his vows was unparalleled." A faint smile touched the monsignor's lips. "Throughout his time in seminary, Giuseppe displayed an unwavering dedication to his biblical studies. His innate aptitude for technology and computers earned him a coveted position at the Vatican's Secret Archive Library—" His voice straining, Giordano paused abruptly, his gaze drifting upwards as if seeking solace in the ancient frescoes above.

The mourners sat in rapt attention, their sorrow intermingling with a sense of pride for the departed young priest's achievements. The monsignor regained his composure and continued. "The day he came to us, his eyes sparkling with excitement as he announced his appointment at the Vatican, was a day of immense joy. We were all so incredibly proud of him. But, a frail heart and the divine timing of God claimed him far too soon." He bowed his head in a silent tribute to the departed. "I firmly believe, Giuseppe, you departed this world content and fulfilled, having realized your dream of serving at the Vatican."

His words once more choked with emotion, Giordano turned to face the casket, his eulogy drawing to a close. "At just twenty-six years of age, you have been called to Heaven far too soon," he murmured, leaning over to plant a tender kiss on the closed casket. "I will miss you, my friend."

As the traditional Catholic rites ended, the Vatican Guard rose in perfect synchrony. They moved to their designated positions beside the casket and, as one, lifted it. Their movements were slow and deliberate as they began their solemn procession down the aisle. The mourners trailed behind, a somber parade of grief making its way towards the waiting hearse that would transport Father Giuseppe Alphonso Benedetti to his final earthly abode.

Once the Mass was concluded, Sister Carlotta, a figure of quiet sorrow, approached the altar. There, she found Cardinal Rosetti and Monsignor Giordano engaged in intense hushed conversation. "Cardinal Rosetti?" she ventured timidly, her voice barely above a whisper. "I'm Sister Carlotta. I appreciate your presence at the service. Father Benedetti would have been deeply honored."

Cardinal Rosetti, visibly irked by the interruption, turned to face the nun. His words were curt, his tone devoid of warmth. "I'm sorry for your loss." With a perfunctory bow, he turned back to Monsignor Giordano.

Undeterred, Sister Carlotta pressed on, her voice trembling with emotion. "I understand that everything happens according to God's plan," she said, oblivious to the cardinal's thinly veiled impatience. "But it's hard for me to accept his time has come so soon."

Rosetti turned to face her once more, his face a mask of forced tolerance. "Were you two close?" he asked, his tone bordering on dismissive.

"He was my friend," she replied, her eyes welling up with fresh tears. "He'd just had a full physical a couple of months ago. The doctor said he was in perfect health. I don't understand how he could die of a heart attack so soon after. How could this be?" She wrapped her arms around herself seeking comfort in her own embrace.

"We cannot comprehend God's timing, my child," Rosetti replied, his words devoid of the solace she sought. "Just know that God's timing is always perfect." His words hung in the air, a cold consolation to the grieving nun. As her tears flowed freely, she looked up at the cardinal, her eyes pleading for a different answer.

Seeing this conversation wasn't going to end, he cut straight to the point. "The pope's personal physician informed me that he conducted the autopsy on Father Benedetti himself. He discovered an embolism, a lethal blood clot that obstructed a vital vessel, leading to heart failure." His blunt voice echoed ominously in the hallowed space.

Sister Carlotta, however, was far from convinced. A nagging suspicion gnawed at her, refusing to be silenced.

"The physician also emphasized that an embolism could remain hidden, striking down even the healthiest individual at any age," Rosetti added, his gaze piercing through the nun. He could sense her growing doubts—a potential threat in the days to come.

"Go in peace, Sister, and remember, everything is under God's watchful eye." The cardinal extended his hand, tracing the sign of the cross on her forehead with a solemnity that belied his underlying contempt.

"Amen," Carlotta whispered, yet her doubts persisted. Beneath her outward sorrow, a troubling suspicion that something was amiss continued to fester.

As Sister Carlotta withdrew from their presence, Cardinal Rosetti nodded at Monsignor Giordano, commanding him towards the tabernacle for a private discussion. He couldn't afford the slightest risk of their conversation being overheard. Only the towering crucifix of Jesus bore silent witness to the cardinal's ominous words.

"Sister Carlotta will be a problem," he seethed, his voice laced with an icy determination as he turned to face the monsignor. "Reassign her to the church in Harare, Zimbabwe."

The monsignor was taken aback by the harsh directive from his superior. Without uttering another word, the livid cardinal abruptly spun around and stormed away in a fury, leaving Giordano to execute the damning order. Monsignor Giordano, ever loyal to the cardinal, would fulfill this command without question.

Turning to gaze out over the sanctuary, he watched as Rosetti made his way down the central aisle. The cardinal roughly brushed past Sister Carlotta, who was kneeling in the first pew, her prayers fervent and earnest. The monsignor looked upon her with a heavy heart, knowing her fate was sealed.

She would never lay eyes on Rome again.

Chapter 2

February 7, 2000
Monday, 8:22 a.m.
Vatican Antechamber

The antechamber in the Vatican was pulsating with centuries of history, each artifact a testament to the past. The marble floor, still in immaculate condition, had borne silent witness to the passage of time since its installation in 1507. Oak shelves, crafted by the renowned Italian carpenter Luigi Bernini, spanned an entire forty-foot wall, cradling volumes of ancient books and priceless artifacts. The grand oak desk situated near the center of the oak shelves, a gift to Pope Benedict III, stood as a symbol of power and authority. Ageless paintings from the sixteenth century adorned the walls, their subjects gazing down from their frames, while sculpted angels dotting the cornices in turn watched over them. At the end of the antechamber, solid oak double doors bore the inscription "PAVLVS III PONT MAX", a tribute to Paul III, the Supreme Pontiff of the Universal Church.

This was the chamber of choice for the pope when it came to conducting special meetings. A room shrouded in mystery and magnificence, its walls echoing with the whispers of countless confidential discussions. The air was thick with anticipation, the room itself seeming to hold its breath in the face of such significant encounters. The pope's chosen setting for these unique gatherings was not just a room, but a stage set for the unfolding of events that could alter the course of history.

Father Mario Marino sat there frozen within the colossal antechamber, his breath held hostage by the impending arrival of Pope John Paul II. The most revered and exalted figure on the globe was about to confer with the young priest in a discussion of paramount significance. The private audience with the pope felt like a surreal dream.

Marino was a whirlwind of emotions —a volatile mix of trepidation and exhilaration. His senses were on overdrive, each noise around him amplified to an almost deafening degree. He could practically hear his own heart pounding like a drum, its rhythm echoing ominously throughout the expansive room. With bated breath, he kept his ears attuned on the formidable oak doors, straining for the faintest whisper of movement that would announce the much-anticipated arrival of the pope.

Father Marino was acutely aware of all the details in the room; he craned his neck about absorbing every nuance, every whisper of history, determined to etch this moment into his memory. *I can't believe I'm here.* That thought echoed incessantly in the mind of the priest ordained Father Mario Eduardo Marino.

The young priest sat in silent contemplation, clad in his usual attire of short-sleeved black shirt adorned with a stark-white clerical collar, along with black trousers and a pair of polished black shoes. His dark-brown hair, freshly trimmed the day before, added to his air of confidence. His tanned hands, resting lightly on the armrests, were in harmony with his overall body. If Mario weren't a priest, his handsome countenance would undoubtedly be the object of many a woman's affection.

The silence in the room did nothing to pacify the young priest's racing thoughts. "Lord, help me ease my heart," Father

Marino implored in a hushed prayer, taking slow, deliberate breaths in an attempt to still his mind. Yet, beneath the surface of his anticipation, a disquieting undercurrent of unease persisted, a nagging that refused to cease.

The massive oak door groaned open in slow motion, the sound reverberating ominously throughout the hushed silence, amplifying its enormity. The cardinal, a figure of authority and reverence who initially ushered him in, stepped into the room, his footfalls echoing in the antechamber like a solemn drumbeat. Father Marino sprang to his feet in an instinctive show of deference.

"Father Marino, it is my esteemed privilege to present to you His Holiness, Pope John Paul II."

The moment of truth was upon him. His heart hammered against his chest like a wild beast trying to escape its cage. *Oh, dear Lord, don't let me throw up now.*

The pope, a figure of serenity, glided through the grand oak doors, his presence filling the room with an overwhelming sense of tranquility. This peace washed over Marino, slowing his racing heart and calming his nerves. He found himself captivated by the pope, his gaze fixed on the holy figure wheeling into the room. Marino, mesmerized by the pope, didn't hear the cardinal exit the chamber. Staring for but a moment, Marino dropped to one knee and bowed in reverence.

"Your Holiness, it is an immense honor to be in your divine presence," he said, his head bowed in respect.

The pope slowly navigated his wheelchair towards him. "Let your heart be at peace, my son," he responded, placing a hand gently on the priest's head. A soothing sensation coursed through Marino's body, further calming his nerves. "You may rise."

Slowly, Father Marino rose to his feet, his gaze meeting the pope's. He was in awe—the moment felt like it was stretching out to eternity.

With a wave of his hand, the pope gestured towards the nearby chair in front of the oak desk. "Please, take a seat. I have been eagerly awaiting our meeting."

The pope has been eagerly awaiting to meet me?

Weak-kneed, Marino sank into the plush leather chair, his eyes never once leaving the pope. He took in every detail: the red papal shoes peeking out from the footrest, the white cassock adorned with the papal coat of arms, the pectoral cross hanging from a gold cord, the wispy white hair peeking out from beneath the white skull cap.

"You look nervous, Father. How do you feel?"

"Yes, Your Holiness, I am indeed nervous. This moment—meeting you—has been a dream of mine since childhood. It feels surreal, like I'm in a dream. I can't believe I'm here. This is the greatest moment of my life," Marino confessed, his words rambling out like a little schoolboy's in a rush of excitement.

"Is it everything you expected?"

"Your Holiness, this is beyond anything I could have ever imagined," he began, his voice trembling with awe. "The splendor of this cathedral, the sheer magnitude of this chamber, the priceless artifacts bestowed upon the popes throughout history . . . it's all so overwhelming. The kindness and grace of the cardinals have been humbling. And being in your presence . . . it's a tranquility I've never known, a sense of awe that's simply indescribable. I—"

He halted abruptly, the echo of his best friend's advice reverberating in his mind. *"Mario! You're talking too much. Even a fool appears wise when he keeps his mouth closed. Shut up!"*

"You were about to say. . . ." the pope gently prodded.

"I . . . I . . . I fear I may be speaking too much, Your Holiness," Mario confessed, his gaze dropping to the floor in embarrassment.

"You're doing just fine, my son. I imagine you have a multitude of questions. I will explain why you were chosen, and should you have any queries once I am done, I will do my best to provide answers."

Pope John Paul II's eyes were soft as he watched the young priest lift his head to listen. "Here in the Vatican, we possess a treasure trove of history, known as the Vatican Secret Archives. It is home to countless books and artifacts. Are you familiar with it?"

The pope paused, observing Mario's nod of affirmation.

"We wish to modernize the preservation of this invaluable information, to safeguard it according to the standards of our digital age by . . . putting it into computerized storage. Is that the correct terminology?"

Once again, Mario nodded, a smile forming on his lips at the pope's use of modern technical language.

"The Vatican II Council recently convened and expressed concern that we risk losing irreplaceable documents if we continue to store them in the traditional manner. A single accident could result in a loss that would be felt for generations to come."

Mario could see the weight of this responsibility literally pressing down on the pope—the aging pontiff was slumping further into his wheelchair as he spoke.

Drawing a deep breath, the pope straightened, his gaze fixed on Mario as he broached the crux of their meeting. "We are hoping you might be able to assist us in this endeavor, by copying these volumes into a digital format. Do you feel capable of undertaking this task for the Vatican?" He paused for a moment, then added, "For me?"

With a surge of confidence, Mario sat up straight. "Your Holiness, it would be my greatest honor to help preserve these historical documents."

An observable sense of relief seemed to wash over the pope, his eyes reflecting the lifting of a great burden. The selection of a trusted priest for this monumental undertaking had clearly eased his concerns.

"Your service to us, Father Mario Eduardo Marino"— the pope's voice echoed throughout the room, each syllable of Mario's full name spoken with profound respect—"is a debt we can never fully repay."

A surge of pride swelled within Mario, making him feel like the most honored man in all of Rome.

"Would you like a personal tour of the Sisteen Chapel?"

The offer left Mario momentarily speechless. "That would be . . . an honor, Your Holiness."

The pope, with a gentle smile, maneuvered his wheelchair forward, extending a trembling hand towards Mario. In a gesture of deep reverence, Mario pushed back his chair and knelt before the pope, taking his hand and kissing the papal ring. A wave of tranquility washed over him as the pope placed his other hand on Mario's head. Yet despite the pope's calming presence, a nagging unease still lurked in the depths of Mario's mind, questioning the reasoning behind his selection for this prestigious role.

After a moment of shared silence, the pope withdrew his hand and turned his wheelchair around heading towards the doors leading out of the room. Mario, following the pope's lead, walked ahead to open the towering oak double doors for them both to exit.

"The Sistine Chapel holds a special place in my heart," the pope said, his wheelchair gliding smoothly over the polished marble floors. "It was within its sacred walls that I was elected pope in 1978," he added, a hint of nostalgia in his voice as they approached the grand entrance to the Sistine Chapel. Mario clung to his every word, captivated by the pope's personal narrative.

On their approach, they passed a tall, imposing man dressed in an ensemble of pitch-black suit, shirt, and tie. An icy shiver coursed down Mario's spine as the man's cold, dark eyes bore into him. A sense of familiarity stirred within him, like a half-remembered nightmare. He couldn't shake off the feeling he had crossed paths with this man somewhere before.

Unfazed by the ominous man's intense gaze, the pope continued to guide Mario into the Sistine Chapel—an exclusive tour for the Vatican's newest recruit.

Chapter 3

February 10, 2000
Thursday Evening
Roberto's Mansion

"Lasagna will be ready in forty minutes," Roberto called out from the kitchen.

"You never make lasagna," Father Mario Marino responded, a hint of surprise in his voice. He knew well Roberto's usual trifecta of indulgences: wine, women, and song.

"Only for special occasions, cherished friends, or romantic conquests. You got two out of three going for ya, buddy," Roberto retorted, his laughter filling the room. Their bond was as strong as blood brothers, having grown up together in the Santa Maria Orphanage since they were infants.

"So, what's the latest conspiracy theory brewing in that wild imagination of yours?" Mario asked, lounging comfortably in the plush leather recliner in Roberto's expansive living room. Mario knew Roberto always had some kind of intriguing theory up his sleeve.

"Global warming," Roberto declared, raising his oven-mitted hand as if taking an oath.

"And what's your take on it?" Mario probed, crossing his arms in anticipation of a fresh perspective.

"What if the scientific consensus is wrong, and it's not cars spewing CO_2 that's the problem, but rather, we're *suffocating*

Mother Earth?" Roberto proposed, his voice filled with conviction.

Intrigued, Mario rose from his recliner and sauntered into the kitchen to better engage in discussion.

Seeing he had Mario's full attention, Roberto leaned against the kitchen island pointing his finger at Mario for emphasis. "Consider this: we've blanketed the Earth with billions of miles of asphalt. If I wrapped you in black asphalt and left you in the sun, wouldn't you overheat, experience severe warming?"

Mario paused, considering this unconventional perspective.

"We're smothering the Earth with roads, highways, and parking lots. If we want to cool it down, we need to find an alternative to asphalt, something that will allow the Earth to breathe." Roberto wrapped his arms around himself to illustrate his point. "*Breathable* asphalt. The Earth needs breathable asphalt."

Roberto reveled in his ability to devise simple solutions to the complex problems plaguing the world, solutions that seemed to elude the masses. After selling his software company for a staggering two hundred million dollars three years ago, he had ample time to ponder humanity's pressing issues, like global warming.

"Hmm, interesting. Where'd you get this one?" Mario asked, his eyebrows raised in curiosity.

"Last week, while I was at Esselunga for groceries. I could feel the heat radiating off the asphalt, and it hit me—the Earth is swaddled in this black, heat-absorbing blanket," Roberto explained, his hands mimicking the act of being warmed by a fire.

"And do the ladies fall for these theories of yours?" Mario asked, a teasing glint in his eyes.

"Oh, God no. I learned the hard way that I can either share my theories or get lucky. Sorry, my friend, I choose sex," Roberto replied, a smug grin playing on his lips as he reminisced about his effortless conquests. "Besides, most of the women I entertain here wouldn't even begin to comprehend the depth of my intellectual theories."

Back when he was a computer programmer living in a cramped one-bedroom apartment, women barely gave him a second glance. The dotcom era changed all that for him. By adding a few zeros to his bank account, suddenly Roberto found himself at the epicenter of female attention. With the steering wheel of his brand-new 2000 Lamborghini Murciélago in hand, a symbol of his triumph, he was now an irresistible woman-magnet. Near limitless time and money at his disposal, he would indulge in the company of those women who were more than willing to exchange their time for intimate moments within the confines of his bedroom.

"You and your conspiracy theories. You think everyone is hiding something, like Mother Superior back at the orphanage," Mario retorted, raising his right hand to his mouth to mimic the act of drinking from an imaginary beer mug.

"I swear I saw her sneak a swig from a hidden flask and tuck it back under her habit when we were in third grade at the orphanage." Roberto's voice hardened at the memory of the stern reverend mother. "You know that's why they call their uniform 'a habit.' It's so they can *hide all their bad habits*." Roberto laughed at his own clever pun. "I just thought of that. Pretty good, right?"

"Sure. Remember that wooden stick she used to discipline you with? It was once a ruler. She struck so many children that all the lines wore off."

"That's because she was a raging alcoholic," Roberto said, rubbing the back of his hand. He'd never shed a tear despite the frequent corporal punishment. He'd refused to give Mother Maria Francis the satisfaction of seeing him cry. "She displayed all the classic signs of an alcoholic."

Mario knew his best friend harbored deep-seated issues from their shared time in the orphanage. His endless parade of romantic conquests after becoming a millionaire was a clear attempt to mask the pain from the harsh treatment he'd received from the nuns and priests. Mario, on the other hand, had found solace in their care.

"Ready for another one?" Roberto asked, eager to share another of his theories.

"What else you got?" Mario said, rolling his eyes in anticipation.

"The LGBT community blatantly snubbing God," Roberto began, his voice dropping into a conspiratorial tone.

"How's that?"

"It's a stroke of genius, really." Roberto paused, building suspense before launching into his argument. "In the biblical tale of Noah and the flood, God presented a rainbow as a covenant to Noah and his family, promising never to unleash such destruction again."

"Yes, I'm familiar with the scripture. 'Never again will there be a flood to destroy all life. When I see the rainbow in the clouds, I will remember the everlasting covenant between God and every living creature on Earth. This is the sign of my covenant with all the creatures of the earth'," Mario quoted from memory, his seminary education serving him well.

"Very good, my young Padawan."

"Who's the Padawan?"

"Just kidding, Anakin."

"You're barely older than me by a few months."

"Yeah, yeah. Details, details," Roberto waved off the comment.

"Continue with your theory please."

"The LGBT community chose the rainbow flag as their symbol to represent them. Did you know it was first created in San Francisco, California in 1978?"

Mario gestured impatiently for Roberto to get to the point.

"Alright, here's the punchline: by flying the rainbow flag at every pride parade, every march, every event, it's as if they're using it as a divine shield. It's like they're throwing God's own words back at Him, saying, 'You can't touch me', all the while wearing broad smiles knowing God will never send another cataclysmic event to wipe out all life on Earth," Roberto finished, looking to Mario for validation.

"That's quite the leap, Berto, though I'll give you points for creativity," Mario conceded, taking a sip of his wine while studying his friend. "Where do you come up with these wild theories?"

"I can't really say. They just come to me, you know. I see something, it sends me down a rabbit hole of thoughts, and voilà: rainbow, Noah, LGBTQ community. Ta-da!" Roberto spread his arms wide like a magician revealing his trick.

"Wow. Your mind truly is amazing." Mario shook his head.

"Enough about my theories—share some details about your new role," Roberto said, transitioning his attention away from his narcissistic thoughts back to Mario.

"What, so you can concoct more outlandish theories?"

"Come on, spill the beans." Roberto appeared anxious to hear about the enigmatic Vatican Secret Archives.

"Let's head over to your computer. I'll show you some information online."

They both sauntered down the corridor towards the second of Roberto's five bedrooms, a space that doubled as his home office and man cave.

"The Archives are exactly as you'd imagine," Mario said, settling into the chair next to Roberto's. "Like something out of a spy movie. Underground, dungeon-esque, secure pass cards, passwords. It's your kind of scene, really."

"Ooh, tell me more about the Dark Side, Obi Wan." Roberto rubbed his hands together, mimicking a mad scientist.

"We're talking about a privileged position. Can we drop the Star Wars references?"

"I'm just messing around." Roberto slid out the keyboard tray.

"Google search 'Vatican Secret Archives'," Mario suggested, familiar with the rising tech startup in Silicon Valley that was gaining popularity for its online search capabilities.

"You realize dogpile.com is the superior search engine, right?" Roberto typed in the URL to the Google competitor's website. "How can a search engine named 'Go Ogle' ever be successful? Sheesh, any time *I* ogle women, I get slapped." Secretly, Roberto was so convinced this latest startup would fail that he was buying thousands of put options against it, betting its stock would crash. He was set to make a fortune, much like George Soros betting against the pound sterling turning him into an instant billionaire.

"Really? You're surprised that behavior gets you slapped?"

"I'm just sayin'."

"Whatever. Just search 'Vatican Secret Archives', will you please?"

Data began filling the monitor, each line populated with newfound knowledge.

"There!" Mario leaned in, his finger tracing a line of information on the screen. "That's the center of my scanning operation—all the diaries, documents, scrolls, and—"

"Wait, they have *scrolls?*" Roberto interrupted, his eyes wide with intrigue.

"You have no idea." Mario swiveled to face Roberto, his expression grave. "Remember. Nothing leaves this room."

"Understood," Roberto nodded.

"No, I need more than an 'understood.' Swear to me this doesn't leave this room."

"Buddy, it's me. I swear. I promise." Roberto raised his right hand, mimicking the solemnity of an oath in court.

Mario turned back towards the screen, his eyes scanning the cascading information. "Now, I've only been granted access to a small section. They trust me, but they're being cautious. They don't want to tempt me. Once I complete this first section, I'll be granted access to the next."

"Incredible," Roberto murmured, his gaze locked on the screen.

"Father Benedetti was also working on this same assignment. Did you know he was only twenty-six years old when his heart gave out?" Mario spoke in a hushed tone, the cold pit in his stomach constantly gnawing at him as he contemplated his new role within the Vatican. The eerie coincidence of Father Benedetti's death cast a long shadow over his prestigious new position. He had recently discovered that Father Benedetti was the second priest assigned to the Vatican Secret Archives who had succumbed to a heart attack.

"Not unheard of, the whole embolism thing and all."

"Hold on. How did you know he died of an embolism?"

"Dogpile.com." Roberto's smile was smug, confident in the superiority of his chosen search engine over Go Ogle.

While Mario had been engaged in his interview process, Roberto had conducted his own investigation into the enigmatic position Mario was vying for. The untimely passing of Father Benedetti could be interpreted as a fortuitous twist of fate opening a golden opportunity for Mario. On the other hand, it could be seen as a curse, drawing him deeper into the perilous depths of the Vatican's sinister web until he was unable to break free. The sole purpose of his quiet search was to safeguard his best friend from falling into a perilous trap. Despite the Vatican's prestigious reputation, Roberto's instincts screamed caution.

The rhythmic tapping of keys filled the room as Roberto continued the online investigation.

"Here it is."

The Vatican Secret Archives, a treasure trove of historical documents and papal records, originated as a dual-purpose repository serving both as an archive and a library for the popes. This dual functionality persisted until 1612 when Pope Paul V appointed a separate custodian specifically for the Archives, marking a significant shift in its management.

The inception of what would later be known as the "Vatican Secret Archives" is attributed to Pope Pius IV. This official designation marked the beginning of a new era in the Vatican's record-keeping. The physical structure housing these secret archives was completed in the early 17th century. For centuries, it stood as a fortress of inaccessible information, its contents shrouded in mystery until the late 19th century. At this point, it was reportedly opened to a select group of scholars, breaking centuries of strict confidentiality.

Pope Pius XII chose his papal name "Pius" in honor of Pope Pius IV, the pope who is credited with the official establishment of the Secret Archives. This choice reflects the enduring significance of the Secret Archives in the Vatican's history.

In an attempt to shed some light on the contents of the Secret Archives, a heavily edited index was published. Alongside this, a comprehensive set of rules was established to regulate access to this privileged information, ensuring its continued protection.

In addition to the Secret Archives, the Vatican also houses an even more confidential collection known as the "Apostolic Penitentiary." This archive contains a wealth of papal documents and canon law, further adding to the Vatican's rich tapestry of historical records.

"Wow, you are in the belly of the beast, my friend." Roberto leaned back, staring at his best friend.

"I am in the secret of secrets."

"You could say you're in the Vatican's most intimate chambers," Roberto laughed, grabbing his crotch with both hands.

"Remember, you can't breathe a word of this to anyone," Mario said, ignoring the crude jab mocking the Vatican.

"I know, I know. I am just so fuc— excuse me, *damn* excited you are in the thick processing the Vatican's deepest secrets." Roberto swiveled his chair around and stood up. "You can tell me more over dinner. The timer's going off."

"Good, I'm famished." Mario followed Roberto out of the office back into the kitchen.

"I got us a delicious DOCG Chianti," Roberto said, referring to the highest classification of Italian wine. "You're going to love this one."

"You didn't skimp on anything, did you?"

"Nope. You've earned it, my friend."

Roberto plated lasagna, salad, and garlic bread for himself and his friend. Gripping a long pepper-grinder, he twisted the wooden cylinder over the salad, knowing how his best friend preferred his meals. He placed the pepper grinder on the island while reflecting on Mario's significant achievement. "Remember how we used to marvel at the Vatican, believing neither of us would ever be part of it?"

Mario watched his friend acknowledging his accomplishment.

"And here you are, entrusted with the most confidential of secrets. I'm super proud of you, Mario."

"I couldn't have done it without your support."

Roberto, cradling two plates of his signature lasagna, led them into the dining room. This was a special meal, a celebration of Mario's new position. Setting down the plates, he lifted his glass of wine in a toast. "To your success, my friend. You've truly made it."

Their glasses clinked together, the sound echoing their shared joy. They both took a moment to appreciate the fine Chianti, a fitting complement to the next chapter of Mario's life.

"Berto, this is truly exceptional," Mario managed to say through a mouthful of lasagna. He wiped at the corners of his mouth with a cloth napkin.

"Thank you."

As they continued to enjoy their meal, the conversation flowed freely. Their friendship, deep and enduring, was nourished by these exchanges. They valued the honesty and openness of their discussions. It was refreshing to take in different perspectives, especially given their contrasting worlds. Roberto, immersed in the high-tech and materialistic world, and Mario, devoted to his faith and religion, provided a balance for each other. Their friendship, forged in the shared experiences of their upbringing in the orphanage, now spanned nearly three decades. Despite their differences, their bond was as strong as blood brothers—it was unbreakable and profound, and they both knew it.

"I got some tiramisu from my favorite patisserie. You interested?"

"Are you kidding? Remember, I have twenty-eight sweet teeth," Mario laughed, flashing a wide grin and pointing to his pearly white teeth.

"I know, I know, everyone else has only one sweet tooth, but you got the full set." Roberto chuckled at Mario's oft-repeated joke. He collected their plates and silverware, stacking them neatly before heading off to slice the delectable Italian dessert.

"Do you want an espresso with that?" he called from the kitchen.

"No, thank you. I have to be up early for morning service."

Chapter 4

March 3, 2000
Friday, 4:45p.m.
Vatican Secret Archives

After three weeks of meticulously scanning delicate documents, Mario's routine in the Vatican Secret Archives had become a well-oiled machine. The Vatican had equipped him with all the necessary tools for the job, mounted on his workstation: a two-foot-by-eight-foot steel workbench on wheels. This compact space held his laptop, scanner, white cloth gloves for handling the fragile documents, a magnifying glass, and various-colored tinted plastic sheets to capture faint markings and details. Mario's meticulous organization showcased his understanding of the weighty responsibility he carried for this crucial assignment, one that would shape future generations for centuries.

The sound of approaching footsteps shattered the deathly silence that enveloped the tomblike atmosphere of the Secret Archives—it was a challenge to remain completely silent in this eerily quiet space. The overseeing cardinal, responsible for ensuring Mario's progress and addressing any queries, would make daily visits to check on him. The cardinal's own dedication to this project was evident; he took his role and responsibility with utmost seriousness.

"Good afternoon, Father Marino," the cardinal's voice resonated in a hushed tone. Despite the absence of any other individuals, the prevailing silence within the Secret Archives demanded a subdued conversation.

"Good afternoon, Cardinal Borelli," Mario replied, matching the cardinal's lowered volume with his own voice.

The scanner hummed as it glided over the document Mario was currently working on. Cardinal Borelli's satisfaction was evident as he inspected Mario, observing the white cloth gloves covering his hands that protected the fragile documents from the oils of human touch. The young priest's performance had exceeded expectations, instilling the cardinal with confidence in his colleagues' decision to entrust Mario with this monumental task.

"I'm checking to see if you have any questions," the cardinal said, his voice filled with anticipation and a hint of mystery.

"Everything is going smoothly. I've developed a foolproof routine leaving no room for error," Mario replied, a sense of pride evident in his voice.

"Excellent."

"Thank you for providing me with this state-of-the-art oversized scanner. It was perfect for that lengthy scroll I had to scan."

"You're welcome. If there's anything else you require, let me know. I'll bring you another requisition form later. Just fill it out and return it to me."

"Thank you. Having the proper equipment on hand is essential for preserving these delicate artifacts," Mario said, determined to impress his superior. He was fully aware of the significance of building strong alliances within the chain of command. Breaching this trust could result in a lifetime of isolation, confined to a confessional booth, forever burdened with the weight of sinners' darkest confessions.

"We are beyond pleased with your exceptional work, Father Marino. This assignment comes directly from the pope himself, and you have surpassed all expectations. Thank you."

Mario bowed his head, feeling a surge of pride at the cardinal's praise. This acknowledgment only fueled his dedication to the Vatican and the pope.

"Thank you, Cardinal Borelli. Your words mean more to me than you can imagine."

"I'll let you get back to it," Cardinal Borelli said, turning and departing from the aisle, leaving an air of anticipation in his wake.

Mario's mind wandered as he watched the cardinal disappear around the end of the aisle. The appreciation the man felt for his work was overwhelming. This was followed by memories of his youth—they flooded his mind, thoughts of the strict Mother Maria, whom Roberto had referred to as "evil." Despite her harshness, Mario couldn't help but feel she too would approve of the man he had become.

He imagined the Holy Mother taking credit for his success, attributing it to her stern discipline. She would have surely disapproved of Roberto and his wealth—for her, money was the root of all evil. *"Yeah, but, money paid for your habit, bitch."* Mario couldn't help but smile at the imaginary debate between his best friend and the "evil Mother Superior" taking place in his thoughts.

His focus shifted back to the task at hand, and he turned towards the shelf to retrieve the next book for scanning. As he reached for it, something caught his eye. Behind the book was a package wrapped in brown paper, seemingly out of place. Intrigued, Mario set the book down on the worktable then carefully removed four more books to access the mysterious package. It was tightly wrapped and secured with crisscrossed twine, resembling a crudely wrapped birthday present. The brown paper bore a wax seal imprinted with a signet ring.

What are you doing back here? Confusion and curiosity filled Mario's mind as he stared at the package.

His eyes remained fixed on the mysterious package as the scanner completed its scan. With utmost caution, he placed the mysterious package on the table. Its presence sent shivers down his spine. As he carefully lifted the book from the glass and returned it to its original resting place on the shelf, his mind couldn't help but wonder about the peculiar package. It stood out like a misshapen puzzle piece, not quite fitting its surroundings. The multitude of books he'd scanned never bore a wax seal, making this discovery all the more intriguing.

Should he skip this item, preserving its seal? Should he break the seal and uncover its hidden contents? He'd been instructed to scan every single item in the Secret Archives, yet common sense suggested this sealed package fell outside that mandate. Opening it would inflict irreversible damage on the precious signet ring stamp.

Contemplating his responsibilities and the instructions he'd received, he resolved that this package was no exception. It, too, deserved to be scanned and preserved for future generations. Who knew what secrets it held? Perhaps this was just the first of many extraordinary oddities that awaited him.

Glancing at his watch, he realized the hour was nearing end of day. Reluctantly, he decided to postpone the unveiling of this mystery until Monday morning. Placing the package back in its original spot, he meticulously returned the other books to their rightful places, concealing the package. He powered down the equipment, leaving the enigmatic package behind, eagerly awaiting its unveiling next week.

Chapter 5

March 3, 2000
Friday, 1:18 p.m.
Harare, Zimbabwe

Sister Carlotta strolled through the bustling marketplace near her newly assigned church in Zimbabwe. Vibrant displays of produce and handmade goods caught her eye, reminding her of the farmers' market near her former church in Rome. As she perused the market's wares, she couldn't help but miss the laughter and innocence of the children she had left behind in Italy. She felt a pang of nostalgia for her daily ritual of purchasing fresh fruit for the children at the school. The fruit salad she made for them was a healthier alternative to candy or gelato. She cherished the joy it brought to their faces.

Little Flavio, what a character he was, the nun thought with a mix of fondness and exasperation. She couldn't help but cringe at memories of him with worm guts plastered around the corners of his mouth. It wasn't that he did it to gross her out—he genuinely enjoyed eating the snails, worms, and bugs he found on the playground. She chuckled at the thought of him growing up to be six feet tall, all thanks to his playground diet. Not to mention the times she'd caught him inside the classroom sneaking bites of paste straight from the container. It wasn't his fault the paste manufacturer made it taste like mint. Of course, the other kids would see Flavio eating it and, being curious, indulging in a taste test of their own. Ew.

Then there was little Cecilia. Her smile could light up an entire room. The nun's heart warmed at the thought of the precious little girl. She was such a joy to hold and talk to. She'd never put up a fuss when Carlotta cradled her in her lap. The little precious darling would go on and on with her stories, all the while enjoying Carlotta's fruit salad. The nun had always noticed how much Cecilia loved the peaches in particular. The little angel would carefully separate out all the peach pieces, eating the other fruits one by one and saving the peaches for last. Carlotta made a mental note to find a Harare vendor who sold peaches, just to remind her of her darling little Cecilia.

The boys, on the other hand, were not ones to be held. They would squirm and wriggle out of Carlotta's grasp within seconds. Their boundless energy made it impossible for them to stay still. Enzo, in particular, was a bundle of excitement. He was thrilled he shared the same name as the legendary founder of the Ferrari brand. The nun had adorned her classroom with posters of various Ferraris. Enzo's favorite was a poster of a 1990 Ferrari F40 with twin-turbo V8 engine Carlotta picked out just for him. The moment he laid eyes on that dream car, he'd declared he would be a racecar driver when he grew up. Watching him zoom around the courtyard on his tricycle, skillfully maneuvering around poles while rearing up on two wheels, it was easy for Carlotta to believe he would fulfill that ambition.

In the bustling marketplace of Harare, she found herself surrounded by a sea of vendors, each displaying their array of goods. Fresh produce, however, was not as readily available as it was back in her beloved Rome. The country's hyperinflation had reached unimaginable levels, making shopping a challenging endeavor with prices fluctuating drastically daily. There were even rumors of a new currency the government was preparing to introduce, merely adding to the chaos. Despite these pressures, the nun refused to live without the simple pleasure of fresh fruit. It was a daily blessing she cherished, a way to hold on to the memories of her wonderful life back in Rome.

She approached an older Zimbabwean lady standing under an oversized sand-colored canopy. The canopy provided much-needed relief from the scorching heat of the day, a stark contrast to the climate she was accustomed to in Rome. Dressed in her black habit, she endured her discomfort, knowing her mission in Harare had been assigned by Cardinal Rosetti himself. She found solace in the fact that she was doing the work of the Lord.

The nun made her way towards this particular vendor selling peaches because the fruit brought back fond memories of little Cecilia back in Rome. She asked the vendor about the cost of the peaches. The elderly woman from Zimbabwe responded by raising two fingers, signifying that the peaches were priced at 2,000,000 Zimbabwean dollars. To Carlotta's surprise, the lady showed kindness and offered a fair price from the get-go, refraining from the usual haggling the locals engaged in. It was evident the woman saw the nun's pleasant face and recognized her genuine nature, understanding she wasn't someone to take advantage of.

Carlotta handed over two 1,000,000 bills for the three peaches she had carefully selected. Placing the precious fruits inside her market bag, she scanned the row of vendors, searching for bananas, apples, lemons, and other fruits to complete her beloved fruit salad. It was important to her to be fair to all the vendors, ensuring that none would benefit more than the others. During her weekly visits to the marketplace, she strived to maintain an even hand with those she met in this struggling and chaotic country. It was simply in her nature to treat everyone with equity and kindness.

* * *

From his distant vantage point, the Vatican assassin meticulously observed the chaotic marketplace through the scope of his rifle. His gaze fixated on the unsuspecting nun weaving her way through the bustling crowd. Every second counted. He glanced at his watch, knowing that the diversion he had orchestrated would soon come into play. The nun was a loose end the assassin had been entrusted to tie up.

Handpicked by Cardinal Rosetti himself, Alistar, the formidable leader of the elite Vatican assassin team, had embarked a week prior on this crucial mission to eliminate Sister Carlotta. Her insatiable curiosity—unfortunate questions she asked at the priest's funeral—posed a grave threat to the dark secrets hidden within the Vatican's hallowed halls. The nun's curiosity could have uncovered the cause behind Father Benedetti's untimely demise.

As a result of the former priest's suspicious behavior, Alistar had arranged a private meeting with the man to discover what he knew. Unfortunately, that discussion ended with an abrupt heart attack. The syringe mark on Benedetti's neck had been expertly concealed, leaving behind no trace of foul play; the young priest's autopsy report, carefully crafted by the Vatican physician, designated an embolism as the cause of death, and that was that.

Peering through the scope of his Remington 700 .308 bolt-action rifle, Alistar scanned the marketplace, making sure that no Zimbabwean police were patrolling the area. With the corrupt government in Harare, it had been a simple matter of bribing the local officials to keep law enforcement at bay for a precious hour.

His gaze returned to the market where the unsuspecting nun was still standing beneath the canopy, exchanging currency for her three peaches. The line of sight between them was clear. With careful precision, he chambered a bullet inside the high-powered rifle equipped with a silencer and flash suppressor, the standard tools of his trade.

The seconds ticked away. The assassin secured the bipod on the windowsill, steadying the rifle against his shoulder as if embracing a fine woman in romantic embrace. His anticipation grew as the seconds ticked away.

From the third-story window, he peered through his scope. His target stood a mere fifty yards away. Such close proximity allowed him to steady his aim without the need to regulate his breathing. The feel of the trigger on his finger brought back haunting memories from his childhood.

All he'd known was the constant abuse his alcoholic father had inflicted on his mother. One fateful night, after witnessing his mother's brutal murder at the hands of his father, Alistar decided to take matters into his own hands. Gripping his grandfather's war pistol, he'd confronted his father, desperate to avoid the same fate that had befallen his mother. His father, consumed by an alcohol-fueled rage, disregarded the gun aimed at him and advanced. Filled with a surge of adrenaline, Alistar pulled the trigger. The bullet found its mark in his father's abdomen. But the nonlethal shot only served to further enrage the drunken man, who lunged towards Alistar with violent intent.

In a desperate act of self-preservation, the fourteen-year-old emptied the entire cartridge into his father's body. The room filled with the sound of gunfire as bullets tore through flesh, leaving his father lifeless on the carpet, blood pooling around him. One final, fatal shot to the forehead ended the nightmare once and for all.

41

With both parents gone and no close relatives to turn to, Alistar found himself in the custody of the Santa Maria Orphanage. The courts ruled his actions as self-defense, but the scars of that night would forever shape him. Now a skilled assassin, Alistar channeled his past trauma into deadly purpose, eliminating those who posed a threat to the Vatican's secrets.

In the distance, he could hear the unmistakable revving of a dirt-bike engine. He glanced at his Tag Heuer watch, knowing the radical terrorist he'd hired was always punctual when there was enough money on the line. Even this ruthless individual would take time out of his busy terrorist schedule for a job like this, once he smelled the Euros waved in front of his greedy face.

The roar of the dirt bike echoed through the narrow alley, sending vendors and locals scrambling for cover. They knew all too well the sound of motorcycles precluded a hit on someone's kill list. It could come from orders given by President Mugabe, the militia, or any number of uprisings in the volatile country.

Alistar watched as the vendors did nothing to help the nun. He couldn't help but feel a twisted sense of satisfaction as he watched the vendors ignore his target. Their inaction toward Sister Carlotta meant his plan was working perfectly.

The chaos paralyzed Sister Carlotta with fear, leaving her vulnerable and exposed. She stood frozen in the crosshairs of Alistar's high-powered rifle, her life hanging by a thread.

The terrorist roared into the plaza on his dirt bike wielding an Uzi, unleashing a hail of bullets into the air above the market stalls. The clay walls behind the tents splintered, raining down debris on the panicking crowd. The screams of innocent bystanders mingled with the deafening sound of gunfire and the revving of the motorcycle.

In the midst of the chaos, Alistar's scope focused on the nun's temple. The single gunshot he needed to complete his assignment would go undetected amidst the cacophony of noise. With the silencer securely screwed onto the end of the rifle, his shot's origin would remain imperceptible to the world, just like the countless secrets hidden within the Vatican's walls.

As the motorcyclist passed, Sister Carlotta's temple remained centered in the assassin's crosshairs. With a steady hand and a heart filled with cold determination, he pulled the trigger. The world fell silent around him.

The bullet soared through the air, destined to fulfill its deadly purpose.

Chapter 6

March 4, 2000
Saturday, 6:04 p.m.
Rome, Italy

"Lasagna again? What's the special occasion?" Mario full of curiosity entering the kitchen.

"Don't get excited, it's leftovers," Roberto replied, a mischievous glint in his eyes.

Mario raised an eyebrow. "Should I even ask who you had over to leave behind this rare treat?"

"How about I just tell you she was blonde. You know I have a thing for blondes," Roberto chuckled, keeping his answer short in respect for Mario's occupation.

Mario sighed, shaking his head. "Will you ever change your ways and settle down with a good Christian girl?"

"Not anytime in the foreseeable future, *Father*."

Mario's tone turned serious. "I'm just looking out for your well-being, you know."

"Hey, you get up on your priestly soapbox and I bring you back down to reality. Let's change topics, shall we?"

With a deliberate pivot, he turned away from Mario to check on the lasagna, signaling he was done discussing his love life.

After enduring the tension hanging in the air, Roberto finally broke the silence. "Ya know," he began still hunched over facing the oven window, "if I were blessed with your striking good looks, I wouldn't have to shell out so much money looking for this elusive soul mate," he chuckled at his light-hearted jest.

Mario retorted with a playful grin, "Well, it's a good thing you're not short on cash then, isn't it?" His response, a cleverly crafted joke, was a welcome relief, effectively diffusing the tension.

"What's the latest on the scanning project?" Roberto's focus consumed by the simmering lasagna.

Mario's countenance transformed, his eyes sparkling with infectious enthusiasm. "You wouldn't believe the discovery that occurred this week."

Roberto's curiosity piqued, he straightened and swiveled to lean against the cool Carrara marble of the kitchen island. "Tell me."

Mario, eager to recount his tale, drew near and pulled out a barstool to sit. "I scanned a significant piece of history involving the Knights Templar. The Chinon Parchment," he said, his voice filled with awe. "The thing was misfiled over three centuries ago. It was just unearthed this week. Finding it was monumental."

Roberto's eyes widened in astonishment. "The Knights Templar? That's amazing."

Mario nodded, his excitement evident. "It took me all week to scan it."

Roberto leaned in, his curiosity growing. "What's on it?"

Mario's voice grew serious, as if sharing a secret. "Pope Clement V's words. He absolved the Knights Templar of heresy back in 1308."

The room fell silent for a moment as the weight of the revelation sank in. The two friends exchanged a knowing look, appreciating the significance of the document.

"The Templars got screwed over by King Philip '*the Fair*' with those false accusations," Roberto intoned, holding up air quotes to make clear his opinion about the king of France.

"But this parchment absolves them of those charges."

Roberto's eyes narrowed in disbelief. "Did you know that's where Friday the Thirteenth comes from?"

Mario leaned in, eager to hear the story.

"The King of France was jealous of the Templars' wealth and power," Roberto began, his voice filled with intrigue. "On the morning of Friday, October 13, 1307, he had over six hundred Templars arrested. They were charged with heresy, devil worship, and even spitting on the cross."

Mario's eyes widened upon hearing this news.

"But that's not all," Roberto continued, his voice dropping. "The King had them brutally tortured until they confessed to things that weren't true. Their bodies were stretched on racks, their limbs dislocated. Some even had their feet dipped in oil and set on fire."

Mario's face twisted in disgust. "That's like something out of a horror movie."

Roberto nodded solemnly. "You know what's even more fascinating? The Templars smuggled out all their treasure before the King could confiscate it. You know what that treasure was?"

Mario nodded side to side, his eyes sparkling with curiosity.

"They had King Solomon's treasure," Roberto revealed, his voice filled with awe.

Mario's jaw dropped. "You mean, the Ark of the Covenant? The Ten Commandments? The Holy Grail?"

Roberto nodded, a mischievous smile playing on his lips. "That's right. The Templars had it all."

Mario's face scrunched in disbelief, but a part of him couldn't help but wonder if there was some truth to the rumors. "Roberto, your endless pursuit of knowledge is incredible."

"Boy, what I wouldn't give to have a look at that treasure." Roberto's gaze drifted away, picturing the invaluable cache of Solomon's riches.

"You've done pretty well for yourself."

"True, I've done well enough." His eyes swept across his opulent abode. "And you too. Remember the safety net I've arranged for us?" He was referring to the special Swiss account he'd set up, a safeguard against any unforeseen circumstances that might befall them. Roberto was a man of caution, always prepared for the worst. This hidden fortune—a cool ten million stashed away in a Swiss bank—was his insurance policy in case anything went terribly wrong.

"I appreciate it, but I have faith in my future. The Church will provide for me when I retire."

"Of course. But remember, I got your back, brother." Roberto turned his attention back to the oven to check on the lasagna. "What other secrets from the Archives?"

"I heard there's a petition from King Henry VIII to the pope seeking an annulment from Catherine of Aragon in 1533."

"No kidding." Roberto checked the thermometer for doneness. "Did you know the pope denying that request led to the birth of the Church of England?" he interjected, flaunting his wealth of knowledge. "Must've hurt the Vatican coffers to lose all that revenue."

"Wow, there's that brain of yours again," Mario said, straightening up and nodding in admiration.

"What else?"

"Records from Galileo's trial."

"Yep. They thought he was crazy; now he's hailed as a genius." Roberto chuckled at the irony.

"Letters from Mary, Queen of Scots. And a grand empress from China. All dating back centuries."

"Holy crap, they're hoarding some serious stuff in there."

Their conversation was abruptly cut short by the oven's insistent beeping.

"Saved by the bell," Roberto quipped, opening the oven door to retrieve the bubbling lasagna. "Let's eat."

After plating the food, they moved to the dining room to enjoy the delectable leftovers. Mario cut his fork through the steaming layers of lasagna. "Mmmm. Even leftover, your lasagna never fails to impress," he said, talking through a mouthful of rich flavors that danced on his tongue.

Roberto chuckled, a hint of pride lighting up his eyes. "I think it actually tastes better the second day."

Mario took another bite, closing his eyes and savoring the rare treat. "I agree. This one *is* better than the last. Did you do anything different?"

"I used a nice bottle of Chianti in the meat sauce as usual, but as a twist I added some truffle sauce. Gives it that earthy flavor. You like it?"

"Delicious. I'll happily be your guinea pig for your experiments any day of the week." Mario consumed another forkful of the signature dish.

"Anything else of interest happening at work?" Roberto probed, his eyes gleaming with curiosity.

"I'm not sure." Mario's gaze dropped to his lasagna, unsure whether to reveal his peculiar discovery involving the concealed brown-paper package.

"What is it?" Roberto had recognized Mario's change in demeanor.

"I . . . um, stumbled upon a rather unusual document in the Archives yesterday," Mario confessed, his voice hesitant.

"I'm sure you are going to find *a lot* of unusual things inside that place. Look at the Templar parchment you just told me about."

"This one . . . this one is different. I don't want you to jump to conclusions and start weaving your conspiracy theories," Mario warned, his tone getting serious.

"Now you *have* to tell me. Spill the beans," Roberto urged, his eyes wide with anticipation.

"Alright, but promise me you'll keep your conspiracy theories in check."

"Enough with the suspense. Out with it already," Roberto demanded, his patience wearing thin.

"I discovered a strange package hidden behind some books on a shelf," Mario revealed, his voice barely audible.

"And . . .?" Roberto's hand gestured for Mario to continue, his impatience growing.

"It appears to be a book wrapped in brown paper, sealed with a wax stamp."

"Ooooo. Oooo. It was Professor Plum in the library with a book wrapped in brown paper," Roberto teased, pointing his finger at Mario in mock accusation.

"Enough with the jokes," Mario retorted, his tone stern.

"Alright, alright. So, what's inside this mystery package?"

"Remember, whatever I tell you stays within these four walls."

"I swear," Roberto promised, raising his right hand in a solemn vow. "Tell me."

"I don't know. I put it back on the shelf," Mario confessed, his voice filled with regret.

"Dude! Now you *have* to open it," Roberto demanded, his anticipation teetering on the edge of mania.

"'Dude'? Really?" Mario retorted, his face scrunched in disbelief.

"Okay, buddy, friend, pal—whatever. You gotta tell me what's in the package," Roberto implored, his voice laced with a raw desperation to know.

Mario hesitated, his heart pounding in his chest. He felt a sudden surge of fear, a fear his esteemed position might be put in jeopardy by revealing too much to Roberto. "You're making me nervous. You can't blow this position for me by using what I tell you to spout off conspiracy theories around others."

"I'm sorry. My imagination goes wild sometimes. I'll let the matter go." Roberto had already decided to back off after seeing the panic on Mario's face. He'd pushed the envelope too far this time. His friend was visibly uncomfortable.

Mario felt only a little relief. He was torn between his loyalty to the Church and his loyalty to his best friend. Roberto had been there his entire life; he'd backed him against the bullies at the orphanage, supported him during the rigors of seminary, and now helped steer him to this honored position in the Vatican Secret Archives. On the other hand, the Church has also been there Mario's entire life. It had raised him, educated him, led him to his calling. He had taken his vows and became a priest, a decision he held dear. Now, carrying out his esteemed position within the sacred walls of the Vatican Secret Archives, his loyalty was coming into question.

Roberto, sensing the tension he'd caused, tried to diffuse it. "You know, it's probably nothing," he said, his voice filled with regret. His mind often ran away through a whirlwind of theories, most of which never materialized. However, this never stopped him from dreaming and imagining the impossible.

"I'm sure it's nothing," Mario agreed, taking another bite of his lasagna. "The Vatican is meticulous in its cataloging. It's probably just an oversight."

"Hey, you'll find out on Monday, right?" Roberto kept his banter light the rest of the night. He was filled with hope that Mario might change his mind in due time.

Chapter 7

May 3, 1982
Monday
Santa Maria Orphanage
Rome, Italy

Alistar took careful aim with the BB gun, his gaze locked onto the pigeon defiling the sacred basilica wall with its droppings. The honor of being assigned extermination duties by Mother Superior was not lost on the fourteen-year-old. As the oldest and biggest child in the Santa Maria Orphanage, Alistar reveled in the sense of authority this task bestowed upon him over the other children. With a steady hand and a sharp eye, he pulled the trigger, nailing the bird with a single precise shot. This marked his fifth pigeon of the morning. His total count had now soared past a hundred since his arrival at the orphanage.

From her vantage point in the window above him, Mother Superior Maria Francis watched with a satisfied smile as Alistar dispatched another pigeon with deadly accuracy. She knew she had chosen the right student for this task. Even though she had bent Church rules by procuring the BB gun for the young boy, she felt justified. Ever since she had assumed the role of mother superior, the pigeons had been a constant nuisance, their presence an affront to her need for cleanliness, not to mention the sanctity of the basilica. The arrival of Alistar at her orphanage had been a serendipitous event. The young man was proving to be a valuable asset in her battle against the pigeon infestation, in addition to his contributions to the orphanage's daily operations.

"Brilliant execution, Al," Mother Superior applauded, her hands resonating throughout the stone-laden courtyard. His knack for shooting the despicable creatures had not gone unnoticed by her. She saw opportunity in the young man, had recommended him to the cardinal who was always on the hunt for promising young recruits for the Vatican's elite Swiss Guard academy. The hefty donations that always found their way back to her church was a bonus that did not go unnoticed.

Alistar remained impassive, his gaze fixed on Mother Superior. He wasn't seeking praise or validation. What he yearned for was liberation from the chains holding him back from purging the world of beings he deemed worthless. This realization had dawned on him after he'd taken his own father's life, a man who had surrendered to his crippling addiction to alcohol.

His father, a man who had once been the family's pillar of strength, had become a pitiful creature staggering home in a drunken stupor night after night. One fateful evening, he'd overstepped the bounds of decency, his alcohol-fueled fury driving him to beat his wife to death. The haunting image of Alistar's mother, lifeless and sprawled on the cold kitchen floor, was forever seared into his memory. As Alistar's finger hovered over the trigger of the BB gun, the chilling memory of his intoxicated father advancing towards him resurfaced. With a steely resolve, he trained the Walther P38 Ruger on his oncoming father.

"Whatcha gonna do, boy?" his father slurred, a malicious grin twisting his drunken features.

Alistar's hold on the pistol intensified. His finger pulled on the trigger relentlessly, the bullets penetrating his father's body but failing to stop the inebriated beast. The fatal bullet to the forehead brought the monster down, spilling a gruesome torrent of blood across the stark black-and-white linoleum floor.

Alistar stared at the lifeless body sprawled before him, a sense of grim satisfaction washing over him. He had finally rid the world of the vile creature. This final act of retribution landed him in the custody of the Santa Maria Orphanage.

The tolling of the church bell echoed through the air, signaling the much anticipated 10 a.m. recess for the eager students of Santa Maria Orphanage. With a thunderous bang, the door leading out to the school yard burst open as a wave of children cascaded down the stairs, their laughter and chatter filling the playground with a lively energy. Alistar, however, took a more measured pace across the school yard, focused solely on returning the BB gun to Mother Maria. He held the weapon discreetly by his side, mindful to shield it from the younger students' curious eyes. Mother Superior had given him explicit instructions not to flaunt the weapon, threatening to confiscate it if he disobeyed. The mere thought of forfeiting this privilege was unbearable to him—it was simply not a choice he could entertain.

Nearby, Mario, his heart filled with the joy of freedom, dashed towards the playground, his best friend matching his stride. Ever since they had come to the orphanage as infants, Mario and Roberto had been inseparable. Lost in the thrill of the moment, Mario didn't notice the older boy striding directly towards him until it was too late.

"Move it, wimp," Alistar growled. Mario tried to run around him but the towering figure sidestepped, blocking his path, and a collision ensued. The blow sent Mario sprawling backwards. The impact of his head hitting the ground was sharp and immediate; his hands instinctively reached back to cradle it and soothe the pain. The sight of blood on his fingers made his heart pound, but he clenched his jaw, determined not to let tears fall.

Roberto stepped up to the much taller boy to defend his friend. "Back off, Al."

"And what if I don't?" Alistar challenged the younger boy, a cruel smirk playing on his lips.

"I'll kick your ass," Roberto shot back, standing on his tiptoes while trying to meet the older boy's gaze.

Alistar slid the BB gun into his left hand before landing a punch on Roberto's face with his right. Roberto staggered backwards, blood streaming from his nose, but quickly regained his footing. With a roar, he lunged at Alistar, toppling the bigger boy to the ground. Roberto rained down punches on Alistar, blood from his nose splattering onto the older boy's face.

The sight of the brawl sent Mother Maria rushing out the door, her ever-present ruler brandished in the air like a weapon. "Stop it! Stop it!" she commanded, her voice echoing across the playground. As she reached the boys, she grabbed Roberto by the collar, yanking him off her favored pupil with a strength that belied her age.

"Roberto! To my office, this instant!" she commanded, her voice slicing through the air like a whip. She brandished her ruler and swatted Roberto with a fervor that echoed throughout the courtyard.

"He started it," Roberto protested, shielding his head from the relentless blows with his arms.

With a final resounding smack on the crown of his head, Mother Maria said, "I've had enough of your lies, Roberto. To my office, now!"

Blood staining his pristine Catholic School uniform, Roberto stormed up the stairs, muttering curses under his breath.

"And you, Alistar?" Mother Maria's tone softened as she turned to help the boy to his feet.

"I'm fine, Mother Maria."

"You're covered in blood. Go to the nurse's office and get yourself cleaned up."

"Thank you," Alistar responded, extending the BB gun towards the reverend mother.

"Put that in my office on your way to the nurse." She gestured with her head, nodding towards the building.

Her gaze then swept over the crowd of students who had gathered to watch the spectacle. "The rest of you, recess is over. Return to your classrooms."

A chorus of disappointed groans filled the air as the students trudged up the stairs to return to their lessons. Mario blended in with the crowd, eager to avoid any blame for the altercation. He was aware of Mother Maria's favorable opinion of him, but he had no desire to explain his involvement with the new kid. If he confessed to the reverend mother and Al found out, Mario would become his relentless target all their remaining years at the orphanage.

Once the school yard was deserted, Mother Maria Francis discreetly reached under her habit and retrieved a hidden flask. She took a generous swig of brandy, the liquid burning a trail down her throat.

Chapter 8

March 6, 2000
Monday
Vatican Secret Archives

With a sense of trepidation, Mario's hand cautiously reached for the four books that served as a veil hiding the enigmatic package. "It's still there," as though he half-expected it not to be. As he delicately placed the quartet of books on the adjacent worktable, his eyes remained riveted on the cryptic parcel. His hand, acting with a mind all its own, reached up to take hold of the mysterious package.

His heart hammered against his ribcage, a silent drum echoing the back and forth of his internal debate—to open or not to open. He was fully aware of the delicate balance of his position within the hallowed halls of the Vatican, a privilege he had no intention of risking.

His fingers traced the edges of the package, curiosity gnawing at his resolve. *I'm just doing my job, right?*

With a deep breath, he placed the package on the cold steel worktable and prepared himself for the delicate operation. He untied the twine with meticulous care before setting it aside. His heart skipped a beat when he noticed the wax seal bore the imprint of a signet ring. He quietly repeated his mantra, "I'm just doing my job," then took a deep, steadying breath.

His finger slipped under the brown wrapping and gently lifted the wax seal to free it from the paper. To his surprise, his finger slid under the seal with ease. It had already been opened.

A wave of relief washed over him. He wasn't the first to discover this package. It was merely another document that needed to be scanned for digital storage.

As he unwrapped the contents, a beautifully crafted journal came into view. Its leather cover was adorned with intricate artwork depicting flowers, patterns, and faces. He carefully picked up the journal, his fingers tracing the soft leather. His heart nearly stopped when he noticed a handwritten note scribbled across the interior of the brown wrapping paper:

Beware!
Do not read!
Your life will be
in danger!
GAB

As the journal slipped from his grasp, a shiver of fear slithered down his spine. *What's this mean? Who is GAB?*

His mind was a whirlwind of thoughts, each more alarming than the last. Roberto's constant chatter about conspiracy theories had seeped into Mario's consciousness, now fueling his wild imagination. The eerie silence of the Secret Archives only amplified his growing fear. Roberto's tales of intrigue and danger painted vivid, spine-chilling scenarios in his mind, scenarios where his own life was at stake.

STOP IT! he internally reprimanded himself, trying to shake off the haunting thoughts. He was in the Vatican Secret Archives, for Pete's sake—one of the most secure places on earth. There was no conceivable way he could be in danger.

GAB? He mulled over the cryptic note. "Someone's initials?" he whispered, speaking quietly aloud. His mind immediately went to a certain deceased priest. He tried to recall Father Guiseppe Benedetti's middle name. "Alberto? No. . . . Alfredo? No, that's white pasta sauce." He grimaced, Roberto's culinary meals intruding on his thoughts. "Alphonso? Yes, that's it. Father Giuseppe Alphonso Benedetti."

He shook his head in disapproval at his predecessor's unprofessionalism. What was Benedetti thinking, defiling an integral part of this fragile document with cryptic graffiti?

Driven by a surge of curiosity, Mario found himself teetering on the edge of disobedience, a mix of fear and exhilaration coursing through his veins. Ignoring the ominous warning, he dared to open the journal. As he did so, a new wave of shivers swept over him; he'd broken his long-standing streak of unwavering compliance to the rules.

His eyes darted nervously over the words etched atop the first page.

Chapter 9

Personal Journal
Eugenio Maria Giuseppe Giovanni Pacelli
1876

Mario exhaled a sigh of relief—the journal was merely a relic from the nineteenth century. The warning, at first so menacing, now seemed less threatening as it stared back at him from the aged wrapping.

With a sense of anticipation, he carefully opened the book to a random page and began to read:

5 December 1923

Rudolf Hess is becoming an invaluable subject, obeying my every direction.

In the aftermath of the botched Beer Hall Putsch, Rudolf and Adolf have been arrested. I have arranged for them to be retained in the same jail cell.

Hess is taking dictation from Hitler about his current struggles. This manifesto will become the foundation o3f Hitler's rise to power.

Cardinal Eugenio Pacelli

Mario was shocked by these words. How could such a document exist within the sacred confines of the Vatican Secret Archives? The name Eugenio Maria Giuseppe Giovanni Pacelli sounded in his mind.

With a trembling hand, he turned the page.

14 March 1924

The Council is concerned about Hitler's temperament. He organizes street brawls and promotes mass meetings. He threatens to kill at the slightest provocation. His training must be swift. I can use his weakness to manipulate him. I will bait him with the spoils of power.

Once he finishes his manuscript, I will have him and Rudolph released from prison. This will mark the beginning of their rise to power through the National Socialist German Workers' Party.

Cardinal Eugenio Pacelli

Mario hastily shut the journal, the warning penned on the wrapping flashing across his vision even when he closed his eyes. He quickly rewrapped the journal with the brown paper, pressing the wax seal into place, and knotted the twine as accurately as he could recall. He returned the journal to its hiding place on the shelf, eager to put distance between himself and the accursed thing. Seizing another book, he pressed on with his duties, trying to forget the disturbing find he'd stumbled upon.

Chapter 10

Throughout the course of the afternoon, Mario found himself enticed by the irresistible allure of the ancient journal; despite his concerns, his thoughts were persistently drawn back to its confusing content. The mundane task of scanning documents served only to fuel his curiosity, his mind frequently straying from his tedium to the cryptic pages of the journal. Thoughts of Roberto's conspiracy theories added fuel to the fire, making it increasingly difficult to maintain focus. Mario found himself constantly having to reel those thoughts back in; otherwise they would run amok with his own wild theories. He had to keep reminding himself it was merely an old journal, a relic from the nineteenth century.

As he lifted the latest book from the scanner, he handled the page with the utmost care, turning it gently before scanning the next. The scanner hummed softly, its glacial pace capturing the highest resolution, securing every detail within its timeless image.

He couldn't take it anymore.

As the scanner worked its magic, he navigated the aisle to where the accursed journal hid. Removing the four books serving as a facade, he placed them on the empty shelf below then reached up to remove the peculiar book once more.

Journal in hand, he made his way to the worktable, his heart pounding in his chest. He took a moment to compose himself, drawing in a deep breath and releasing it slowly. With trembling hands, he untied the twine and peeled back the brown wrapper. The warning inscribed within seemed to leap out at him and bounce around in his head, its message clear and ominous.

Knock it off! Mario commanded his thoughts.

With a sense of trepidation, he began to read the first entry.

3 March 1888

Grandfather gave me a special book for my birthday yesterday:

The Art of War
by Sun Tzu

We spoke privately for an hour about the Council's decision. I'd been looking forward to this private meeting; he has it with each of us upon reaching our twelfth birthday.

He told me he has an especially important mission for me. I didn't understand everything he told me, but he said I will in time. The Council will guide me.

I do not know what wisdom this book holds, but I will cherish it for the rest of my life.

Thank you, Grandfather. I will not let you down.

Eugenio Pacelli

Chapter 11

2 March 1888
Pacelli Residence
Rome, Kingdom of Italy

"Happy birthday, mio nipote!" Marcantonio Pacelli called out, his voice full of a profound warmth as he bestowed his birthday blessings upon his grandson, Eugenio Pacelli.

"Thank you, Grandfather," Eugenio responded, his face lighting up upon hearing the deep, resonant voice of his respected patriarch drawing near.

Today marked his twelfth birthday, a day of significant importance in the Pacelli family. It was the day when a boy was ushered into the realm of manhood through a sacred conversation with his grandfather. This was a rite of passage Eugenio's older brother and cousins had experienced; to the man they'd emerged from the cloistered meeting with their faces glowing with newfound maturity and pride. Such was the power of a private meeting with the revered patriarch of the Pacelli family.

Eugenio had been yearning for this moment since his eleventh birthday, counting down the days with a mix of anticipation and anxiety. Now the wait was finally over.

"Nipote, let's go to your father's study. There are matters we need to discuss." The grandfather's voice was gentle yet firm, guiding the young man down the grand hallway of the house he'd grown up in.

"Yes, Grandfather," Eugenio responded, his heart pounding with excitement and a hint of trepidation. This was it, the moment he had been eagerly awaiting all day. He was ready. His brother and cousins had guided him, prepared him for this pivotal meeting with the eldest patriarch of the family.

"Do not dare interrupt him," Francesco had commanded, his voice laced with the authoritative tone of an elder brother.

"Listen to every word he tells you," another cousin advised, his voice heavy with the gravity of the impending meeting.

Eugenio felt a surge of readiness; his preparation for this moment was thorough and complete.

As he stepped into the grandeur of the study, he was acutely aware this private audience with his grandfather would mark a pivotal moment in his life. It was destined to be a meeting that would forever etch itself into his memory.

"Take a seat, nipote," the patriarch said. His voice boomed throughout the room.

Eugenio complied, his eyes never leaving his grandfather as the older man moved with a dignified grace towards the fireplace.

Marcantonio stood before the dancing flames, his eyes closed as if he was gathering his thoughts; indeed, he was preparing himself to impart wisdom and instructions that would shape his grandson's destiny—and the world at large. The Council of the Black Nobility had convened and unanimously chosen Eugenio, Marcantonio Pacelli's own flesh and blood, to undertake their mission. After five years of careful observation and scrutiny, they had concluded that Eugenio was the only suitable candidate within the vast Pacelli lineage capable of undertaking this prestigious and daunting task.

Eugenio watched as his grandfather stood tall and resolute by the fireplace, anticipation building within him over the words that would irrevocably alter the course of his life. The esteemed patriarch's prolonged silence only served to amplify the gravity of the moment.

Marcantonio turned slowly, his face etched with a seriousness that was impossible to ignore. "I trust you are aware of the long-standing tradition I conduct with every young man of the Pacelli lineage," he began.

"I do, Grandfather," Eugenio responded, his voice steady despite the anticipation coursing through his veins.

"I must tell you, Eugenio, that the conversation we are about to have is unlike any I've had with your predecessors," Marcantonio continued, his gaze unwavering.

Eugenio remained silent, his posture rigid as he braced himself for the unprecedented revelation.

"The Council has reached a definitive decision. One that I had a significant hand in shaping." Marcantonio paused, ensuring that Eugenio was fully engaged in the moment. "It is a great honor that this commission has been chosen from our bloodline."

Eugenio held his breath, hanging onto his grandfather's every word, his heart pounding in his chest.

"Eugenio, it is with immense pride that I announce the Council has chosen you for the path to the papacy," Marcantonio Pacelli declared.

The boy was taken aback. He was at a loss for words, unable to formulate a response. He could see the pride radiating from his grandfather at this supreme appointment.

Eugenio was well aware of his grandfather's unwavering dedication to the Vatican, a commitment that spanned decades, long before Eugenio was even born. Marcantonio had been part of the entourage that accompanied Pope Pius IX into exile, serving as a political consultant and lawyer, managing Vatican affairs from a distance. The Black Nobility, recognizing the severity of this exile, decided that a new leader in Rome was needed. The Vatican's financial stability was hanging by a thread, and without immediate intervention, the Holy See risked losing its independence and falling under Italian rule once again. The fate of the Vatican now rested upon the shoulders of Marcantonio Pacelli's grandson.

Eugenio bowed his head and closed his eyes. "As it shall be, Grandfather."

Marcantonio exhaled a sigh of relief upon hearing his grandson's words. He had been certain of Eugenio's loyalty and admiration for him, and was confident the boy would accept his destiny—however, he'd needed to hear that acceptance from Eugenio himself.

Marcantonio was filled with a sense of satisfaction knowing he could relay to the Council their chosen one had willingly accepted the monumental task. The Council had meticulously crafted a timeline for Eugenio's ascension to the papacy, a path that would secure the Vatican's financial stability for generations to come.

Over the course of the next hour, patriarch and grandson delved into the intricate plans and strategies the Council had devised for the boy's future. As their meeting neared its conclusion, Marcantonio ambled towards the fireplace, his eyes fixed on a package lying on the mantel. It was wrapped in nondescript brown paper.

"This tome was unearthed in the far reaches of the Orient and recently translated into our native tongue. I want you to have it," he said, crossing the room to hand the gift to Eugenio.

With careful hands, Eugenio unwrapped the package, revealing a copy of *The Art of War* by Sun Tzu. The book was an oddity, its cover adorned with Chinese characters and its contents filled with ancient wisdom about warfare. Eugenio was intrigued yet puzzled as to the relevance of such a book.

"This book will serve as a guide for the mission the Council has entrusted to you. I want you to read it, study it, understand its teachings," Marcantonio instructed, his gaze intense, ensuring his grandson grasped the importance of his words.

Eugenio met his grandfather's gaze. "I will. Thank you, Grandfather," he said, rising to his feet to shake the hand of the esteemed patriarch. He'd remembered Francesco's advice to conclude the meeting with a handshake, resisting his natural inclination to embrace the beloved man who had just entrusted him with such a significant responsibility.

"I shall leave you to your thoughts now," Marcantonio declared, his footsteps echoing ominously as he moved towards the office door. He paused, casting a final glance over his shoulder at his grandson. "I will inform the Council of your decision, Eugenio."

The use of his birth name, rather than the usual affectionate "nipote", sent a shiver down Eugenio's spine. It was a clear indication of his transition from boyhood to manhood, a rite of passage that placed him on par with his older brother and cousins. He was no longer just a grandson; he was a man, a part of the elite group that held the fate of the Vatican in their hands.

As the door closed behind Marcantonio, Eugenio was left alone in the grand study. He would not emerge as his kin had prior, not yet—he was on a different path now. The weight of his choice pressed heavily upon his young shoulders. He knew the Council did not make such decisions lightly. This was a lifelong commitment, a path of servitude that would lead him into the priesthood, into the heart of the Vatican, and into the intricate web of the Black Nobility.

In his hands he held the book his grandfather had given him—*The Art of War*. A strange gift from the Orient. Its significance was lost on him. What did war have to do with priesthood, with the papacy? Confusion swirled in his mind, but he trusted in his grandfather's wisdom, in the guidance that had led him to this pivotal moment in his life.

With a deep breath, he opened the book, his eyes scanning the first page as he began to read.

The Art of War

Warfare is the greatest affair of state, the basis of life and death, the Tao for survival or extinction. It must be thoroughly pondered and analyzed. Therefore, structure it according to the following five factors, comparatively evaluate it through estimation, and seek out its true nature. The first is termed the Tao, the second Heaven, the third Earth, the fourth generals, and the fifth the laws for military organization and discipline.

Warfare is the greatest affair of state? The opening sentence left Eugenio in a state of bewilderment. What possible connection could there be between the brutalities of war and the sanctity of the papacy? With a sense of trepidation and curiosity, he turned the page, delving deeper into the enigmatic text.

Warfare is the Tao of deception. Thus:

- Although you are capable, display incapability.
- When committed to employing your forces, feign inactivity.
- When your objective is nearby, make it appear distant.
- When your objective is far away, make it appear nearby.
- Display profits and entice them.
- Create disorder and take them.
- If they are substantial, prepare for them.
- If they are angry, perturb them.
- Be deferential to foster their arrogance.
- If they are rested, force them to exert themselves.
- If they are united, cause them to be separated.
- Attack where they are unprepared. Go forth where they will not expect it.

These are the ways military strategists are victorious. They cannot be spoken of in advance.

Eugenio found himself grappling with the enormity of the plans the Black Nobility had meticulously crafted for him. The certainty of his ascent to the papacy, as chosen by the Council, was the only clear aspect in this whirlwind of information. He had unwavering faith in his grandfather, a man of wisdom and experience who had served the Vatican in various capacities, including Under Secretary in the Papal Ministry of Finance and

Secretary of the Interior. Eugenio was confident his grandfather would never steer him onto a path that wasn't in the best interests of the Pacelli family, the Black Nobility, or Eugenio himself. He was ready to embrace his destiny with honor, guided by the wisdom of his revered grandfather and the Council of the Black Nobility.

Closing the book, he rose from his seat, a newfound sense of purpose radiating from him. He exited the study, his stride full of pride and determination. While he couldn't fully grasp every detail of the intricate path that had been laid out for him, he was committed to following his elders' guidance with unwavering discipline and diligence.

Eugenio Maria Giuseppe Giovanni Pacelli was certain of his destiny. He would be pope.

Chapter 12

March 6, 2000
Monday, 6 p.m.
Rome, Italy

Mario approached the imposing double doors of Roberto's palatial mansion, his eyes widening in awe at their magnificence. They never failed to impress him. He gently pushed open a door and poked his head inside the opulent foyer. "Berto, are you in?"

"I'm in the kitchen," came the distant reply.

As Mario ventured further into the house, the tantalizing aroma of garlic sautéing in butter, the earthy scent of mushrooms, and the rich, hearty smell of sausage and ground beef wafted through the air. Taken with the subtle hint of pasta boiling in the background, it made for an olfactory symphony that caused his stomach rumble in anticipation. He hadn't intended to stay for dinner, but with every step the heavenly smells were becoming increasingly difficult to resist—provided there wasn't a lady guest already being entertained.

Mario often marveled at the paradox that was Roberto—a man who cooked like an angel but lived a life that was anything but angelic. He held onto the hope that with enough gentle persuasion, he could steer his best friend away from his hedonistic lifestyle. Roberto was a man of immense potential, but he seemed to prefer the pleasures of the flesh. And who could blame him? With his wealth and leisure, why not indulge in the finer things in life—wine, women, and song?

Rounding the corner into the exquisitely designed kitchen, Mario was greeted by the familiar sight of the sprawling seven-foot-by-twelve-foot island, its white Carrara-marble top streaked with black veins littered with the remnants of dinner preparation.

Roberto stood in front of his commercial-sized refrigerator retrieving a bottle of Perrier. "It's like you have a sixth sense when I'm making one of my signature dishes," he quipped, handing the bottle to Mario.

"I was hoping you weren't entertaining tonight."

"Everything okay?"

"Um, yeah. Hey, would you mind if I stayed for dinner?"

"For you, anything," Roberto replied, turning back to the six-burner stove to stir the simmering sauce. "What brings you out to my neck of the woods?"

"Can we check out some stuff on the internet?"

"Ah, the pasta's done. Sure, but can we look after we eat?" Roberto suggested, the aroma of the cooked pasta wafting through the air. "I research better on a full stomach."

"Good idea. I'd rather search on a full stomach too," Mario agreed, his stomach growling in anticipation. "I'll set the table while you dish out the food."

Seated at the robust oak table, on chairs fit for royalty, the pair indulged in another of Roberto's culinary masterpieces: spaghetti. After numerous visits to trattorias, bistros, and ristorantes across Rome, Roberto had been unable to find a spaghetti dish that satisfied his desire. Frustrated, he decided to create it himself. After several trials with fresh local ingredients sourced from farmers' markets and butchers, he finally concocted the perfect spaghetti sauce. Everyone who tasted his signature dish was enamored by it—especially Mario, who had a particular fondness for spaghetti.

"What's bothering you, bro?" Roberto asked, noticing Mario's distracted demeanor.

Mario paused, savoring the mouthful of spaghetti before swallowing, then said, "This spaghetti is incredible."

"Thank you," Roberto responded, noting Mario's evasion. "But you're avoiding my question. What's troubling you?"

"Do you remember the mysterious brown package I mentioned last week?"

"Of course, but I wasn't going to bring it up. You got your panties all in a wad last time."

"I opened it," Mario admitted sheepishly, a wave of shame washing over him for his indiscretion.

"No way!" Roberto's eyebrows shot up in surprise. His friend was not one to break rules. "Whatcha find?"

"A journal. A beautiful one, with a leather cover adorned with artwork the likes of which I've never seen before. It's truly remarkable. You should see it, Roberto."

"Forget the artwork—what was on the inside?" Roberto asked, his hand gesturing impatiently for Mario to get to the crux of the matter.

"I read an entry about Adolf Hitler and a man named Hess."

"*Rudolf* Hess?" Roberto asked, his interest intensifying.

"Yes, that's right. The entry mentioned both of them being in prison."

"Incredible. A journal talking about Hitler and Hess. What else did you find?" Roberto asked, his eyes wide with intrigue.

"I got scared and put it back," Mario admitted, his voice shaky.

"Scared? By a journal? How does a journal scare you?"

"There was a warning written on the inside of the wrapping paper. It said 'Beware! Do not read! You'll be in danger!' or something like that."

"It's just an old journal, Mario. That warning probably doesn't mean anything," Roberto said dismissively. His hand drifted towards his wine glass to indulge in a generous gulp; his initial enthusiasm was clearly waning.

"The warning was signed with the initials 'GAB'," Mario revealed, his voice laced with intrigue.

"And?" That tidbit alone did not pique Roberto's interest.

"The priest who served in the Vatican Secret Archives before me shared those very initials."

"What was his name again?"

"Giuseppe Alphonso Benedetti. GAB."

"Perhaps it's a coincidence," Roberto suggested, setting down his wine glass and reclining in his chair. Despite his casual motions, there was a sense of foreboding creeping over him. He had a hunch this journal held more secrets than Mario was letting on. "What else did you uncover in your reading?"

"I read the first entry, dating back to 1888. The author spoke of a meeting with his grandfather and being designated as a successor in line for the papacy."

"Ah ha," Roberto exclaimed, pointing an accusatory finger at Mario. "So, the popes *are* handpicked, not democratically elected." He mused over this revelation, a conspiracy theory brewing in his mind. "Even within the sacred walls of the Vatican, it's about who you know, not what you know." He took another sip of his Chianti, his mind racing. "And to whom does this alleged future pope's journal belong to?"

"I don't know. That's why I came over to research it with you."

"Then let's go. I gotta know who this dude is." Roberto gathered his plate and wine glass and swiftly headed towards the kitchen.

"Alright, alright. Let me finish up here." Mario consumed the remainder of the delicious dish faster than he would have liked.

By the time Mario joined him, Roberto was already seated at his desk, ready to search deeper into the mystery.

"Search 'Eugenio Pacelli'," Mario instructed.

Roberto inputted the search query into dogpile.com, and a plethora of search results flooded the screen:

Eugenio Maria Giuseppe Giovanni Pacelli, better known as Pope Pius XII, held the esteemed position of the head of the Catholic Church and the sovereign of the Vatican City State from 2 March 1939 until his death in October 1958. Prior to his ascension to the papacy, Pacelli held several significant roles within the Church:

1) secretary of the Department of Extraordinary Ecclesiastical Affairs, a role that saw him involved in the Church's most pressing matters;

2) Papal nuncio to Germany, acting as the diplomatic representative of the Holy See to the German State right after World War I;

3) In his capacity as the Cardinal Secretary of State, Pacelli worked tirelessly to conclude treaties with various European and Latin American nations. Among these

> was the notable Reichskonkordat with the German Reich, a treaty that marked a significant moment in the Church's history.

"Fascinating. He got entangled in the Nazis' web," Roberto mused, his eyes reflecting a spark of intrigue.

Mario's brows furrowed in confusion at Roberto's statement. "Where'd you get that from?"

"'German Reich' is synonymous with the Nazis."

Mario fell into a stunned silence. This glaring piece of information had somehow been disregarded from the curriculum in seminary.

As Roberto's finger flicked the mouse wheel scrolling through a sea of related articles, his excitement grew palpable. "Hold on! Oh, we have to look at this one."

> **The Botched Embalming of Pope Pius XII:** In line with long-standing customs, the task of embalming Pope Pius XII fell to the papal physician, Riccardo Galeazzi-Lisi. Despite his prestigious position, Galeazzi-Lisi was notorious for his lack of medical competence. This deficiency was glaringly evident in his disastrous attempt at embalming the pope. As the funeral procession moved from Castel Gandolfo to Rome, the pope's body began to decompose in full view of the public. The spectacle was horrifying, with the pope's chest collapsing, his nose and fingers detaching, and his body taking on an alarming "emerald-green" hue.

"Oooooh, that is just disgusting," Roberto bellowed, his laughter coarse and unrefined as he cringed at the grotesque blunder.

"Truly nauseating," Mario grimaced, his face contorting as he visualized the cadaver decaying under the relentless gaze of the public.

Roberto clicked on more articles, his eyes darting across the screen, absorbing the information. "You're saying you found this guy's personal diary?"

"The diary supposedly belongs to that man there." Mario's finger tapped the name displayed on the monitor. "Eugenio Pacelli."

"There's something suspicious about this priest-slash-cardinal-slash-pope guy," Roberto surmised, suspicion creeping into his voice.

Despite the vast wealth of information available online today, there are certain limitations when it comes to accessing the Vatican Secret Archives. Specifically, documents dated post-1939 are generally off-limits to researchers. Additionally, a whole segment of the Secret Archives, which pertains to the personal matters of cardinals from 1922 and beyond, remains inaccessible.

"Well, isn't that just *convenient*." Roberto's tone dripped with skepticism. Any potentially damning evidence was safely locked away within the walls of the Vatican's formidable fortress, shielded from the public's prying eyes.

The Vatican, a colossal entity in Rome, cast an imposing shadow over the city's populace. It was as if the Holy See had its eyes on every move you made, whether in the public sphere or in the privacy of your own home. There was no escaping its omnipresence. Every Roman citizen could feel the Vatican's power, its influence seeping into their lives. The commandments were clear: Thou shalt not lie, steal, or cheat. Thou shalt not kill nor envy. Thou shalt not covet thy neighbor's wife. Thou shalt not pick thy nose. The fear of condemnation, the guilt instilled by the Vatican's all-seeing power, was a constant companion to the city's inhabitants.

Mario's discovery of this journal could potentially shatter the Vatican's image of purity. Roberto knew his friend was a stickler for rules, but could Mario, just for one night, dare defy the rules once again? The thought was thrilling yet filled with uncertainty.

"Do you think I could take a look at it?" Roberto ventured.

"Are you out of your mind? If I'm caught smuggling anything out of the Archives, I'll be more than out of a job—they could impose laicization!" Mario's voice was laced with both conviction and fear.

Roberto's confusion at the unfamiliar term was evident on his face.

"*Laicization.* It's when the authority strips me of my lawful position as a priest."

"Got it. Wasn't aware of that one," Roberto conceded, understanding that Mario was a man of unshakable loyalty to the Catholic Church. There was no breaking the iron grip the Church had on his best friend. He might not agree with it, but Roberto respected Mario's wishes that he not interfere with his faith and principles.

To defuse the tension, Roberto quickly scrolled down the search results, eager to uncover more information.

Eugenio Pacelli, who would later become Pope Pius XII, was born into a distinguished Roman family on March 2, 1876. The Pacelli family, part of the "Black Nobility", had a long-standing connection to the papacy. Marcantonio Pacelli, Eugenio's grandfather, held significant roles in the Papal Ministry of Finances and the Interior under Pope Pius IX, and was the founder of the Vatican's newspaper, *L'Osservatore Romano*, in 1861. Ernesto Pacelli, Eugenio's cousin, was a trusted financial advisor to Pope Leo XIII. Filippo Pacelli, Eugenio's father, was the dean of the Sacra Rota Romana, while Eugenio's brother, Francesco Pacelli, was a lay canon lawyer who played a crucial role in negotiating the Lateran Treaty in 1929, resolving the Roman Question. Despite the family's legal tradition, Eugenio, at the tender age of twelve, declared his intention to join the priesthood.

"See this guy, Marcantonio?" Mario said, pointing at the name glowing on the monitor. "He's the one who revealed to Eugenio on his twelfth birthday that he would ascend to the papacy."

"The pope, huh?" Roberto's interest rose as he rapidly skimmed through the entries. "Seems to align with this detail of him entering the priesthood at the tender age of twelve." His finger paused the mouse on the screen, highlighting a peculiar term. "And what is this 'Black Nobility'?"

The term "Black Nobility" refers to a group of Italian aristocratic families who remained loyal to the papacy during the reign of Pope Pius IX. This period was marked by significant political upheaval, as the Kingdom of Italy's army invaded Rome on September 20, 1870, effectively ending the Papal States and seizing control of the Apostolic Palace. In response to this, the pope retreated to Vatican City for the next 59 years, claiming to be a prisoner within the Vatican to avoid acknowledging the authority of the Italian government. Those aristocrats who had received their titles from the Holy See symbolically kept their doors closed in mourning of the pope's confinement. This act of solidarity earned them the moniker of the "Black Nobility".

Roberto's fingers flew over the keys, anxiously digging deeper into the vast expanse of the internet.

The Influence and Continuity of the Black Nobility in the Catholic Church: Numerous individuals from Black Nobility families, distinguished by their ancestral connections to the papacy, have ascended to prominent positions within the Church, including the papacy itself. Notable examples of such families that continue to exist today include Eugenio Pacelli, who ascended to the papacy as Pope Pius XII; Ernesto Pacelli, a significant financial figure; and Prospero Colonna, who served as a mayor of Rome.

"Eugenio Pacelli knew from age twelve he would become the pope because of his ties with this Black Nobility group.

Almost like the mafia where your life's path is chosen for you at a young age," Roberto summarized, his voice heavy with the weight of the revelation of Eugenio Pacelli's clandestine rise to the papacy.

Mario, sinking back into his chair, felt a wave of disbelief wash over him. His decision to join the priesthood had never been about power or status. His vocation was a commitment to serve God and mankind, utilizing his God-given talents and abilities in the most impactful way he could. This shocking revelation was a jarring contradiction to his deeply held beliefs and understanding of selfless service. He had always followed the teachings of the Church hierarchy, striving to be a faithful steward and servant of Jesus Christ. His convictions were firmly anchored in the teachings of the Catholic Church. Was there more going on behind the scenes he was completely oblivious to? How had he been so blind to this covert deception?

Roberto broke his train of thought. "You need to dig deeper into that journal."

Mario met Roberto's gaze with a determined look. "I'll get to it tomorrow."

Chapter 13

March 7, 2000
Tuesday, 8:23 a.m.
Vatican Secret Archives

With heightened anticipation, Mario activated the complex array of equipment, its hum filling the aisle with an electric tension. He stretched his arm up, reaching for the four ancient books that stood sentinel before the journal. With a sense of reverence, he placed the books on the worktable, their dust-laden covers whispering tales of forgotten lore.

His hand moved to the journal—its presence commanded his attention. He placed it beside the quartet of books, his gaze locked onto the papal stamped-wax seal. A sense of trepidation gripped him. The prospect of unearthing a truth that could shatter his belief in the Catholic Church was daunting.

The truth was a double-edged sword. On one side, the allure of knowledge was irresistible. On the other, the fear of irrevocable change felt paralyzing. Once seen, the eyes could not unsee. Once learned, the mind could not unlearn.

With a deep breath, he untied the twine, its coarse texture a stark contrast to the smooth brown paper it bound together. The moment of truth was upon him. He opened the book, revealing the next journal entry, a gateway to a world unknown.

8 September 1894

I started my theology studies at Almo Collegio Capranica this week.

Following the direction of the Council, I also enrolled at the La Sapienza State University to study language and history. Grandfather instructed that I will need to acquire extensive knowledge of languages and history for my mission.

There is much work required of me. However, I am honored to have been chosen.

I will not disappoint you, Grandfather. I will make you proud.

Eugenio Pacelli

21 June 1895

Latest instruction from the Council:

It is necessary I drop out of seminary to continue my studies from home. The Council says I need more focus under the tutelage of father and mother; they along with other tutors will help me complete my studies. I will graduate and be ordained a minister according to schedule.

This strategy follows the teachings in The Art of War:

Although you are capable, display incapability.

I have been preparing the professors and the dean for my departure by feigning intolerable stomach pain after eating the food in the cafeteria the past several weeks. They have given me a special dispensation to continue my studies from home.

Eugenio Pacelli

2 April 1899

I was ordained a priest today by Monsignor Romeo Cassetta. Romeo has been a family friend for a long time. I was honored to have him conduct the private Easter ceremony for my ordination with only my family in attendance.

The private ceremony is imperative to keep up the ruse of my special needs as spoken of in the The Art of War:

Although you are capable, display incapability.

I shall soon begin my postgraduate studies in canon law. I am honored to follow in Grandfather's footsteps; he too received his doctorate in canon law.

I will not disappoint you, Grandfather.

Father Eugenio Pacelli

8 June 1902

Grandfather died today. I am heartbroken.
He is the reason I am following this path.
I loved him so much, and now he is gone.
I will miss you.
I will not disappoint you.
I shall make you proud, Grandfather.

Father Eugenio Pacelli

Mario continued reading the newspaper clipping glued on the opposite page of Eugenio's journal:

OBITUARY

In loving memory of Marcantonio Pacelli who passed away peacefully on June 8, 1902, at the venerable age of 98. Born on April 15, 1804, in the picturesque town of Onan, Italy, he was the cherished son of Gaetano Pacelli and Maria Antonia Caterini.

Marcantonio Pacelli was educated in Rome, Italy and received a doctorate in canon law in 1824. Pacelli was a valuable advisor to Pope Pius IX. His dedication to the pope helped ensure the careers of his children and grandchildren.

On 24 November 1848, Marcantonio Pacelli accompanied Pope Pius IX to Gaeta, as part of the pope's entourage in exile. During this period, Marcantonio Pacelli served as a political consultant and lawyer for the management of Vatican business from afar.

In 1851, Marcantonio Pacelli was appointed the Deputy Minister of the Interior for Vatican City. He held this venerable position until 1870.

In 1861, Marcantonio Pacelli initiated the publication of the Vatican's newspaper, *L'Osservatore Romano*.

As we mourn the loss of Marcantonio, we also celebrate a life well-lived. His memory will forever be etched in our hearts, and his spirit will continue to guide us. Your journey on earth may have ended, but your legacy will live on forever.

Marcantonio Pacelli was a loving husband, father, and grandfather to his wonderful family. He is survived by four sons and two daughters: Ernesto, Filippo, Teresa, Giuseppe, Vincenzo, and Mary Rose.

1 June 1917

The Black Nobility maneuvered my promotion through the Vatican with stunning swiftness, influencing the pope to elevate my position to Apostolic Nuncio of Bavaria. Pope Benedict XV consecrated me as cardinal in the Sistine Chapel two weeks ago. Without delay, I departed for Munich to fulfill my duties as the Vatican's ambassador to Bavaria.

There is no other Vatican representation in Germany due to all the turmoil surrounding the Great War.

I met with King Ludwig III and Kaiser Wilhelm II. Both received my appointment from Pope Benedict XV positively. I will build relationships with both for I will require favors of them in the future. This will advance the Black Nobility's directive to expand my influence in Munich.

Cardinal Eugenio Pacelli

27 September 1919

Adolf Hitler called on me unannounced last night. General Ludendorff instructed him to come seek my council and guidance. The general knows very well my loathing for Communism and attacks on the Catholic Church.

Hitler will be the perfect pupil for the Council's plan. I will entice him with his lust to fulfill his utmost desires, guiding him to rule over the entire German Empire.

Before sending Hitler on his way, I gave him a large cache of money. Enough to fund his early revolution and support his efforts to gain notoriety in Munich.

Cardinal Eugenio Pacelli

Chapter 14

26 September 1919
Munich, Germany

"Your Excellency, thank you for meeting with me at this ungodly hour," Adolf Hitler began, his voice meandering with a humble reverence. In his hands he held a letter written by none other than General Ludendorff himself. He extended the letter towards the cardinal, a silent request for him to review its contents.

Pacelli accepted the letter, his eyes scanning the words with an intensity that reflected his anticipation of the general's commendation. Once he had read the contents, he gestured for Hitler to follow him towards the library where they could speak privately, without fear of interruption.

"Your general speaks highly of you, Herr Hitler," Pacelli began, his voice echoing in the quiet room. "What is it you seek from me?"

"Germany is under siege, Your Excellency," Hitler replied, his voice heavy with concern. "The Communists are gaining ground."

"I am aware of their expansion," Pacelli responded, his tone reflecting his loathing for the ideology that threatened Germany. "They are making their presence felt here in Munich and Berlin."

"That is why I am here, Your Excellency," Hitler continued, his gaze steady on the cardinal. "General Ludendorff believes you can help."

A slow smile spread across Pacelli's face as he realized the potential that lay before him. "Then it seems we may be able to help each other," he mused, his mind already spinning with possibilities.

"How might that be?"

"I am in the process of devising a grand strategy, a plan of such magnitude that it will eradicate communism from Germany," Pacelli revealed, his eyes gleaming with determination. "And I believe, Herr Hitler, you could be the leader who will bring this plan to fruition."

Hitler, his body taut with anticipation, leaned in, his eyes gleaming with the prospect of hearing the cardinal's grand scheme. He harbored grandiose dreams of leading Germany out of the shadows and into the glory it rightfully deserved. The global community's relentless persecution of Germany, holding it solely accountable for the atrocities of the Great War, was a grotesque display of injustice and cruelty. That his fellow Germans were being driven to the brink of starvation was a cruel and inhumane act. Hadn't the Geneva Conventions been established to prevent such atrocities, safeguarding citizens of the world's nations from such torment?

"I have the necessary connections to elevate you to the position of Chancellor of Germany," Pacelli revealed, his voice barely audible. To expose this confidential information was to take a great risk—this secret, if leaked, would jeopardize the Council's mission were Hitler to betray him. "But you must understand, this is not something that can be accomplished overnight. It demands time and patience."

A smile of satisfaction spread across Hitler's face at the prospect of such a future. But then, doubt crept in. "But how can this be? President Von Hindenburg will never allow it, Your Excellency."

"This will be a process that spans decades, my friend. Rome wasn't built in a day," Pacelli explained, his voice steady and reassuring.

"You're right. You have higher powers than I could ever imagine. Please, share your vision with me."

"I need your absolute assurance that our discussions will remain confidential. Can I trust you, Adolf?" Pacelli's gaze bore into Hitler, searching for any signs of deceit. He needed to be certain that Hitler was the right man to execute the Council of the Black Nobility's grand plan.

"You have my unwavering loyalty, Your Excellency."

"Excellent, my son. Now, let me share our vision with you."

Hitler, in his naivety, believed that "our vision" referred solely to the shared aspirations of himself and the cardinal. Little did he know it implied a grander scheme, a master plan conceived by the Black Nobility. The Council's aim was to bolster the Vatican's financial reserves, and they planned to use Germany as the primary instrument to achieve this monumental task.

"As I mentioned earlier, Adolf," Pacelli began, his voice steady and resolute, "this is not a task that can be accomplished overnight. It will require decades of meticulous planning and unwavering commitment. Are you prepared to dedicate yourself to the cause?"

"Again, I give you my solemn word, Your Excellency," Hitler responded, his voice echoing his determination.

"Excellent," Pacelli replied, his gaze scrutinizing Hitler, gauging his reaction to the daunting timeline. He was reassured when he saw the man, the decorated soldier, listening attentively, unfazed by the prospect of a decades-long commitment. "We both know who was responsible for Germany's defeat in the Great War."

"The Jews." Hitler spat out the word with substantial disdain.

"Indeed. The Jews betrayed Germany, driven by their insatiable greed. They sought profits at any cost, and now the entire nation of Germany is paying the price—a staggering one hundred thirty-two billion gold marks."

Hitler's eyes darkened with memories from the front lines. "I've seen the horrors of war firsthand. Those money-grubbing traitors will never comprehend the sacrifices we made, the atrocities we endured. They have never set foot on the battlefield, never experienced the camaraderie of the trenches." Hitler's voice was laced with bitterness and longing. He yearned for the unity he'd experienced with his fellow soldiers, the respect he had earned for his bravery. His act of valor—dragging a wounded comrade to safety—had earned him the Iron Cross and the admiration of his peers. He yearned to feel that bond again.

"There's already a simmering undercurrent of anti-Semitism in Munich and Berlin," Pacelli noted, steering the conversation back on track.

"Yes, I've heard the whispers in the beer halls. I attended a meeting a few weeks ago led by an anti-Semite. His views mirror my own," Hitler admitted, referring to a recent gathering of the German Workers Party. "The war reparations are bleeding us dry. The people know who's to blame—the Jews. Those damned traitors," Hitler spat again in contempt.

"It's high time the Jews made amends to the German people for the atrocities they inflicted upon them."

"But how can that be achieved?" Hitler questioned, his brow furrowed in thought. "The Jews won't willingly part with their ill-gotten wealth. Have you ever tried to pry a pfennig from a Jew's hand? They haggle over every last cent."

Hitler, despite his cunning, had always found himself outmaneuvered by astute Jewish businessmen, never managing to secure the upper hand in any deal. The thought of retribution consumed him. He was prepared to go to any lengths to finally triumph over the influential Jewish community who seemed to have it all—the grandest estates, thriving businesses, powerful connections, and most enviable of all, the finest art collections. Hitler coveted their art, yearned to be part of this exclusive circle, but was always kept at arm's length, his non-Jewish heritage a barrier he couldn't overcome. The prospect of turning the tables, of holding the reins of power, was an intoxicating thought.

"The winds of change are on the horizon, I assure you. But first, I need your unwavering loyalty. Can I trust you with this mission?" the cardinal confirmed a third time.

"I am at your disposal, Your Excellency."

Hitler's thoughts drifted back to his days in the war. He had learned the value of obedience, of following orders from his superiors while serving as an infantryman during the Battle of Ypres. This brutal conflict had claimed the lives of 80 percent of his comrades, reducing his company of two hundred fifty men to a mere forty-two. Despite the devastating losses, Hitler's loyalty to his leaders remained unshaken.

"What do you need me to do?"

"Keep your eyes open for any opportunity to make your mark within this Workers Party group. This could be the first stepping stone to you becoming the leader of the Third Reich."

This new political phrase resonated with Hitler, stirring a sense of pride and ambition within him. "Leader of the Third Reich," he repeated, sitting up straighter as he envisioned the prestige that came with it. "Germany will rise to greatness once again."

Hitler had always held the Germanic people in the highest esteem; their strength and resilience resonated deeply within him. To lead them, to become their beacon in the storm, was the apex of his aspirations. Born an Austrian, he had always felt like an outsider, a spectator peering in through a frosted window. It was only when he enlisted in the German army, fighting shoulder to shoulder with his German brethren in the Great War, that he felt a profound sense of belonging. But then a tragic incident: a British gas shell temporarily blinded him, leaving him confined to a hospital bed until the war's bitter end. Isolated there, Hitler became convinced that the German government had betrayed him, his comrades, the entire nation. And beneath this conviction, a deeper truth gnawed at him—it was the Jews who had truly betrayed them all.

"I will summon you for another meeting," Pacelli declared, his tone grave. "It is of utmost importance that our discussions regarding this divine mission remain strictly between us. Can I count on your unwavering commitment and loyalty?" he repeated a fourth time, cementing Hitler's allegiance.

"You have my loyalty, Your Excellency."

"To initiate your mission, you will require financial support." Pacelli rose from his seat and strode towards a large painting hanging on the wall. With a swift movement, he swung the painting aside, revealing a hidden safe. He deftly manipulated the tumbler, and the safe door swung open to reveal a substantial cache of Church funds stored within. This money, destined to fuel Hitler's burgeoning revolution, would forever bind him to the cardinal.

A smile spread across Hitler's face as he realized the magnitude of the opportunity lying before him. His meeting with the cardinal had not only secured the funding he needed to pursue his ambitious path, but had also opened the door to a future he had only dared dream of—becoming the leader of Germany.

As the clock chimed 2 a.m., Pacelli subtly gestured to Hitler, a silent indication that their clandestine meeting had reached its conclusion.

"You must go. Be swift and silent. It is of utmost importance no one ever learns this meeting took place," Cardinal Pacelli whispered, leading the way towards the library's exit. Hitler rose from his seat, following the cardinal in a hushed manner. "Our conversation tonight must never be spoken of. Do you understand?" Pacelli cautioned, pressing a finger to his lips in the universal sign of silence.

Hitler responded with a silent nod, understanding the gravity of their secret rendezvous as they exited the library.

Upon reaching the front door, Pacelli handed him the bag filled with money. His eyes darted toward the shadows, a subtle warning to Hitler that they were not alone.

The household was deep in slumber, oblivious to the clandestine meeting taking place. The only exception was Pacelli's devoted aide, Sister Pascalina, who remained vigilantly awake. Her constant worry for the cardinal's health often led the nun to wake at odd hours of the night, checking on Pacelli's wellbeing.

"Go, quell the devil's works. Help spread the love of Almighty God." Pacelli gave Hitler a look, his words a cryptic directive for Hitler to follow suit. His gaze was intense, a silent command that left no room for misinterpretation.

Quick to comprehend, Hitler cast a glance over the cardinal's shoulder, his eyes catching sight of a shadowy figure concealed in the darkness. "For the love of Almighty God," he echoed, before turning to leave the residence of the Nuncio of Germany, eagerly anticipating his next orders.

Pacelli would need to be more cautious in the future, ensuring his discussions with Hitler remained confidential. The grand mission of the Black Nobility could not be exposed, not even to his loyal aide. Despite her decade-long loyalty to him, he did not want Sister Pascalina entangled in the mission entrusted to him by the Council.

Closing the front door behind him, Pacelli retreated to his library and sank into the comfort of his high-back leather chair. His mind began to weave the intricate web of his next moves with the young revolutionary who had serendipitously fallen into his lap. Eugenio's progression of the mission would undoubtedly bring a smile to his brother's face.

Chapter 15

28 September 1919
Sunday, 7:03 a.m.

In the secrecy of his private quarters, Cardinal Eugenio Pacelli initiated a secure line of communication with his brother, Francesco Pacelli. His heart pounded with an intensity that echoed the gravity of the situation. The secure phone line was his only connection to his brother; he dared not put their communications in writing. The conversation that was about to take place had the potential to change everything. Eugenio's voice, a low murmur, echoed through the line:

Cardinal Eugenio Pacelli:
    "Brother, I believe I have found the man who could act as the linchpin for the Council's grand scheme."

Francesco Pacelli:
    "Excellent work. Who is this person?"

Cardinal Eugenio Pacelli:
    "An Austrian. A man by the name of Adolf Hitler."

Francesco Pacelli:
    "An *Austrian*? How could he possibly lead the German people?"

Cardinal Eugenio Pacelli:
"He has proven his allegiance in the German military. His superior officer brought him to my attention. Hitler's fervor for the German people is nothing short of extraordinary."

Francesco Pacelli:
"What are his ambitions? He will need an immutable drive to endure the inevitable hardships."

Cardinal Eugenio Pacelli:
"He harbors a profound aspiration to become a celebrated artist."

Francesco Pacelli:
"An *artist*?"

Cardinal Eugenio Pacelli:
"He has expressed his deep disappointment in not being accepted into the Vienna art school on multiple occasions. Art seems to be his ultimate passion, above all else."

Francesco Pacelli:
"Then we must lure him with a grand vision that will sustain him as he ascends to power in Germany."

Cardinal Eugenio Pacelli:
"I've just had a remarkable thought: Hitler could construct the largest museum in Germany, surpassing the grandeur of the Louvre, the British Museum, even the Smithsonian."

Francesco Pacelli:

"A splendid idea, brother. Present this to Hitler at your next encounter. I will relay this information to the Council and keep you updated with further directives."

Cardinal Eugenio Pacelli:

"Agreed, brother. Excellent."

Francesco Pacelli:

"The Council and I are also working with a potential leader here in Italy. A Fascist by the name of Mussolini. I will keep you informed of any new developments."

Cardinal Eugenio Pacelli:

"A Fascist?"

Francesco Pacelli:

"The Council is exploring every possible avenue."

Cardinal Eugenio Pacelli:

"I will continue my work with Adolf. I am convinced he is the one."

Francesco Pacelli:

"Well done, Eugenio."

Cardinal Eugenio Pacelli:

"Thank you, brother. You as well."

Chapter 16

13 December 1919
Munich, Germany

In the confines of the cardinal's library in Munich, a private meeting was taking place. Pacelli leaned forward, his voice a low murmur. "Adolf, your leadership skills have not gone unnoticed. They are truly remarkable."

Hitler, standing tall and imposing, said, "Anton Drexler has been a great ally. His trust in me has led to my appointment as Party Speaker of the National Socialist German Workers' Party."

Pacelli nodded, his gaze steady on Hitler. "Your unwavering loyalty and adherence to directives have caught not only my attention but also that of my esteemed Council."

Hitler's eyes gleamed with a sense of accomplishment. "Your guidance has been instrumental. The transformation from the old German Workers' Party to the NSDAP has given us a distinct identity. The unanimous acceptance of our new flag has elevated my status within our party." He moved to take a seat in the cardinal's library. The air was heavy with anticipation.

Pacelli said, "To make a global impact, you require a symbol that will instill terror in the hearts of the people. The Swastika on the Nazi flag will serve as that symbol."

Hitler's gaze bore into the cardinal. "The flag is indeed a sight to behold. Its blood-red background is a powerful symbol."

The room fell silent as both men thought dark thoughts.

"To aid the continuance of your mission, I am assembling a formidable team of leaders for you." Pacelli's eyes gleamed with a fierce determination. "They will be your loyal subjects as we strive to restore Germany to its rightful place on the world stage. Are you with me?"

Hitler's gaze, steady and resolute, bowed his head in deference. "You have my unyielding loyalty, Your Excellency."

Pacelli continued, his voice a low, commanding rumble. "I am assigning you an aide-de-camp, a trusted confidant who will shadow every step of your ascension within the Third Reich, Adolf. Through him, I will relay my directives. Do you understand?"

"I understand, Your Excellency," Hitler affirmed, his voice steady.

Pacelli extended a piece of paper towards him. "Here are the names of the individuals I am enlisting on your behalf."

Hitler's eyes scanned the paper. He read out the first name. "Rudolf Hess."

"Hess will be our primary liaison. He will be the conduit through which I relay my directives. He will be your steadfast companion, always by your side throughout your rise to power."

"Hermann Göring," Hitler continued, his eyes flicking to the next name.

"Göring will be the commander of your Luftwaffe," Pacelli declared, his voice unwavering.

"But the Treaty of Versailles forbids Germany from having an air fleet," Hitler interjected.

"Göring will build the Luftwaffe in secret. The world does not need to be privy to the resurgence of the German Air Force," Pacelli retorted, a sly smile playing on his lips.

"Heinrich Himmler," Hitler said, moving on to the next name.

"Himmler will command your police force. The current SA are nothing more than rabble-rousers." Pacelli's voice dripped with disdain for the current Sturmabteilung Brownshirts. These stormtroopers were reckless, unfit to serve the grand vision of the Black Nobility. "Your leadership is far too crucial to be associated with those ruffians."

"Reinhard Heydrich."

"Heydrich will serve under Himmler and be tasked with rounding up any dissenters. Anyone who dares defy your mission will be rounded up and incarcerated. No exceptions."

"This is an impressive roster, Your Excellency."

"Only the finest for your rise to power within the Third Reich," Pacelli concluded.

With a sense of profound confidence, Hitler carefully folded the letter and tucked it securely inside his shirt pocket as if it were a priceless artifact. This was no ordinary list—it was a meticulous roster of allies handpicked by the cardinal himself. It was far too valuable to be misplaced.

"Adolf." Pacelli's voice sliced through the silence, a stern command wrapped in a velvety tone. "There must never be any evidence of our private meetings. Do you understand?"

"Yes, Your Excellency," Hitler responded, his voice echoing the solemnity of Pacelli's.

"Commit those names on the list to memory, then destroy it," Pacelli decreed. This would set a precedent the two men would continue throughout all their future communications, and would also become the unspoken rule for the entire Nazi Party: obliterate any and all incriminating evidence, no matter what.

With a nod of understanding, Hitler took out the list. His eyes scanned over the names one final time, etching each into memory. Then, ever the obedient soldier, he strode over to

Pacelli's grand oak desk, his hand reaching for the gold lighter adorned with an embossed cross. The lighter sparked to life with a flick of his thumb. He held the list to the flame and watched as it consumed the paper, reducing it to ashes that fell neatly into a metal trash can.

"Remember this, Adolf," Pacelli's said, his voice low and urgent. "Our communication must always remain a secret. Any leak could jeopardize your ascension to power. You wouldn't want that to happen, would you?"

"No, Your Excellency," Hitler replied, his voice firm.

Pacelli's insistence on secrecy was not merely to safeguard Hitler's reputation; it was a shield to protect himself and the Vatican from any potential fallout resulting from the rising Nazi leader's actions. There would be no evidence, no trace of the machinations that were set in motion. Never.

"I will be in contact with you soon," Pacelli intoned, a clear signal that their meeting had reached its end.

With a final bow, Hitler exited the library, leaving behind the smoldering remnants of the list and the weight of the secrets it once held.

Chapter 17

22 November 1919

Francesco, my dear brother, has been counseling the Fascist in Rome. The Council is carefully evaluating both Hitler and Mussolini to see who will spearhead their mission.

Mussolini appears to have great attributes, but I believe Hitler will become the ultimate leader. He possesses the great oratory skills necessary to lead both Germany and Italy combined.

Yet collaboration between Hitler and Mussolini would result in a formidable force that could reshape the world as we know it.

I will continue with the Council's plan to shape Hitler's path to power.

Cardinal Eugenio Pacelli

Chapter 18

17 November 1919
Rome, Italy

In the grand, intricately decorated halls of the Vatican, where the administrative heart of the Holy See beats, the office of legal affairs was the stage for a duel of titans. The highly respected Francesco Pacelli, the Vatican's unwavering legal advisor, found himself locked in a gripping battle of words with the fiery Fascist, Benito Mussolini. The Council, with their profound wisdom and strategic vision, had entrusted him with the daunting task of transforming the passionate Italian nationalist into a formidable contender for their clandestine mission.

"Do not let this electoral setback cloud your vision, signor," Francesco said, attempting to soothe the storm brewing within Mussolini.

"But this was to be my triumphant moment, counselor!" Mussolini's voice filled with rage at the counselor's indifference. Francesco had foreseen a victory for Mussolini in the Italian Parliament, but the votes had cruelly betrayed their expectations.

"Patience, signor. As the Good Book teaches us, patience is a virtue," Francesco reminded him, his voice steady and calm. Under his guidance, Mussolini had founded the Italian Fascists of Combat earlier that year, a strategic move in line with the Council's grand plan. This newborn party was the ideal weapon for the Black Nobility's aim to disrupt the status quo, especially in the wake of World War I, with Italy teetering on the brink of chaos and desperately seeking a leader.

"I fail to see how this defeat can be acceptable to you, counselor," Mussolini challenged, his anger unabated.

"This setback is but a minor obstacle in our grand design, Benito. We have allies in high places, and a myriad of strategies at our disposal," Francesco reassured him, his tone firm.

"Why weren't these strategies employed for this election, counselor?" Mussolini's voice laden with contempt, his eyes narrowing suspiciously questioning the credibility of the counselor's network.

"Sometimes, one must lose a battle to ultimately win the war. You understand this analogy, don't you?" Francesco rebuking the Fascist, his gaze penetrating and unrelenting.

Mussolini found himself at that moment in deep introspection, pondering his fate under the guidance of the esteemed Vatican counselor.

The room was thick with tension, the silence deafening. Francesco allowed the Fascist time to make a final decision: embrace the Council's grand plan or forsake his destiny.

"I trust you have a plan to ensure my success," Mussolini finally conceded, rising to leave the counselor's office. His faith in Francesco was evident, despite the recent setback.

These confidential meetings with the young Italian rebel were bearing significant results. Challenging the Fascists was not only cementing, but fortifying his allegiance to the Vatican counselor. Mussolini was shaping up to be the leader the Black Nobility sought. The Council's plans were unfolding precisely as they had envisioned.

Chapter 19

15 February 1920

The Art of War
All warfare is based on deception.
Appear strong when you are weak.

Hitler has ascended the ranks of the Nazi Party.

Anton Drexler, captivated by Hitler's oratory skills, has appointed Hitler as the main speaker at every meeting. Each meeting is electric with anticipation and thick with promise.

Cardinal Eugenio Pacelli

28 February 1920

Hitler organized the largest meeting in Nazi Party's history, with over 2,000 people in attendance. He is gaining notoriety within Munich among the locals.

As I instructed, Hitler has announced the 25-point Programme that the Council prepared. This programme will give hope to the German people and induce them to rise out of the hardships imposed by the Treaty of Versailles.

The German people are looking for a leader. Hitler will be their leader, their savior, their Führer.

Cardinal Eugenio Pacelli

Chapter 20

24 February 1920
Staatliches Hofbräuhaus
Munich, Germany

I n the heart of Munich, a city steeped in history and culture, an event of unprecedented magnitude was unfolding. Hitler, the rising star of the Nazi Party, had orchestrated a gathering that was nothing short of colossal. Over 2,000 citizens, their blood pumping in anticipation, filled the hall to its brim, their eyes fixed on the charismatic figure at the podium.

His name, once a mere whisper in the city's bustling beer halls, was now on the lips of every citizen, reverberating throughout the cobblestone streets of Munich. His fiery speeches and magnetic persona were drawing the locals towards him like moths to a flame. He was not just a leader, but a savior. The stage was set, the pieces moving; the future of Germany was about to be irrevocably altered.

Before the large gathering, Hitler unveiled the Council's meticulously crafted program. This manifesto, a beacon of hope piercing the gloom of despair, had been designed to lift the German people from the crushing weight of the Treaty of Versailles. The German populace, wearied by the harsh penalties of the treaty, were yearning for a leader to sail them out of their stormy sea of despair. Hitler, with his electrifying charisma and compelling oratory, announced the Nazi Party's 25-point Program:

- The Treaty of Versailles and the Treaty of St. Germain shall be abolished.
- Unification of all German-speaking people must occur, uniting them into one country. Common utility precedes individual utility.
- All German citizens receive equal rights and obligations.
- Only a member of the German (Aryan) race, of German blood, can be a citizen. No Jew can be a citizen.
- All non-Germans must leave the Reich immediately.
- Those whose activity is judged injurious to the general interest shall be punished with death without consideration of confession or race.
- Roman Law, which serves a materialistic world order, shall be replaced by German common law.
- Control the German press must be established, with only members of the German race allowed to work for the newspapers and other media. Publishment of non-German newspapers requires express permission from the State.
- Demand the creation of a strong central state power for the Reich, including the unconditional authority of a centralized Parliament over the entire Reich and its organizations.

The atmosphere was electric, the crowd pulsating with excitement as they absorbed the words that promised the restoration of Germany's strength. The Treaty of Versailles and the Treaty of St. Germain had left the German economy in tatters; unemployment had skyrocketed, and the nation's pride was severely wounded. The Treaty of Versailles, a punitive document that held Germany responsible for the horrors of World War I, was a bitter pill to swallow. The German populace seethed with resentment towards their government for agreeing to the astronomical sum of one hundred thirty-two billion gold marks in war reparations. It was a debt so colossal, it threatened to shackle the nation for a century to come. Hitler, along with the rest of the German people, felt a deep sense of betrayal.

The aftermath of World War I and the Treaty of Versailles had plunged the country into a pit of despair and destitution. Thousands of Germans, their bodies wasting away from hunger, queued up at food kitchens, their hollow eyes filled with desperation. Some had not tasted food in days, their bodies so frail that they collapsed while waiting in line for a morsel of food.

As Hitler's voice echoed through the beer hall, a wave of fervent agreement swept through the crowd. Each person present was united in their support, their hearts resonating with the words barked out by the man on the stage. The treaties' oppressive weight were a crushing burden that had sown the seeds of stress, depression, and destruction among the German people. But now, Hitler's announcement acted as a torch of optimism piercing through the gloom. His bombastic delivery of the 25-point Program was like a clarion call, rallying the masses and bolstering their support for the Nazi Party. The prospect of granting complete, unconditional authority to the Reich struck many as a welcome relief compared to the harsh conditions they had endured since the Great War.

Chants of "Heil Hitler! Heil Hitler!" reverberated through the beer hall, growing in intensity with each repetition. The man stood tall, basking in the adulation of his fellow Germans. This was the recognition he had yearned for, reminiscent of the camaraderie he had shared with his fellow soldiers in the trenches. Crippling reparations for the Great War had eroded the hope of the people, but out of the ashes of despair he emerged as their leader. Their Führer. Their Savior.

The 25-point Program also provided a foundational blueprint for the removal of the Jewish population from Germany. With the widespread belief that the Jews had betrayed the German people in World War I, anti-Semitism ran rampant throughout the country. Belief that Jewish influence had led the country to lose the war had fueled a rapid growth in hostility towards the Jewish population.

As a tide of anti-Semitism surged in Germany, the Black Nobility's choice of leader remained uncertain. The question hung in the air: who would be the one to fulfill their mission?

Chapter 21

30 October 1922

Francesco's candidate has been appointed Prime Minister of Italy. This Fascist is the youngest person in history to be appointed prime minister. My brother has done well grooming Mussolini to be the leader the Council is searching for.

Congratulations, brother. You have done well.

Cardinal Eugenio Pacelli

Chapter 22

CORRIERE DELLA SERA

Anno 46 – *N. 71*	*Roma – Lunedi,* *30 Ottobre 1922*	*Edizione del* *Pomeriggio*

MUSSOLINI ELECTED
PRIME MINISTER

Signor Mussolini, the leader of the Italian Fascists, after an interview with King Victor at the Quirinal yesterday, assumed the premiership and formed a cabinet. He himself has taken over the Ministry of the Interior and Ministry of Foreign Affairs, and appointed seven other Fascists to office.

30 October 1922
Rome, Italy
March on Rome

I n a bold and audacious move, Benito Mussolini, flanked by a formidable force of 30,000 Fascist "Blackshirts", descended upon Rome, their demands resounding throughout the ancient city's streets—the resignation of the liberal Prime Minister Luigi Facta. King Victor Emmanuel III, in a desperate bid to avoid bloodshed, capitulated, surrendering power to Mussolini and thus crowning him prime minister. At the tender age of thirty-nine, he became the youngest prime minister in Italy's storied history. His ambition was as grand as it was chilling—the establishment of a totalitarian state with himself at its helm, the supreme leader.

His brother, wielding the power of the press as the editor of the Fascist newspaper *Il Popolo d'Italia* was instrumental in disseminating the message of Il Duce ("The Leader") throughout Rome. In a remarkably short span of time, Il Duce established a legal dictatorship, earning himself the ominous title of "the founder of Fascism".

"Our program is simple," Mussolini declared, his voice reverberating across a crowd of 60,000 militants gathered at a Fascist rally in Naples. "We want to rule Italy."

The crowd erupted in a roar of approval. The newly formed Fascist Party was gaining momentum in Italy, a snowball growing larger and more unstoppable with each passing day. With this much momentum, it seemed inevitable that Mussolini would soon rule all of Italy. The Council's plan was unfolding with a precision and elegance that was almost poetic.

* * *

"History has been made today, Il Duce," Francesco Pacelli lauded Mussolini, his voice oozing pride and admiration. "You are the youngest to ever hold the mantle of prime minister in our beloved Italy." Their meetings had become a regular occurrence, a necessary ritual to keep Francesco's candidate tethered to the Council's grand vision.

Mussolini reclined in an imposing leather chair in Francesco's Vatican office, a room that breathed power and influence. The scent of Cuban cigars wafted through the air, a tangible symbol of their shared triumph. Mussolini was a maelstrom of emotion, brimming with confidence yet humbled by the magnitude of the mission entrusted to him just eighteen months prior. His destiny was clear, his role in this grand scheme pivotal; he was ready to play his part to perfection.

"Your guidance has been invaluable, counselor," Mussolini confessed, his voice laced with gratitude and a hint of regret over his past doubts. "I underestimated the reach of your influence in our great city."

"Our connections are not just vast, Prime Minister—they are effective," Francesco replied, his tone hinting at the power his organization wielded.

"I am, and will forever remain, in your service."

"To your success, Prime Minister," Francesco proposed, striding over to the bar to pour two glasses of his finest Cognac. Mussolini rose and crossed the room to accept the glass of exquisite Hermitage Grande Champagne Cognac from Francesco's prized collection. They raised their glasses in a toast and the clink of crystal echoed throughout the room, a symphony of celebration for Mussolini's greatest achievement yet.

Chapter 23

20 October 1923
Tuesday
Munich, Bavaria, Germany

"Do you have everything prepared for the rally?" Cardinal Pacelli probed Hitler, his voice laced with anticipation and a hint of urgency.

"Every detail, as per your instructions, Your Excellency."

"As you know, last year's uprising in Rome was a triumph. Mussolini now holds the reins of power in Italy. The liberal Italian government has been effectively decapitated," Cardinal Pacelli declared, thrusting a year-old newspaper towards Hitler as evidence.

"Do you foresee us seizing control of the Bavarian government in a comparable manner?"

"That is the goal. However, regardless of the outcome, I anticipate this uprising will catapult you into the public eye. That is of the utmost importance, Adolf."

"I trust your guidance, Your Excellency."

Hitler's loyalty to the Nuncio of Germany was unshakable—he had witnessed the cardinal's influence permeating throughout the whole of Germany. Hitler understood that his own climb to the pinnacle of power within Parliament was a game of endurance, a test of his personal patience. As Cardinal Pacelli continued to fortify his position, weaving his influence deeper into the fabric of the German hierarchy, Hitler knew that his own ascension to power would inevitably follow.

With the cardinal subtly manipulating the German elite, it wouldn't be long before he was facilitating crucial introductions for Hitler. He saw Pacelli's predictions materializing before his eyes. He could almost taste his rise to power in the Third Reich, so long as he just clung to the cardinal's coattails.

His destiny as the Führer, the ultimate leader, seemed all but guaranteed.

8 November 1923
Friday Evening
Bürgerbräukeller Beer Hall
Munich, Germany

Hitler, backed by a formidable force of 600 members from his Sturmabteilung paramilitary organization, stormed into the bustling beer hall meeting of three thousand attendees. Enraged by Gustav Ritter von Kahr's decision to call off the revolution, Hitler and his associates seized the moment, capitalizing on the burgeoning unrest and the populace's support. Hermann Göring, the formidable leader of the Sturmabteilung, spearheaded the audacious intrusion into Bürgerbräukeller Beer Hall.

Hitler, flanked by the likes of Rudolf Hess and his six other loyalists, navigated through the sea of startled faces in the crowded auditorium. Struggling to command the attention of the crowd, Hitler, in a dramatic display of authority, climbed onto a chair with his pistol raised. The deafening sound of a gunshot echoed through the hall as he fired a round into the ceiling. His voice boomed, "The national revolution has broken out! This hall is surrounded by six hundred men. Nobody is allowed to leave."

With the crowd now hanging onto his every word, his voice gnashed with authority. "The Bavarian government has been deposed. There is now a new government, under the command of General Ludendorff."

Then Hitler, flanked by the unwavering Rudolf Hess and his loyal associates, herded Kahr and associates into a secluded room and demanded their support for the putsch. After enduring hours of intense negotiations stalled by Kahr's stubborn refusal to comply, Hitler re-emerged into the cavernous beer hall. Addressing the restless crowd, his voice reached every heart and soul. "Outside are Kahr, Lossow, and Seisser. They are struggling hard to reach a decision. May I say to them you will stand behind them?"

The crowd responded with an overwhelming, deafening roar of approval signaling their unanimous agreement to proceed with the putsch.

Hitler masterfully manipulated the crowd's emotions, his voice resonating with passion and determination. "You can see what motivates us is neither self-conceit nor self-interest, but only a burning desire to join the battle. We are in the grave eleventh hour in the fight for our German Fatherland." He paused, letting his words sink in before delivering his final chilling statement. "One last thing I can tell you: either the German revolution begins tonight, or we will all be dead by dawn!"

The crowd's response was an earth-shaking roar of approval. The sheer volume of their support did not go unnoticed by the three holdouts. They could not ignore Hitler's skill in swaying the crowd. They knew they had no choice but to comply.

As the clock struck 11:00 p.m., General Ludendorff emerged from the shadows, his presence a beacon of influence and power. His mission was clear—to sway Kahr, Lossow, and Seisser to join the brewing revolution. With his persuasive prowess and commanding aura, he managed to extract a reluctant agreement from the trio.

For the next several hours, confusion and unrest permeated the air. Government officials, armed forces, police units, and ordinary citizens all found themselves at a crossroads, torn between their loyalty to the crumbling government and the allure of a radical uprising led by the nascent Nazi Party. The question hung heavy in the city—remain faithful to a failing regime, or join the clamor for change demanded by the German people?

As dawn broke, the disorganized coup, lacking strong leadership, crumbled under its own weight. State police and armed soldiers descended upon the rebels, their ambush heralded by a hailstorm of bullets, leaving four state police and sixteen Nazis dead. The remaining Nazis either scattered or were rounded up and arrested. Hitler, Hess, and Ludendorff fled Munich, narrowly escaping the authorities' clutches.

10 November 1923
Sunday Evening
Munich, Germany

The late-night shadows seemed to pirouette on the ancient walls, casting an eerie glow around the room. Hitler, shrouded in a cloak of anonymity, had managed to infiltrate Pacelli's residence, skillfully eluding the relentless pursuit of the state police and officials who were tirelessly hunting him down.

The city was a cauldron of clashing emotions and simmering tension. A substantial segment of the population, disillusioned by the current government's surrender to the Versailles Treaty, were rallying behind the insurrection against the established political regime. Yet there was an overbearing fear of the unknown, a reluctance to embrace the emergent Nazi Party. Could these Nazis truly provide a panacea for the citizens' hardships? There were even hushed murmurs of support for the rebellion within the sacred corridors of Parliament itself, yet none were audacious enough to speak up in public for fear of risking their esteemed positions for the sake of this unproven Nazi Party. Their loyalty, albeit begrudgingly, remained tethered to the weakened and defunct government.

"I have failed you, Your Excellency," Hitler confessed, his whisper piercing the hushed silence of Cardinal Pacelli's private study.

"This is merely a bump in the road, Adolf, a stepping stone on our path," Pacelli reassured him, his voice steady and comforting. "We will seize this opportunity to launch you into the limelight. Trust me, Adolf."

"I don't see . . ." Hitler began, but his voice trailed off, uncertainty clouding his words.

"Envisioning the future of Germany isn't about what you can see with your eyes," Pacelli interjected, his tone firm yet encouraging. "Use this time to hone your public-speaking skills. I shall ensure the press is present at your trial to grant you the notoriety we seek."

"As you wish, Your Excellency," Hitler responded, his voice filled with newfound resolve.

"Despite the considerable sway I hold in Munich, Adolf, it seems you will have to face some time behind bars," Cardinal Pacelli expressed, his voice laced with regret yet firm in determination. "I have already negotiated with the presiding judge. You and Hess will serve your time at Landsberg Prison. There you will be granted the privilege of receiving visitors without question. I will visit you personally to give you your next directives." Pacelli's steady gaze comforted Hitler. "Do not let your heart be troubled, my friend. You are destined to be the Führer of the Third Reich."

Hitler straightened his posture, his eyes gleaming with newfound determination. "Thank you, Your Excellency."

"During your time in prison, Herr Hess will assist you in writing your manifesto. Its contents will springboard you into the public eye. Spare no detail. In this time of oppression brought about by the Treaty of Versailles, the public will cling to your manifesto as if it were the new Bible. Get this manuscript written quickly. Then I will orchestrate your release from prison."

His instructions delivered, Cardinal Pacelli rose from his seat, a silent indication that their clandestine meeting had reached its conclusion. Hitler mirrored his actions, rising to follow the cardinal out of the secluded study.

With a sense of renewed purpose, Hitler left the residence and made his way directly to the police station to surrender himself.

26 February 1924
Tuesday
Munich, Germany

A dolf Hitler's trial commenced on the 26th of February, 1924, a date that would be etched in the annals of history. As assured by Pacelli, the event was not just a trial but a spectacle, a grand stage meticulously covered by the press, the details of which were splashed across the front pages of the nation's newspapers the very next day.

Hitler, known for his fiery rhetoric and anti-Semitic tirades, surprisingly tempered his tone. Guided by Pacelli's strategic advice, he pivoted his defense, focusing not on his usual targets but on his unwavering dedication to the welfare of the German people and the necessity for audacious measures to rescue them from their plight.

Pacelli's own influence over the local press was evident. Hitler's defense speeches, carefully crafted and passionately delivered, were printed verbatim. This not only amplified his voice but also significantly boosted his popularity among the Munich populace, turning the tide in his favor.

28 February 1924
Munich, Germany

Adolf Hitler and Rudolf Hess were declared guilty of high treason, a verdict that led to a five-year sentence in the relatively lenient confines of Landsberg Prison. This was the most lenient punishment available for those perceived as honorable, albeit misguided. The prison was known for its comfortable cells and generous visiting privileges extended to its inmates, who could receive visitors on a daily basis. So it was that Cardinal Eugenio Pacelli visited Hitler and Hess to hear their confessions.

"Your Excellency, I am grateful for your visit," Hitler expressed from the confines of the austere prison visitation room.

"Adolf, do not let this situation concern you. We will turn this setback into an advantage," Pacelli replied, his voice steady and reassuring. "Dictate your struggles to Rudolf. They will serve as the foundation for the manifesto the German people crave. You have already caught the eye of numerous officials who are sympathetic to your plight and align with the principles of the Nazi Party."

Hitler absorbed the cardinal's directives with rapt attention—he understood the strategic advantage his prolonged incarceration could offer. The German populace, much like him, were shackled by the oppressive chains of the treaty. However, his circumstances were comparatively better. Unlike them he was guaranteed meals and decent living conditions, not to mention the luxury of daily visitation. Outside the prison walls, citizens grappled with food shortages and the relentless onslaught of hyperinflation. In this context, Hitler was in a favorable position to concentrate on crafting his manifesto, and thereby guide the beleaguered German people from their plight.

"I will continue talking with the judge to mitigate your sentence. Given his pro-Nazi leanings, I am confident I can orchestrate the desired outcome," the cardinal assured.

"Thank you, Your Excellency."

"Begin working on your manifesto. Once the German people read it, they will embrace you as one of their own."

"Manifesto . . ." Hitler echoed the word, envisioning the waves of adulation from the German populace that would greet it.

Pacelli observed Hitler caught up in his self-indulgent reverie and vowed to make it a reality. Each German household would possess a copy of the manifesto. It would become the most sought-after book in Germany, perhaps the world, surpassing even the Bible.

"I may not be able to visit again in the immediate future. From here on, I will relay my instructions through Herr Hess." Pacelli paused as he heard the guard's footsteps nearing the door. "May you be blessed, Herr Hitler. Your sins have been forgiven." He rose as the guard unlatched the door, indicating their time was at an end.

"Thank you for hearing my confession, Your Excellency."

Hitler returned to his cell and explained Cardinal Pacelli's directives to Rudolf Hess. Requesting a typewriter from the prison warden, the man destined to lead the Third Reich began to narrate his life's tribulations, every word meticulously typed out by Cardinal Pacelli's trusted confidant.

13 September 1924
Landsberg Prison
Munich, Germany

"How goes the progress on Hitler's manifesto?" Pacelli questioned Rudolf Hess in the austere confines of the Landsberg Prison visitor cell. The cardinal was cautious to limit his visits, wary of arousing suspicion from the ever-watchful guards or their stern warden. His connections within the Munich community were extensive, and he had to be meticulous so as not to arouse suspicion and jeopardize these valuable ties.

"The dictation is a challenging affair, Your Excellency. I must constantly steer Adolf back on course, or else he veers off into one of his impassioned diatribes of rage."

"Has he chosen a title for the book yet?"

"He refers to it as *Four and a Half Years of Struggle against Lies, Stupidity, and Cowardice: A Reckoning.* It's quite long if you ask me."

"You are correct in your assessment." Pacelli paused, mulling over a more fitting title. "Advise him to truncate the title to simply *My Struggle.* That will be more palatable to the masses. We cannot risk alienating the German people with an overly complex title."

"I will relay your suggestion to Adolf. I hope he will not object, once he learns it comes from your wise counsel, Your Excellency."

"I will arrange for another meeting in the coming weeks. In the meantime, continue your dictation with the man who is destined to become the leader of the Third Reich." Pacelli rose to his feet and extended his hand in a firm shake. "You are proving to be a most loyal servant, Herr Hess."

"Thank you, my lord," Rudolf said, bowing in deference to Cardinal Pacelli.

November 1924
Munich, Germany

I n the chilly November of 1924, Hitler dictated the final words of his monumental manuscript *Mein Kampf*. Concurrently, Cardinal Pacelli was meticulously weaving his web of influence among political leaders, power brokers, and high-ranking officials, all in a bid to secure the release of Hitler and Hess from their confines. Already possessing considerable sway over the Munich judiciary, Pacelli masterfully wielded the weapon of persuasion to orchestrate Hitler's release from prison just a week before Christmas.

"Consider the man's intentions, Your Honor. Hitler's devotion to Germany surpasses even that of the most patriotic Bavarian natives," Pacelli argued before the judge in the latter's private chambers. Pacelli was confident the judge would employ discretion in keeping their meeting confidential; after all, he held a trove of compromising information that could potentially ruin the judge's reputation. It was practically impossible for him to deny Pacelli's request.

Judge Schmidt sat in an uncomfortable silence, his unease growing with each word the cardinal spoke. He was beginning to regret the favors he had sought from the Nuncio of Germany. Their cost was proving to be exorbitant.

"Besides, it's the holy season, Your Honor. Can't you find it within your heart to release this war hero from his chains?" Pacelli added, his voice laced with a persuasive charm dripping with exploitation.

"I will see what I can do, Your Excellency," Schmidt responded, a sense of unease creeping into his voice as he grappled with the Nuncio of Germany's intimidating tactics. He was well aware of Pacelli's reputation for manipulating the political chessboard, bending Parliament members and high-ranking officials to his will. The judge just never imagined he would find himself on the receiving end of the cardinal's manipulative prowess. The man's interest in this Viennese-born soldier-turned-German-nationalist was disturbing, and it gnawed at the judge's conscience. The favors he had accepted from the cardinal now felt like shackles, forcing him to comply with his every demand.

"I appreciate your consideration, *Your Honor.*" Pacelli's voice dripped with a smug satisfaction. He rose, prompting the judge to follow suit. Pacelli extended his hand across the desk, and the judge reciprocated the gesture. The cardinal withdrew, leaving the judge with his dreadful sense of inevitability. He knew he had no choice but to grant Pacelli's request. The stakes were too high, the potential exposure too damning for him to dare defy the Vatican diplomat.

As the door closed behind the departing cardinal, the judge felt a chill run down his spine. It was as if he had just struck a deal with the devil himself. Even the lingering warmth of the cardinal's handshake seemed to burn his palm. An ominous feeling settled in his gut. He couldn't pinpoint why, but he was certain that his compliance would set in motion a series of unfortunate events.

Hitler, meanwhile, served only eight months of his sentence before being released on December 20, 1924, on the grounds of good behavior. A few more private meetings, and Rudolf Hess too was free a mere ten days later.

Chapter 24

March 7, 2000
Tuesday, 5:22 p.m.
Vatican Secret Archives

"Father Marino?" Cardinal Borelli called out as he rounded a corner inside the Vatican Secret Archives, only to find Mario engrossed at the scanning worktable, bathed in the soft glow of the lamplight while hunched over some ancient manuscripts.

The priest jolted, the sudden interruption shattering his deep concentration on the journal, causing his heart to race. Time had slipped away. How many hours had he been captivated by this heretical artifact?

"It's after five o'clock, Father."

"Oh, uh, I . . . um, I lost track of time, Cardinal Borelli," Mario stammered, his heart pounding in his chest.

"What are you working on that has you so enamored?" The cardinal's gaze fell on the journal sprawled open on the worktable.

"Just the, uh . . . uh, the next piece I'm working on. I'm trying to figure out the best way to scan it without causing any damage." Mario's voice shook as he tried his best not to lie.

"May I take a look?"

"It's nothing, really." Mario's pulse quickened, beads of sweat forming on his forehead. He was a terrible liar, and his nervousness manifested itself through him profusely sweating.

With an air of authority, the cardinal began his measured stride down the aisle. Fear gripped Mario; his heart pounded like a drum in his chest. He quickly turned around and closed the journal, but not before Borelli caught a glimpse of its exquisite leather cover.

"That's a beautiful cover. What's inside?"

"Just more fragile documents. You know, same old stuff," Mario managed to utter, pivoting to face the cardinal. His voice wavered, betraying his nervousness. Sweat was now visibly pooling on his forehead, each droplet a testament to his escalating fear.

Borelli's eyes narrowed, his suspicion piqued by the sight of the sweat glistening on Mario's forehead. Something was decidedly off. "Are you feeling alright, Father Marino?"

"I, uh, seem to be under the weather," Mario stuttered, the words struggling to escape his lips.

Cardinal Borelli, a notorious germaphobe, instinctively recoiled. "Then you must go home. We cannot afford a contagion within these sacred walls," he declared, retreating until he was at the far end of the aisle.

"Okay. Sorry, Your Eminence. I'll shut down the equipment and head home." Mario got busy at the worktable, doing his best to avoid Borelli's penetrating stare.

"Call in sick tomorrow if you're not feeling better," the cardinal advised before disappearing around the corner.

Mario pulled out a handkerchief and mopped up the beads of sweat clinging to his forehead. He glanced over his shoulder to make certain the cardinal was gone. Hands trembling, he carefully rewrapped the journal, pressing the wax seal into place with a reverence that belied his anxiety. Reaching up, he deftly nestled the journal on the shelf, replaced the quartet of nondescript books in front masterfully concealing its presence.

Heart still pounding in his chest, he powered down the equipment, slung his backpack over his shoulder, and made his way for the exit of the Secret Archives' hallowed confines.

The revelations contained within the journal continued to echo in his mind. A clandestine cache of deceit and corruption, a myriad of secrets begging to be untangled. He had no choice but to let them linger in the shadows of the Secret Archives until tomorrow.

Chapter 25

March 7, 2000
Tuesday, 6:59 p.m.

"Roberto," Mario croaked as he passed through the unlocked front door to Roberto's residence, his breath ragged from his brisk walk. A fear, alien and chilling, had taken root in his heart, a sensation he had never experienced before, especially in the sanctuary of the Catholic Church. The revelations gleaned from Pacelli's journal had shattered that peace.

"In my office," came Roberto's response down the hallway.

With a sense of urgency, Mario navigated through Roberto's home, beelining for the office. As he appeared in the office doorway, Roberto could immediately sense his friend's emotional disarray—Mario looked like a man haunted, his eyes wide with fear.

"Whoa! What's the matter, bro?" Roberto rose from his desk to meet Mario at the doorway.

"You won't believe what I found out today," Mario managed to say as he moved to sit on the room's leather couch, his heart pounding like a drum.

"Do you need a glass of water or something?"

"No, no, just sit down."

"Bro, what's happening?"

"That journal I mentioned"—Mario's gaze bore into Roberto—"it's Pacelli's journal. It details how he puppeteered Hitler into becoming the Führer of the Nazi Party."

"Wait, what?"

"The journal, Pope Pius XII's journal. He was secretly behind Hitler's rise to power."

Mario's unblinking stare was making Roberto increasingly uncomfortable. He had never seen his best friend in such a state. Yet it was hard to believe what he was hearing. He reached over, placing his hand on Mario's shoulder.

"What exactly did you read in that journal?"

"I poured over it for . . . I can't even tell you how long. It was filled with entries detailing Pacelli's orders from the Black Nobility. From his own grandfather. They orchestrated some grand scheme involving both Hitler and Mussolini."

Roberto sat there, his hand still resting on Mario's shoulder, his mind reeling as he tried to piece together the conspiracy unfolding before him. His concern for Mario, his lifelong friend, superseded his usual suspicious tendencies. Mario was, and would always be, his top priority. He would move heaven and earth to ensure his friend's safety.

"Hitler had a meeting with Pacelli in Munich in 1919. Pacelli handed Hitler a bag— no, a *cache* of money to fuel Hitler's revolution. That was the genesis of the Nazi Party."

"Let's search this." Roberto rose from the couch, his silhouette cast against the room's dim light as he moved towards his computer. "You good with that?"

"Yeah, yeah," Mario agreed, trailing after Roberto to the desk.

With a sense of urgency, Roberto dragged a chair beside him for Mario to sit in. He was concerned his friend, still reeling from the shocking revelations, might collapse or something.

His fingers swiftly danced over the keyboard with practiced ease and soft clicking filled the room. His eyes focused, his mind racing as he typed into his favorite search engine:

```
Pacelli and the Nazis
```

A torrent of over a thousand search results flooded the screen, each one a potential key to the mystery. Roberto's hand hovered over the mouse before selecting the first entry.

```
Reichskonkordat: a treaty negotiated between
the Vatican and the emergent Nazi Germany. Signed
on 20 July 1933 by Cardinal Secretary of State
Eugenio Pacelli, who would later ascend to the
title of Pope Pius XII. The treaty promised to
safeguard the rights of the Roman Catholic Church
in Germany.
```

Mario's patience was wearing thin. "We already read this before."

"What was the name of that shadowy group? Black something?"

"Black Nobility."

As Roberto typed in the name, a deluge of hits cascaded onto the screen.

"It looks like the Black Nobility's shadowy past seems to have had a profound influence on the Vatican. The Pacelli family was deeply intertwined with the Vatican's strategic operations." Roberto skipped through the information on the screen. "The patriarch, Marcantonio, remained loyal to Pope Pius IX during his exile from the Vatican. Francesco served as the Vatican's legal counsel. And it appears your Eugenio character ascended the ranks with an eerie smoothness—all masterminded by the Black Nobility, based on what you've told me. It was a grand scheme, meticulously planned from the beginning."

"That matches what's written in the journal. Eugenio's grandfather told him the Black Nobility predestined him to be the future pope."

Roberto swiveled around to face his friend, his voice laced with a chilling undertone. "What the hell have you stumbled upon?"

"I'm not sure, but it's giving me the heebie jeebies. Roberto, this is not the Catholic Church I've known and loved my whole life."

Roberto held his tongue, choosing to remain a silent pillar of support. Now was not the time to voice his own opinions about the Catholic Church. His best friend's world was crumbling, his faith being tested in the most brutal of ways. Roberto's primary concern was to shield Mario from the harsh reality that the institution he'd devoted his life to was not the sanctuary he believed it to be.

"I think you should stay here tonight. The guest bed is all made up." He paused for a moment, his mind briefly wandering to the room that had previously hosted some of his blond guests. "With fresh, clean sheets."

Mario sat in silence, his mind replaying his history with the Church. The orphanage. His time as an altar boy. The seminary. His ordination as a priest. He had always felt secure within the walls of the Catholic Church. That sense of safety was rapidly evaporating.

Looking over at Roberto, he said, "Thank you. I'll take you up on that."

Chapter 26

March 8, 2000
Wednesday, 6:29 a.m.

"Roberto?"

Roberto's eyes flicked up from the glow of the monitor, catching sight of Mario's silhouette framed in the office doorway. His voice was gravelly and thick with early morning haze as he said, "Dude. You won't believe what I've unearthed about the Pacelli family."

Mario's eyebrows furrowed, his gaze drifting to the clock on the wall. "Have you been up all night?" His footsteps clacked on the hardwood floor as he crossed the room to join Roberto, piqued by his friend's enthusiasm.

"Check this out."

Mario leaned in, his body casting a shadow over Roberto as he steadied himself on his friend's shoulder, his eyes scanning the information displayed on the screen. Roberto remained silent, allowing Mario time to absorb the shocking revelations.

"I remember reading in the journal about Eugenio's deep admiration and respect for his grandfather," Mario murmured, his eyes never leaving the screen.

Roberto nodded in agreement, his finger tracing the lines of text on the screen as if to underline their significance. "Marcantonio, the patriarch, wielded immense influence over the whole family. He masterfully paved their way within the

Vatican's intricate power structure, enabling several Pacellis to ascend to positions of considerable importance."

Roberto's finger paused, pointing at a particular piece of information. "Did you see this? Marcantonio earned a doctorate in canon law. Then Eugenio did his thesis focusing on concordats and the functions of canon law. The apple didn't fall far from the tree." His voice was laced with a hint of sarcasm. "Canon law is the laws that govern the Catholic Church as decreed by the pope himself. They're essentially laws that legalize the Vatican to behave like a dictatorship, Mario."

Mario continued to read, his eyes darting across the screen, absorbing the information while listening to Roberto's commentary.

Mario's voice dropped to a disheartened whisper. "The journal had entries about how the Black Nobility orchestrated missions to ensure the Vatican's financial stability. To bolster its financial reserves, they chose Eugenio Pacelli to become pope and execute the master plan They never elaborate on this master plan though."

Engrossed in the damning revelations, Mario felt a wave of despair washing over him. The faith that had been his guiding light, the sacred institution to which he had pledged his life—was it all just an elaborate facade of deception and corruption? His entire belief system was being shaken to its core, leaving him to grapple with a harsh reality. What was the truth? His mind raced to the countless faithful around the world, blindly pledging their allegiance to an institution steeped in lies and treachery. The thought of how they would react upon learning this horrifying truth about the Vatican sent shivers down his spine.

"Yeah. Marcantonio, the family patriarch, was the mastermind behind it all. Look at this: Francesco was the pope's canon lawyer and confidant. He was the one who brokered the

Lateran Treaty of 1929 with Mussolini." Roberto paused, the weight of his words hanging in the air. "Mussolini compensated the Church handsomely for the loss of the Papal States. He essentially paid for the Vatican's independence, and gave them a ton of money on top of that."

Mario's eyes widened. "There was a journal entry where Francesco conspired with Mussolini, aiding his ascent to power. It was a power play between Eugenio and Francesco, each vying to shape the next leader."

"Are you serious? It really said that?" Roberto's eyes mirrored the shock in his voice.

"Yes. Eugenio was grooming Hitler, and Francesco was grooming Mussolini."

Roberto's fingers danced across the keyboard, pulling up images of Hitler and Mussolini. The image of Mussolini in his military uniform being saluted by an Italian officer with a Heil Hitler sent a chill down his spine. "The Italians adopted the Nazi salute rather quickly, it seems. Look at that picture." He jabbed his finger at the screen.

Both men stared at the images scrolling down the monitor, a grim tableau of history unfolding before them. "They joined forces in October 1936 as the Rome-Berlin Axis," Roberto murmured. An image showed Hitler and Mussolini marching together in their infamous "goose step" march, a stark reminder of the past.

Mario glanced at the clock in the corner of the monitor. "I have to get ready for work."

"Shouldn't you call in sick?" Roberto asked, concern etched on his face.

"I have to go in," Mario replied, his voice firm. Despite the shocking revelations, he remained a loyal servant of the Church.

"Do you think you could get a copy of that journal for me?" Roberto asked, his eyes eager. The prospect of seeing Pope Pius XII's actual notes with his own eyes was just too enticing.

"Really? You want me to *steal* from the Vatican, Roberto?" Mario asked, incredulous.

"You're right, bro. I'm sorry," Roberto said, his voice softening.

"I'm staying at home tonight. I need some time alone to pray about this." Mario's voice was heavy with the weight of their discovery, the implications of their findings still sinking in.

Chapter 27

March 9, 2000
8:08 a.m.
Vatican Secret Archives

Mario trod down the aisle towards his worktable, a sense of urgency to his stride. He set down his backpack and reached up for the books concealing the journal. As he pulled down one of the books, Cardinal Borelli appeared at the end of the aisle, catching Mario just as he was about to commit the clandestine act.

"Father Marino. Are you feeling better today?" the cardinal said, maintaining a safe distance, his fear of contracting an illness from the young priest evident.

His fixation on maintaining an environment devoid of germs had been the cardinal's primary concern throughout his ascension within the Vatican's hierarchy. The cardinal's well-known distaste for socializing with the masses, a potential breeding ground for a plethora of diseases, was as notorious as his rank. The confessional, a veritable hotbed of microbial combat, was his personal hell. The mere thought of physical contact—handshakes, embraces, or even proximity to others—was abhorrent to him. The confessional was perceived as an adversary, a potential assault on his immune system. He was not about to jeopardize his well-being by interacting with this priest, who had likely been exposed to a myriad of illnesses during his commute that morning.

"Thank you, Cardinal. I'm feeling much better today. I believe the extra rest last night worked wonders," Mario responded, taken aback by the unexpected encounter so early in the morning. He resolved to be more aware of his surroundings from now on—he couldn't afford to let his superiors catch on that he knew about the sinister journal.

"I was discussing that journal you were reading yesterday with another cardinal. Do you have it on you?"

"Oh, uh, I guess I . . ." Mario turned back to the worktable, his hands clumsily shuffling through various books and papers. "I must have put it away. Could I get it to you later today?"

"Where is it?" The cardinal's suspicion rose in tandem with Mario's hesitation.

Mario's pulse began to race, sweat beading on his temples. "I'll have to locate it."

The cardinal's gaze bore into the young priest. "I'm beginning to question if we've chosen the right person for this task, Father Marino. Do you have the journal or not?"

Recalling the cardinal's germaphobia, Mario coughed into his hand a few times, feigning the remnants of his "illness" while wiping the sweat from his forehead.

The cardinal recoiled, hastily putting distance between himself and Mario—the threat of germ warfare swiftly overpowered his suspicions. "Very well. Later today." His gaze lingered on the sweat glistening off the priest's forehead. Borelli turned around and exited the aisle, leaving Mario to his tasks. "If you feel the need to go home, do so," he called beyond the bookshelves.

Mario's heart pounded like a drum. The early-morning encounter with the cardinal had left him breathless. *Dang it! I can't let him see this journal.*

He darted to the end of the aisle, his eyes tracking the cardinal as he strode briskly towards the exit. He needed to devise a plan to delay handing over the journal to the cardinal— but the question was, how?

He retraced his steps back to the worktable. Peeking down the aisle to ensure no one was watching, he reached up and removed the quartet of books that continued to serve as makeshift camouflage for the journal. He took down the journal and carefully placed it on the table to unwrap it. His mind raced with a single desperate thought: *How do I prevent them from laying hands on this?*

His own hands trembled slightly as he began to unwrap the sinister journal. The warning on the wrapping paper, penned by Father Benedetti, leapt out at him once more:

Beware!
Do not read!
Your life will be
in danger!
GAB

The words echoed ominously in his mind, a chilling prophecy that sent shudders down his spine. Was it truly an embolism that had claimed Father Benedetti's life, or was there a more sinister truth lurking beneath the surface? Was it possible this journal's discovery had resulted in his untimely demise?

The influence of Roberto's conspiracy-driven mindset began to make Mario's head whirl. Except this was different— Mario had truly stumbled onto something substantial. The evidence was right there, glaring at him in black and white. In this new light, Roberto's outlandish theories, once dismissed as crazy ideas, suddenly didn't seem so far-fetched.

Mario had been too naive, too trusting in his belief that the Catholic Church was a haven of peace and tranquility. The proof was undeniable—those in power had hidden their corruption behind the glory and honor of basilicas, cathedrals, and churches.

The word 'basilica' echoed in Mario's mind. An honored title, bestowed upon a church of special spiritual, historical, or architectural significance. Now the term dripped with hypocrisy. The pope himself granted this title, a mark of honor that remained with the church in perpetuity. Could this too be a cunning ploy by the Vatican, a means of concealing something within these specially titled churches scattered across the globe? Nothing seemed too far-fetched now.

Mario's unwavering faith in the Catholic Church had been shattered and replaced by a newfound skepticism. He was seeing the Church with new eyes. Critical eyes. Roberto's eyes.

With a newfound determination, he opened the journal. He was no longer a mere pawn in a grand chess game orchestrated by an institution claiming to be his protector; he was now a player in a game of subterfuge and deceit that had far-reaching implications, affecting billions of unsuspecting souls across the globe. The magnitude of the deception was staggering. How many years, decades, or even centuries had this charade been going on? Was it still happening today?

Taking a deep, steadying breath, Mario prepared himself for the revelations that lay ahead. He began to read where he'd left off the previous day, his eyes scanning the pages with a newfound intensity.

14 September 1924

The Art of War
#23 Pretend inferiority and encourage his arrogance.

The seed has been sown. Hitler's obsession with the Führermuseum shall be the catalyst that propels the Council's mission.

Cardinal Eugenio Pacelli

Chapter 28

"Your collection of art is truly magnificent," Hitler said, his eyes drinking in each piece of artwork adorning the cardinal's library.

"Thank you. I've devoted considerable effort amassing this collection," the cardinal responded, a hint of pride in his voice.

Art had always held a magnetic pull on Hitler, even as a child. Despite the brutal beatings from his abusive father, young Adolf's rebellious spirit never wavered from wanting to nurture his artistic talents.

Hitler scrutinized every detail of the Monet hanging on the wall. He was captivated by its intricate brushstrokes, the masterful interplay of light and shadow, the spatial imprecision. A pang of jealousy stirred within him at Monet's natural skill.

"I see you're quite taken with my Monet. It's an original, naturally."

"Very impressive, Your Excellency. Art has always been a passion of mine."

"Tell me about this passion," Pacelli urged, sensing the opportunity to gain more of the leverage he needed over Hitler. With Hitler's deepest desires exposed, Pacelli could manipulate him along the path to power, thereby advancing the Council's grand plan.

"My father never permitted me to chase my dream," Hitler confessed, his voice tinged with a melancholic remembrance of that oppressive chapter of his life. "When I was about seven, he enrolled me in a technical school. But I yearned to attend a classical school and become an artist. I thought that my poor grades would force him to withdraw me from the technical school and enroll me in the classical one instead."

"Did you ever make it into the classical school?"

"No. My father passed away when I was just thirteen. After that, my inclination towards that art school dwindled," Hitler confessed, a shadow of sorrow crossing his face.

"And then what happened?" Pacelli probed, eager to delve deeper into Hitler's hidden desires.

"When I turned sixteen, I passed the final exam and bid farewell to my school days, vowing never to return," Hitler shared, his voice heavy with the weight of his past. Suddenly tiring of standing, he moved away to seek the comfort of the leather chair in front of Pacelli's desk.

Pacelli's gaze followed Hitler, observing his somber demeanor as he sank into the chair. The cardinal remained silent, providing a safe space for Hitler to continue his narrative.

"At the age of eighteen, I applied to the Academy of Fine Arts in Vienna only to face rejection twice," Hitler confessed, his gaze dropping as he relived the crushing disappointment of his dreams.

"That must have been traumatic."

"Nothing compared to the devastation of losing my mother that Christmas," Hitler admitted, his voice barely more than a whisper.

Still, in the presence of the cardinal, Hitler felt a sense of security. It was as if he could share his deepest secrets without fear of judgment. Pacelli seemed to truly listen and understand him, much like his mother had.

"After that, I embraced a bohemian lifestyle," he said, his posture straightening as he recalled this transformative phase of his life. "I believed that was how true artists should live, and I wanted to experience it firsthand." He looked up at Pacelli, searching for any signs of disapproval, but all he found was empathy and understanding in the eyes of the esteemed diplomat. It was clear why Cardinal Pacelli was a respected ambassador of the Vatican in Germany.

"I attended Wagner's opera production, *Lohengrin*, ten times," Hitler said, a hint of enthusiasm creeping into his voice. This opera was one of his favorites by the renowned German composer.

"Is that so? Amazing. I had the extraordinary honor of attending his awe-inspiring opera *Tristan and Isolde*," Pacelli said, sharing his reverence for the brilliant composer.

Hitler, visibly moved, leaned forward in his seat, his eyes sparkling with exhilaration. "Then you understand my sentiment. He is not just a composer, but the epitome of musical genius," Hitler proclaimed, perched on the edge of his seat, his eyes gleaming with the thrill of discovering a shared passion with the esteemed cardinal.

"You mentioned earlier the Academy in Vienna rejected your application not once, but twice?"

"Yes." Hitler's demeanor hardened, his face a mask of stoicism at the painful reminder.

"What if the Vienna Academy of Fine Arts wasn't the only path to recognition?"

"I'm afraid I don't understand, Your Excellency."

"What I'm suggesting is, what if you were to establish your *own* museum?" Pacelli watched as the gears in Hitler's mind began to turn, his face illuminated by the tantalizing prospect.

"My own museum," Hitler echoed, the words slipping from his lips like in a dream.

"Envision it, surpassing the magnificence of the Louvre in Paris, the British Museum—even the Smithsonian in the United States."

Hitler's gaze drifted off into the distance, his mind lost to the vision of a museum of such monumental scale.

"All the world's most influential leaders boast impressive art collections, Adolf. But yours, yours would be unparalleled, the most expansive collection the world has ever seen." Pacelli's voice tolled like a bell throughout the room, his words painting a vivid picture in Hitler's mind. Hitler found himself entranced—his gaze remained fixed on the world outside the window yet his mind was elsewhere, lost in the gloriousness of this vision.

"Now, picture your own work, Adolf. Visualize the prized pieces *you* painted hanging in the same space as the masterpieces of Monet, Degas, Van Gogh. Imagine the awe and respect that would command."

Envisioning a world where he was the curator of his own grand museum, Hitler found himself entranced by the idea. He could almost hear the soft whispers of visitors, their reverence marveling at his masterpieces. He could feel the cool metal of the barrier keeping crowds at a safe distance from his gems. Their gaze captivated by the vibrant colors and delicate brush strokes of his artwork. A surge of pride, potent and intoxicating, coursed through his veins. This dream, so grand and audacious, was beyond anything he'd ever dared to imagine. And now it was within his grasp. He knew, with a fierce certainty, he would stop at nothing to make this dream a reality.

"Consider it the 'Führermuseum'," Pacelli suggested, his eyes keenly observing Hitler devouring the tantalizing prospect laid before him. Everyone had their Achilles' heel, their irresistible lure. For Hitler, it was art. Pacelli was well aware of this, and so he'd masterfully fanned the flames of this passion. It was the ultimate bait, a desire so potent it eclipsed all others in Hitler's heart.

"Why not erect this monumental edifice right in the heart of Linz?" Pacelli suggested, his voice echoing with a sense of splendor.

"Linz," Hitler murmured, his mind's eye painting a picture of a colossal museum, a testament to his vision, standing tall amidst the cityscape of his childhood. Despite the bitter memories Linz held for him, the idea of exacting a form of poetic justice by constructing the world's largest museum there held a certain appeal.

"To fill the halls of your Führermuseum, you would need to amass an unprecedented collection of artwork, Adolf," Pacelli continued, his tone matter-of-fact.

"That's right, Your Excellency. How might I acquire such a vast collection?" Hitler questioned, the image of his grand Führermuseum disappearing in the face of this daunting obstacle.

"The answer lies with the Jews. Remember those who betrayed the Germans in the Great War?" Pacelli's words hung heavy in the air.

"The Jews," Hitler echoed, his voice laced with bitterness as he recalled the greed of the Jews, their betrayal of the Germans for personal gain.

"Wouldn't it be fitting for the Jews to bear the cost of the retribution imposed on the German people by the Treaty of Versailles?"

Hitler nodded, his mind filled with images of the priceless artwork that adorned the opulent mansions of the Jewish elite.

"Of course, you wouldn't *sell* the artwork to repay the treaty's demands, Adolf. You would seize it for your Führermuseum, for the world to marvel at," Pacelli clarified, his vision of the future clear and compelling.

Hitler looked at Pacelli. His mind reeled from the enormity of the dream being woven before him. In the presence of this great man, his ambitions soared to heights he had never before imagined.

"Adolf, you must understand that this museum, this dream, can only become a reality if you are the leader of Germany," Pacelli said, his gaze steady on Hitler.

"I understand, Your Excellency." Hitler's voice was firm with newfound resolve.

"Your primary objective must remain crystal clear, Adolf: you are destined to become the leader of the German empire. Once you are appointed as the Führer of the Third Reich, you will command the respect of global leaders. Your word will be law." The authority girding Pacelli's voice sent shivers down Hitler's spine.

He found himself entranced by the cardinal's vivid depiction of this potential future. The idea of being Germany's Führer, guided by Pacelli, was intoxicating. He saw his future self, a figure of awe and respect showcasing the monumental museum in Linz to leaders from around the globe. His would be the envy of the world.

Pacelli's voice broke through Hitler's reverie. "But in exchange for this vast collection of artwork, there will be a price to pay."

"You never mentioned any cost, Your Excellency." Hitler's voice wavered, the fear of his dream being too expensive creeping into his mind.

"Consider it an extension of your tithes and offerings, my friend. I propose that the gold you extract from the Jews be discreetly funneled to the Vatican on a regular basis." Hitler was oblivious to the fact this was one of the Council's core aims, to bolster the Vatican's financial stability.

"What is this you speak of? What gold am I to extract from the Jews?" Hitler asked, confusion etched on his face.

"When you seize their artwork for your Führermuseum, you will also seize their gold." Pacelli's voice was steady and direct. "You will then transport this gold covertly to the Vatican." He extended his hand towards the meticulously rolled map resting at the corner of his imposing desk.

"The Jews' gold in exchange for my Führermuseum?" Hitler echoed, trying to comprehend the magnitude of the deal.

"And your ascension as Führer," Pacelli added, unfurling the strategic battle map that had been meticulously crafted by the Council.

"The 'cost' is the gold I seize from the Jews. That's it?" Hitler questioned, his voice dropping to an unusual hush as he grappled with the bewildering intricacies of the deal.

"Yes. Allow me to show you how this will work," Pacelli said, placing paperweights on the corners of the expansive map.

Hitler moved to Pacelli's side of the desk, his eyes scanning the intricately detailed map of the railway routes running from Eastern Europe to the Vatican. The plans outlined how he was to transport the confiscated Jewish gold to Rome.

Pacelli watched Hitler with a satisfied smile, confident that the Council's mission to fortify the Vatican's financial reserves was on the brink of fruition.

Chapter 29

18 July 1925
Munich, Bavaria, Germany

M ein *Kampf* Volume 1 is published. 9,473 copies sold.

Mein Kampf

by
Adolf Hitler

Chapter 30

2 February 1926

The Art of War
#4 Moral Influence
That which causes the people to be in harmony with their leaders, so that they will accompany them in life and unto death without fear of mortal peril.

The Council is still deciding between Hitler and Mussolini.

Italy's population is below forty million. Not enough to engage in full-scale war. The German population of sixty-two million, on the other hand, is sufficient.

Brother, we shall see whose leader will be victorious.

Cardinal Eugenio Pacelli

Chapter 31

21 January 1926
Rome, Italy

"Prime Minister, it's good to see you," Francesco Pacelli greeted Benito Mussolini, ushering him into his office with a warm, welcoming smile.

Mussolini strode across the polished floor to firmly grasp Francesco's outstretched hand. "Thank you. I came as soon as I received your summons, counselor."

"I've been speaking with my directors, and they have informed me we have a small issue."

Mussolini, sensing the gravity of the situation, took a seat. The prime minister's eyes locked onto Francesco's, ready to grapple with the impending complication.

"It appears our beloved Italy lacks the *numerical* strength to pose a significant threat on the global stage."

"What are you implying, counselor?"

"The population of Italy currently hovers around forty million. To expand our influence, Italy will need to seize control of neighboring territories, which will in turn require a formidable military. To wage a significant war, Italy would need a population of at least sixty million to be powerful enough to annex the neighboring lands."

"And how do you suggest we increase our numbers?" Mussolini asked, leaning forward in anticipation of the counselor's great wisdom.

"You, Prime Minister, have the power to enact natalist policies designed to stimulate a population boom. You must increase the birthrate in Italy."

Mussolini's attention was riveted on Francesco as he meticulously outlined the decree, a directive handed down from the Council that would shape Italy's future. Presently, Mussolini's popularity among the masses was soaring, thanks to his numerous public policies that had significantly improved civilian life. The once chaotic and unreliable railway system was now a model of punctuality, with trains arriving and departing with clockwork precision. This newfound order and consistency in transportation had fast become a vital aspect of the citizens' daily lives, helping win over the hearts of the Italian people. Mussolini had been hailed as a hero, his title "Il Duce" reverberating across the length and breadth of the peninsula. The populace was ready to follow their prime minister's lead, no matter the ask.

"You are to issue a decree promoting family growth. Tax exemptions will be granted to large families, while bachelors will face tax penalties," Francesco instructed.

Selling such a policy to the House of Commons would be a monumental task for Mussolini. Yet, to ascend to the status of a global superpower, it was crucial for Italy to increase its population to a staggering sixty million people. A 50 percent population increase was a lofty goal, but Mussolini was prepared to impose this ambitious target on his people.

"I will mobilize my team to implement this immediately, counselor," Mussolini affirmed, his voice resolute. "Consider it done."

Chapter 32

16 February 1929

The Art of War
#5 The Moral Law causes the people to
be in complete accord with their ruler,
so that they follow him regardless of their lives,
undismayed by any danger.

The Black Nobility successfully orchestrated and executed the Lateran Treaty between the Kingdom of Italy and Vatican City.

Francesco, my brilliant brother, acted as Lead Council between the king and the pope, securing Vatican City's independence. Mussolini, who signed on behalf of the king, played an essential role in compensating the Vatican for its loss of the Papal States.

In a grand gesture of recognition, Mussolini commemorated the successful negotiations by commissioning the Via della Conciliazione, a symbolic stre'et linking the Vatican City to the heart of Rome. This subtle act was a silent nod to everything my brother has done for the prime minister.

Brother, I commend you on this triumphant treaty. You continue to be a great role model that inspires me.

Cardinal Eugenio Pacelli

8 *February 1930*

The Art of War
#16 While heading the profit of my counsel,
avail yourself also of any helpful
Circumstances over and beyond the ordinary rules.

Pope Pius XI has appointed me Vatican Cardinal Secretary of State. I am now responsible for foreign policy and state relations throughout the world.

The Council has faithfully enacted my rise through the Vatican hierarchy. My mission to assume the papacy is on schedule. I believe Grandfather would be proud of my progress fulfilling his vision.

My brother and I are working together once again in the Vatican. In carrying out the Council's mission, we shall be victorious.

Secretary of State,
Archbishop Eugenio Pacelli

Chapter 33

21 January 1930
Munich, Germany

"Herr Hitler."

"Is there a problem, Your Excellency?" Hitler's voice was laced with apprehension as he entered the cardinal's study.

"Quite the opposite, Adolf. My mission is progressing as planned, in tandem with yours."

"And might I ask, have there been any new developments?"

"I have been elevated to the position of Vatican Secretary of State, Adolf," Pacelli announced, his voice carrying a note of triumph.

"Congratulations, Your Excellency." Hitler's voice betrayed a hint of surprise.

"Ah. Do not concern yourself thinking *your* mission has been derailed in any way," Pacelli reassured him.

It was only when Pacelli mentioned this that Hitler began to worry Pacelli's promotion might hinder his own ascent to power. Without the cardinal guiding his every move, he feared he might lose the momentum he'd been building towards becoming the leader of the Third Reich.

"You mean to return to Rome? How will I proceed without you, Your Excellency?" Hitler's voice was filled with frustration; he could feel his dream of becoming Führer, his Führermuseum, and the adoration of the German people all slipping away from him.

Pacelli had anticipated this reaction. Hitler seemed oblivious to the influence, connections, and power that Pacelli and the Council wielded across Europe. Didn't he recognize all that Pacelli had done for him so far? Had Pacelli not fulfilled all his promises?

"I understand the anger boiling within you, Adolf. However, for you to ascend to the esteemed position of Führer, it is imperative that I, too, ascend to the pinnacle of power within the Vatican. I must occupy the highest seat of authority to ensure your triumph, Adolf."

Hitler's mind churned with the realization that his own political ascension in Germany was inextricably linked to Pacelli's rise within the Vatican. As the Nuncio of Germany representing the Vatican, Pacelli was merely that: a representative. For Hitler to claim the highest echelons of German power, Pacelli would need to ascend to the ultimate position within the Vatican—the papacy. The mechanics of this ascension were unclear to Hitler, yet every prophecy the cardinal had made in their meetings had come to fruition. How could Hitler now doubt the cardinal's foresight? It immediately became clear to him that Pacelli's promotion within the Vatican was a pivotal stepping stone on his path to becoming Führer.

"I understand, Your Excellency. Please accept my apologies for my lack of faith," Hitler articulated, his body bending forward in a profound act of deference towards the distinguished ambassador of the Vatican. In that instant, Hitler's allegiance to the cardinal crystallized, deepening like iron bonds tempered in the furnace of faith.

"You are destined for greatness, mein Führer," the cardinal's voice echoed in the room, a prophecy hanging in the air.

Hitler maintained his bowed position, absorbing the weight of the cardinal's words.

"I have already informed Herr Hess about my promotion. He will serve as our intermediary, relaying my instructions to you." The cardinal's voice was steady and reassuring.

"I understand, Your Excellency." Hitler straightened, his eyes meeting the cardinal's, waiting for any additional instruction. Pacelli's silence filled the room, a clear indication their meeting had reached its conclusion. With a final nod, Hitler turned and exited the study. Both men got back to their busy work of changing the world.

Chapter 34

4 February 1933

The Art of War
#23 Pretend inferiority and encourage his arrogance.

My phone conversation with President Paul von Hindenburg convinced him to name Hitler Chancellor of Germany. The extensive collection of incriminating and compromising pictures made the president's decision not only inevitable but obvious.

Hitler's promotion to the second highest rank in Germany is exceeded only by the president himself. Having this newfound position of authority, Hitler ordered the immediate and rapid expansion of the Gestapo, putting Hermann Göring in charge. The Gestapo will put a swift end to any opposition that challenges the Nazi Party's supremacy.

Hitler is implementing the Council's plans flawlessly. Our mission is on the brink of being fulfilled.

Secretary of State,
Archbishop Eugenio Pacelli

3 March 1933

The Art of War
#21 When he concentrates, prepare against him;
where he is strong, avoid him.

The German Parliament Reichstag building burned to the ground after our covert arson attack. Hitler is using this as propaganda blaming the Communist Party.

By Decree of President von Hindenburg, the Schutzstaffel (SS) Stormtroopers can arrest and imprison opponents without specific charges, eliminate any political opposition, and control all publications. This gives Hitler's government the authority to overthrow state and local governments.

The Nazi Party has taken control of the government.

Secretary of State,
Archbishop Eugenio Pacelli

23 March 1933

The Art of War
#4 Moral influence
That which causes the people to be in harmony with their leaders so that they will accompany them in life and unto death without fear of mortal peril.

Hitler successfully maneuvered the Enabling Act through Parliament. He and his Reich government can now issue laws without Parliament's approval. These laws cannot be cancelled even by a vote in the Reichstag. This Act shall serve as the foundation to carry out the complete Nazification of Germany, a testament to the absolute power wielded by Adolf Hitler.

Secretary of State,
Archbishop Eugenio Pacelli

24 March 1933

The Art of War
#21 When he concentrates, prepare against him;
where he is strong, avoid him.

SS Protection Squads have built the first concentration camp in Dachau, Germany. This is the first of many such camps to come that will incarcerate Hitler's political opponents.

Secretary of State,
Archbishop Eugenio Pacelli

174

4 April 1933

The Art of War
#17 All War is based on deception.

Hitler began his anti-Jewish campaign, boycotting all Jewish owned businesses.

Secretary of State,
Archbishop Eugenio Pacelli

Chapter 35

21 July 1934
The Vatican
Rome, Italy

"Brother," Eugenio Pacelli's voice echoed ominously, welcoming Francesco into his austere office.

"It's good to see you, brother." Francesco planted a kiss on each of Eugenio's cheeks in a familial gesture of affection.

"Please, make yourself comfortable," Eugenio said, nodding towards a chair, his voice laced with an undercurrent of urgency. "I met with the Council yesterday. They are quite satisfied with Hitler's rise to power."

"So I've heard, brother. What's their next move regarding Hitler?" Francesco's eyes reflected a keen interest.

"He occupies the second highest position of power in Germany. The Council needs him to ascend to the highest rank so he can initiate the next phase of their grand scheme."

"What about my candidate?" Francesco's voice held a note of concern.

"The Council has yet to finalize their choice for the ultimate leader, brother. They are strategically positioning both candidates, keeping all options open."

"Do you think they might consider merging the two into a single figurehead?" Francesco hinted. He was strategically maneuvering Mussolini, preparing him to propose the Four

Power Pact between Italy and Britain, France, and Germany. Francesco felt that gaining France as a strategic partner would be especially beneficial, thereby elevating Mussolini's standing with the Council.

"I'm not sure. Their immediate concern was Hitler's current number two position," Eugenio said in a grave voice. "President von Hindenburg is proving to be a great hindrance to Hitler's mission."

"What does the Council want me to do?" Francesco's own voice was steady, revealing no trace of emotion.

"President von Hindenburg needs to be removed from the equation. They want you to arrange for his assassination."

"Oh. Is that all?" Francesco's voice was laced with derision.

"I know it's a minor task, brother, but until I ascend to the papacy, I am at your mercy."

"It shall be done, brother." Francesco rose from his chair, his arms encircling his brother in a firm embrace, a silent promise of loyalty.

"You know I always strive to emulate you," Eugenio breathed.

Francesco's smile was a tacit acknowledgment of his younger brother's compliment.

"Grandfather always held you in high regard, Franco."

"He thought the world of you too, brother."

A moment of silence ensued, a testament to their unbreakable bond and mutual respect. Their brotherhood was paramount, superseding any mission from the Black Nobility. Yet together, they were unstoppable—they held the world's fate in the palm of their hand.

Chapter 36

2 August 1934

The Art of War
#26 Attack where he is unprepared.

President Paul von Hindenburg has died. His already declining health simplified the process for the assassin who administered the overdose of morphine, sealing the president's fate.

Upon his death, Hitler abolished the Office of the President and declared himself both Chancellor and Führer of the German Reich. He has become the absolute dictator of Germany. Nothing can stand in his way.

Secretary of State,
Archbishop Eugenio Pacelli

Chapter 37

21 September 1936
Vatican City

Francesco rushed into his brother's office and said, "Your Excellency, there's been a change in your itinerary."

"Francesco, we are brothers. There's no need for such formalities."

"It is out of respect, brother." Francesco's voice carried a note of reverence.

"Yes, well. What is this change?"

"Your summer retreat to Switzerland has been cancelled. Instead, you will go to the United States for a series of high-stakes meetings." Francesco's words hung heavy in the air.

"Is this the Council's doing?"

"Yes. Your unofficial American tour will include private meetings with influential archbishops. We are also orchestrating a potential meeting with President Roosevelt, although that confirmation is still pending."

Eugenio's gaze held steady on his brother. "And what is my mission there?"

"Your mission is three-pronged. First, you will rally the support of President Roosevelt and the United States. Second, you are to extend an invitation to the U.S. government to establish formal diplomatic relations with the Vatican and accept a papal nuncio. This will forge a direct line of communication between the Vatican and President Roosevelt. Last, you are to reassure President Roosevelt that Reverend Coughlin's recent verbal onslaughts by were not sanctioned by the Holy See. There will be a private discussion with Coughlin, instructing him to cease his tirade over the airwaves against the U.S. president."

"When do I leave?"

"The first of October. A team of your most trusted allies is being meticulously selected and briefed on the tasks at hand."

Eugenio's eyes reflected the weight of the impending task; he studied his brother, his mind engrossed in the intricate details of this monumental undertaking.

"When you arrive in New York, you will be staying at the Grand Inisfada Estate in Long Island, the home of Genevieve Brady."

Eugenio furrowed his brows. "I am unfamiliar with this woman."

"She is the late wife of Nicholas Brady, a duke of the Holy Roman Church. She will act as your bridge to the influential and powerful elite of America."

Eugenio nodded. "I appreciate you orchestrating this crucial mission, Franco."

Francesco paused, his gaze intense and penetrating. "This assignment, brother, is a turning point for the Vatican's future. Do you comprehend the sheer scale of this visit?"

"I do understand the gravity of the situation. I assure you, I will not let you down, brother."

"Excellent. If you should have any questions, do not hesitate to summon me."

Chapter 38

8 October 1936
New York Harbor

The majestic SS Conte di Savoia ocean liner sliced through the waters of the Hudson River, making its grand entrance into the bustling New York harbor. Awaiting its arrival was an esteemed apostolic delegation led by a formidable assembly of bishops, high-ranking clergy, and distinguished civic representatives. The Vatican Secretary of State was not just greeted by these dignitaries, but also a buzzing swarm of journalists, photographers, and Catholic reporters, all eager to document this momentous occasion and probe Pacelli about the intentions behind this unprecedented visit to the United States.

The six-foot tall, slender Archbishop, with an austere countenance that commanded respect, delivered a succinct yet impactful statement to the audience of reporters. As he opened the floor for questions, Pacelli's piercing dark eyes surveyed the eager press corps shouting out questions.

"Are you here to support President Roosevelt in his reelection?" one reporter managed to ask, his voice rising above the others.

Pacelli responded in his plaintive voice with a calm and measured tone, "As I explained in my brief, I am here on my first visit to the United States to see with my own eyes this country and feel the pulsations of its life and its labor. My desire is to know firsthand this great and powerful nation which holds such a unique and important place among all the peoples of the world."

Another journalist, eager to stir controversy, asked, "What is the Vatican's stance on Reverend Charles Coughlin's scathing criticism of President Roosevelt?"

Pacelli, maintaining his composure, replied, "I am afraid I don't have a response from the Vatican on that matter."

Bishop Spellman boldly interposed himself between Pacelli and the throng of reporters. "Gentlemen, thank you for coming out today. Archbishop Pacelli has just arrived from a long voyage. Let's offer him his privacy so he can get to his lodging and get settled in. Thank you, gentlemen." With a firm hand, Spellman guided Pacelli away from the voracious crowd of journalists towards a waiting vehicle.

"Your assistance is invaluable, my friend." Pacelli expressed his gratitude by firmly shaking Spellman's hand.

"Think nothing of it, Your Excellency. Your schedule is packed, and I didn't want those relentless hounds to exhaust you on your very first day. I haven't forgotten your health concerns."

With the protection of a police escort, Pacelli, Spellman, and their entourage swiftly departed en route to the first of many meetings with U.S. Cardinals during Pacelli's momentous visit to the United States.

8 October 1936
Afternoon
New York City

"Cardinal Hayes, let me get right to the matter at hand," Pacelli's voice sliced through the air, his gaze fixed on Cardinal Patrick Joseph Hayes. The Cardinal of New York, a seasoned veteran of the Church, felt a chill run down his spine. Whispers of Pacelli's relentless demands had reached his ears through the sacred corridors of the Church. He knew that any command from Pacelli—the Vatican's iron fist sheathed in a velvet glove—was not to be taken lightly. Any defiance could result in catastrophic repercussions. Hayes was acutely aware that the Vatican Secretary of State's unprecedented visit to America was no casual affair—the stakes were high, the air thick with anticipation.

"President Roosevelt's success in the upcoming election is of paramount importance. I demand that you steer the Archdiocese of New York to rally behind FDR." Pacelli's words hung heavy in the room.

Cardinal Hayes, despite his initial shock, understood that this was not a request, but an ironclad command. "May I ask the reason behind this directive, Secretary?"

"That it is of the highest importance is all you need to know. Do I make myself clear?" Pacelli's patience was wearing thin; his annoyance with the New York cardinal's probing question was undeniable.

"It shall be done."

"Ensure the faithful understand that a vote against FDR is a vote against God himself."

"I will personally relay this command." Hayes hastily scribbled down the instructions, mentally preparing to summon an emergency meeting of all the priests, bishops, and deacons of the district.

"Furthermore, I want you to reinforce America's commitment to isolationism with your entire archdiocese."

Hayes, his pen still moving across the paper, remained silent.

"If these directives are ignored, well, it would be a shame if the press were to stumble across your *indiscretions*, Cardinal." Pacelli's voice was icy as he slid a series of incriminating photographs across the table towards Hayes. The sight of his own face caught in compromising positions with the parish youth sent a wave of icy dread coursing through him. The whispers of Pacelli's ruthless tactics clearly had not been just rumors. If Roosevelt were to lose the election due to Hayes's district, it would spell the end of the cardinal's esteemed position. The photos would undoubtedly find their way to the press.

Pacelli rose, his movement a clear dismissal. Hayes pushed himself up, his legs trembling as he glared once more at the damning photos on the table. He hastily gathered them up and trailed after Pacelli to the door.

Pacelli extended his hand, his grip cold and unyielding. "Let nothing escape these walls." Hayes felt a chill slither up his arm as he was ensnared in Pacelli's grasp.

"Nothing leaves this room," Cardinal Hayes echoed, his head lowered in submissive surrender to the Vatican Secretary of State.

Once the door closed behind Pacelli, Cardinal Hayes moved to the trash can and set the photos ablaze. As the flames consumed the incriminating evidence, a bone-chilling dread gnawed at his core: Pacelli had more copies in his possession ready to shatter his revered status should FDR's reelection fail.

8 October 1936
Evening
Inisfada Estate
Manhasset, Long Island

"Duchess Brady, it is an absolute honor to make your acquaintance," Eugenio Pacelli murmured within the atrium of the Tudor Revival mansion, his eyes meeting those of the duchess's. As a duchess of the Holy Roman Church, a title bestowed upon her by Pope Pius XI, Genevieve Brady was a woman of significant influence—her connections ran deep into the political heart of the U.S. It was these connections that had led Francesco to arrange Eugenio's stay at the opulent estate.

"Your Excellency, the honor is entirely mine," Genevieve Brady responded, her voice filled with genuine warmth as she addressed the esteemed Vatican Secretary of State. "Bishop Spellman, it is always a pleasure to see you. You appear to be in good health."

"The pleasure is indeed mine," Spellman replied, his gaze shifting to his left. "Duchess, allow me to introduce Count Enrico Galeazzi."

"A pleasure to meet you, Count." Genevieve offered him a graceful curtsy.

Count Galeazzi, a trusted friend and confidant of Eugenio Pacelli, often accompanied the Secretary of State on sensitive diplomatic missions. Although this visit to America was officially labeled "informal", the underlying agenda was of paramount importance to the Black Nobility's mission.

Once the formalities were concluded, Bishop Spellman wasted no time in getting down to business. "Duchess, might

185

there be a private space where we can discuss the itinerary for Archbishop Pacelli's visit to the U.S.?"

"Of course. My staff will ensure your entourage is comfortably accommodated," Genevieve assured, her hand subtly gesturing to her dutiful servants. They promptly attended to the guests, ensuring their luggage was transported to their designated quarters. With a graceful turn, Genevieve led the way towards the library, a sanctuary of knowledge nestled within the vast mansion. The archbishop, the bishop, and the count trailed behind, their footsteps echoing through the opulence of the eighty-seven-room mansion. Cradled within three hundred acres of lush landscape, the Inisfada Estate stood as a testament to architectural genius and at present was the fourth largest mansion in the United States.

"May I offer you a drink, Your Excellency?" Genevieve inquired upon entering the library.

"Under normal circumstances I would decline, but that onslaught by the media has left me somewhat drained. A Cognac would indeed soothe my spirit," Pacelli responded.

"And for you, Bishop?"

"The same, please."

"And you, Count?"

"Cognac as well, thank you."

Once the Cognac was served, Spellman wasted no time in addressing the most pressing matter at hand. "Have arrangements been made for Archbishop Pacelli's meeting with President Roosevelt?"

"We are in the process of coordinating that," Genevieve explained. "As you are aware, President Roosevelt is in the throes of his reelection campaign. His itinerary has him crisscrossing the United States rallying support in key cities."

"This meeting is of utmost importance. Have you received any feedback from his staff regarding his availability?" Spellman pressed.

"We have been in contact with Joseph Kennedy, a close advisor to Roosevelt. They maintain regular communication, speaking at least twice a week without fail," Genevieve assured.

The bond between FDR and Kennedy had been forged in the crucible of political ambition, solidified during the tumultuous period of FDR's 1932 presidential bid. Kennedy's financial support, both personal and procured, was instrumental to Roosevelt's campaign, a fact that did not go unnoticed by the future president. This led to Kennedy's appointment as the chairman of the Securities and Exchange Commission in 1934. Despite his brief tenure from 1934 to 1935, Kennedy's leadership proved pivotal in establishing the SEC as one of the most respected institutions resulting from the New Deal, a testament to Roosevelt's ability to fulfill his campaign promises. This shared history had deepened the men's mutual trust and respect, creating a bond that was unshakable.

"What's your read on Joseph Kennedy?" Pacelli asked.

"Mr. Kennedy is orchestrating a luncheon here in New York towards the month's end. I am confident he can secure a meeting with the President for you then, Archbishop," Genevieve assured.

Eugenio's gaze shifted to Count Galeazzi, silently seeking confirmation that the proposed timeline would be workable with his calendar. The count's nod was all the affirmation he needed. His visit to the United States was only supposed to last for two weeks, but this crucial meeting warranted flexibility.

"I am deeply grateful for your efforts, Duchess. I eagerly await your confirmation of this pivotal meeting," Pacelli expressed, his head bowing in a gesture of gratitude for Genevieve's tireless work on his behalf.

"I've also arranged a meeting with Joseph Kennedy for you, Your Excellency."

"Mr. Kennedy's reputation precedes him. I appreciate your efforts."

With a gentle clink, Pacelli placed his glass on the coffee table then rose from the plush couch. This subtle gesture was a clear signal the meeting was concluded. Galeazzi, Spellman, and Brady followed suit, rising in unison.

"My staff will guide you to your accommodations," Genevieve offered, gesturing towards the waiting staff ready to attend to their every need. "Should you require anything, please do not hesitate to call for me."

9 October 1936
Inisfada Estate
Manhasset, Long Island

I n the seclusion of the study, Galeazzi, Spellman, and Pacelli convened, their minds focused on the intricate web of the archbishops's upcoming itinerary. This was no ordinary schedule, but a strategic chessboard of meetings with cardinals stationed throughout the country's pivotal swing cities that held President Roosevelt's political fate in the balance. These encounters were designed to underscore the importance of the president securing another term. The Vatican's alliance with Roosevelt and the United States would prove to be yet another critical chess piece in the grand game of global politics.

13 October 1936
New York City

The archbishop, the bishop, and the count embarked on their journey from the Inisfada Estate, their destination being Boston for Pacelli's inaugural meeting. Their route took them through the heart of Hartford, Connecticut and included a strategic pitstop at St. Joseph's College where they were to rendezvous with Bishop Maurice F. McAuliffe. Hartford was important in its own right, with its potential to sway the upcoming election in FDR's favor.

The meeting with Bishop McAuliffe mirrored the one with Cardinal Hayes, a dance of power and manipulation. This bishop, too, was presented with incriminating photographs, a ticking time-bomb that threatened to explode his reputation if he dared defy the archbishop's demands.

Spellman and Galeazzi, the architects of this intricate web of control, had gathered damning evidence against all the key swing states' cardinals and bishops, making Pacelli's task of securing loyalty at these personal meetings a smooth operation.

Pacelli, a staunch advocate of absolute leadership, propagated the doctrine of autocratic control, extending his iron grip even to the far reaches of the United States. This pattern of dictatorial extortion acted as the blueprint for every encounter he had with the cardinals and bishops during his so-called "informal" tour of America.

21 October 1936
Washington, DC

"Eugenio," Count Galeazzi began, his tone heavy with the weight of the news he was about to deliver, "due to the president's relentless campaign schedule, our initial meeting plans have been cancelled."

Pacelli's brow furrowing in concern. "Have alternative arrangements been made?"

"Unfortunately, FDR will not be available to meet until after the election. If we are to accommodate, this will extend your visit to nearly a month."

"That's quite the significant extension," Pacelli noted, his mind already racing from the implications.

"Spellman and I have devised a plan: we propose you embark on an air tour of the United States, a press tour that will herald you as the highest-ranking Vatican official to ever grace American soil. The media will be in a frenzy over your extended visit," Galeazzi explained, a glimmer of excitement in his eyes.

"Ah. You've already scheduled these meetings in key voting districts, I presume?"

"Indeed. Chicago, Cleveland, South Bend, St. Paul, Minnesota, San Francisco, Los Angeles, St. Louis, Cincinnati, Syracuse—and finally back to New York City where you will meet with FDR at his residence," Galeazzi detailed, his voice steady and confident.

"That's quite an extensive itinerary," Pacelli mused, his mind whirling with the enormity of the task ahead.

"Your presence in these pivotal voting blocs will undoubtedly secure President Roosevelt's reelection."

"When do we depart?" Pacelli asked, ready to face the challenge head-on.

"Tomorrow."

22 October 1936
Chicago, IL

"Cardinal Mundelein." Archbishop Pacelli's voice dripped with a feigned reverence that was as hollow as it was insincere. "I bring warm greetings from the Vatican and His Holiness." The words were laced with an unmistakable disdain for the cardinal.

Mundelein, taken aback by the unexpected visit and the thinly veiled scorn in Pacelli's voice, responded with a hint of unease, his voice wavering slightly. "The honor is all mine, Archbishop. Do extend my humble blessings to the pope." This abrupt, unofficial visit from the Vatican Secretary of State had caught him off guard. Given Pope Pius XI's precarious health, it was highly unusual for Pacelli to venture out of the Vatican on such short notice.

The Chicago cardinal couldn't help but feel a sense of unease, a nagging suspicion that there was a hidden agenda behind this sudden visit. Pacelli's rapid ascent within the Vatican hierarchy hadn't escaped the notice of his fellow clergymen. Mundelein couldn't shake off the feeling that there was more to this visit than met the eye.

"I'll cut to the chase," Pacelli said, his gaze steady on Mundelein. "The upcoming election is of utmost importance. It's absolutely vital that President Roosevelt clinch another term in the Oval Office." He paused, allowing the weight of his words to permeate the room, the silence amplifying the tension. "Reverend Coughlin's radio broadcasts have been escalating in their criticism of the president. Over the past few years, they have contributed to steadily chipping away at the president's approval rating, resulting in a significant and worrying decline."

"We are not ignorant of the reverend's broadcasts, Archbishop," Mundelein retorted, his voice trembling slightly, betraying his fear. "But we've taken care not to provoke him, terrified that his venomous words might be directed towards us. As a close personal friend of Roosevelt, I take these insults to heart."

Pacelli remained stoic, his gaze piercing through Mundelein as he absorbed the cardinal's feeble justifications.

"The United States leans more Episcopalian than Catholic. We simply cannot risk alienating any of our devoted followers," Mundelein added, his voice laced with a tone of defensiveness.

"I assure you, the Vatican understands the delicacy of the situation."

Mundelein felt a surge of disgust at Pacelli's words. The Vatican Secretary of State was acting like a privileged son who had been handed the reins of a company without ever having toiled for it. His swift promotion to the second highest position in the Vatican had been a little too convenient, raising suspicion among the clergy that there were unseen forces at play.

"Do not worry. We possess the means to silence that reverend's inflammatory rhetoric."

Mundelein was somewhat aware of the "influence" the Vatican held over Coughlin's life if he did not cease his critical radio broadcasts against the President. Whispers of persuasive conversations with the Vatican had circulated among the cardinals, leading to a suppressed atmosphere of terror.

"Cardinal Mundelein, we require your unwavering support in promoting President Roosevelt within your diocese and parishes. It is of utmost importance that your flock cast their votes for Roosevelt in this imminent election. The future of America hangs in the balance. Do I make myself clear?"

Pacelli's words were as sharp as a blade, leaving no room for misinterpretation.

Cardinal Mundelein gave a silent nod of agreement. The archbishop's veiled threat hung in the air like a guillotine blade, its implication clear—the same "influence" being brought to bear against Coughlin could just as easily be directed towards him.

"Also, it is crucial that the United States maintain its isolationist stance. This nation cannot afford another setback like the aftermath of the Great War or the crippling Great Depression," Pacelli continued, his voice cold and unyielding as he outlined the Council's directives.

Cardinal Mundelein remained silent, absorbing Archbishop Pacelli's words with the obedience of a disciplined pupil, his mind racing from their implications. The peaceful facade Pacelli portrayed in public was a stark contrast to the malevolent aura he exuded in private.

Pacelli rose with Mundelein following suit. The tall, slender Pacelli locked eyes with Mundelein, his gaze piercing, ensuring the Cardinal of Chicago grasped the gravity of this meeting and the actions that were to follow. Mundelein stared back into the abyss and saw a deep-rooted evil lurking there. Without uttering another word, Pacelli turned and exited the cardinal's office. Bishop Spellman was waiting outside to escort him to his next appointment. Hesitating for but a moment, Mundelein followed. He trailed behind the pair, feeling as though he had just struck a deal with the devil.

In the weeks that followed, similar private meetings and directives and threats were issued to the cardinals in charge of the most important cities throughout the United States.

5 November 1936
Hyde Park, Roosevelt's Home
New York City

"Mr. President, I bring heartfelt greetings and warmest regards from His Holiness," Pacelli said, extending his hand with a gracious smile as he began his coveted meeting with President Franklin Delano Roosevelt.

"The honor is entirely mine, Archbishop," FDR responded, his hand firmly clasping Pacelli's. The president leaned heavily on his cane; the polio had taken its toll. Despite the pain, he stood tall, a testament to his resilience and his respect for his esteemed guest.

"Please, Mr. President, let's sit," Pacelli suggested, gesturing towards the elegantly set dining table. As they moved to their seats, the wait staff glided in to present the first course of their luncheon—a velvety cream of asparagus soup, adorned with a dollop of sour cream.

"Congratulations on your sweeping victory in the election. I understand you claimed all but two states. Quite the achievement," Pacelli remarked, his eyes reflecting genuine admiration.

"Well, it seems Maine and Vermont aren't quite taken with my New Deal program," FDR chuckled, his humor undiminished by the landslide victory.

A moment of silence fell between the two men as they savored the rich, creamy soup.

Pacelli broke the silence, his tone sincere. "I am grateful for your time, Mr. President. And may I say, we deeply appreciate the efforts of your friend Joseph Kennedy in arranging this luncheon.

He is indeed a man of great character. You are fortunate to have him as a confidant."

"Joe is a trusted ally. We talk frequently. When he deems a meeting important, I move mountains to make it happen," FDR responded, his voice filled with respect.

They continued their meal, each spoonful of the asparagus soup savored before it could cool.

"Mr. President, I must confess, I am quite an admirer of yours. Your exploits and achievements have not escaped me."

"Is that so?" Roosevelt responded, a hint of surprise in his voice. "And what have you heard?"

"Well, I understand you are somewhat of a *treasure hunter*," Pacelli revealed, a glint of intrigue in his eyes.

Roosevelt was momentarily taken aback by the Vatican Secretary of State's comment. It seemed Pacelli had done his due diligence before their meeting—a refreshing change from the usual diplomatic chatter he was accustomed to.

"It seems you've done your homework, Your Excellency. I'm flattered," Roosevelt replied, a hint of amusement in his voice. Pacelli responded with a slight bow of his head.

"As you can see from these photographs"—Roosevelt gestured towards the wall—"I did indulge in a bit of treasure-hunting in my younger days. However, once I entered public service, that all came to an end."

"Would you mind sharing some of your exploits? I must admit, I too have a penchant for treasure-hunting," Pacelli confessed, his interest piqued.

"I was part of a team on Oak Island, part of the Old Gold Salvage and Wrecking Company in Nova Scotia," Roosevelt reminisced, his gaze distant as he recalled his time in 1909. "We were on the hunt for a mysterious lost treasure."

"What was this treasure you sought?" Pacelli asked, his curiosity evident.

"Well, there were many rumors," Roosevelt began, a hint of embarrassment creeping into his voice. "The most popular was that the Knights Templar had buried their treasure on the island when they fled France in 1307."

"And did you ever uncover any Templar treasure?"

"Unfortunately, we didn't find anything groundbreaking. However, I have kept up with the story over the years," Roosevelt admitted, feeling at ease discussing his youthful adventures. "The Knights Templar were rumored to have found King Solomon's treasure. The same King Solomon from the Bible."

Pacelli nodded, engrossed in Roosevelt's tale.

"Early explorers stumbled upon a peculiar indentation on the island, a telltale sign of a possible pirate's cache. The island turned out to be a labyrinth of cunningly designed booby traps and flood systems, a fortress designed to safeguard some buried treasure from prying eyes." A shadow crossed Roosevelt's face as he recalled a tragic incident. "We lost a brave soul to the island's deadly secrets. The company eventually succumbed to bankruptcy, and I found my calling in public service."

"I'm sorry to hear about your loss. It seems like a bitter memory," Pacelli sympathized.

"The thrill of the hunt was intoxicating," Roosevelt admitted, his eyes gleaming with the memory of the adventure. "Until the accident, of course. But imagine if we had unearthed King Solomon's treasure, a prize that has eluded treasure hunters for centuries?"

"Indeed, I can only imagine," Pacelli replied, captivated by the tale.

"Allow me to share a piece of history with you," Roosevelt said, his hand reaching into the depths of his suit pocket to retrieve a well-worn photograph he always carried on him. It was a memento from his past, a silent testament to the unyielding spirit of adventure that still pulsed within his veins. "This was the fearless team I was a part of on Oak Island."

"A fine-looking group of men. You all look so proud. It must have been an exciting time."

"A time like no other. But destiny put me on a different path," Roosevelt said, his hand gently patting his leg, a stark reminder of the polio that had irrevocably changed the trajectory of his life. "I was summoned to serve my country."

"Thank you for sharing, Mr. President. I always enjoy a good treasure-hunting story."

"Might I ask, what is it about the Templar treasure that so intrigues you?"

"Treasure-hunting has always been a passion of mine, especially when it comes to the Knights Templar. Do you know the superstition surrounding the number thirteen traces back to the Templars?"

"I do. I avoid traveling on the thirteenth day of the month, or hosting thirteen guests for a meal," Roosevelt admitted with a chuckle. "A strange fear for a president, isn't it?"

"Not at all, Mr. President. We all have our fears," Pacelli said, his tone turning serious. "For instance, I worry about the Vatican's financial stability."

Roosevelt's brows furrowed at the mention of the Vatican's financial woes.

"The Vatican is in the process of establishing the Institute for the Works of Religion—a Vatican bank, if you will," Pacelli revealed, hinting at the Vatican's future plans. "Given the current turmoil in Europe, we want to ensure the Vatican's financial security for centuries to come."

"I've been closely monitoring the unsettling events unfolding in Europe," FDR confessed, his eyes reflecting the weight of being responsible for the world's affairs. He was a man who understood the importance of staying informed, especially in these tumultuous times. "You mentioned plans for financial security. Could you elaborate?" Roosevelt's interest was piqued. The United States, still nursing the wounds of the Great Depression, also pined for guarantees of financial stability. FDR's New Deal programs had provided some relief, but the nation's financial reserves remained far from robust.

Pacelli nodded. "The Vatican, along with Catholic churches worldwide, will serve as a fortress of hope in these dark times. But even a fortress needs to fortify its reserves to withstand the storms of the future. I can't divulge all the details at this moment, but rest assured, the financial gains we envision are . . . staggering."

Roosevelt leaned forward, trying to comprehend the implications.

"This is sensitive, a hypothetical, if you will. . . . Do you have a facility in America where we could secure such an immense treasure?"

"We have Fort Knox," Roosevelt replied, a hint of pride creeping into his voice. "Why do you ask?"

Pacelli's gaze hardened. "The turmoil in Europe may necessitate a secure location for safekeeping the Vatican's invaluable artifacts. I fear Europe may not provide the security we need."

Roosevelt nodded, understanding the gravity of the situation. "Fort Knox is the most heavily fortified military base in the United States. It's probably the most secure place on the planet."

Pacelli appeared relieved. "If necessary, can I count on you to safeguard our priceless treasures were they to be transported here, Mr. President?"

"How much are we talking?"

"Think vast. Templar Treasure amount."

Roosevelt's response was immediate and firm. "I can assure you, Archbishop, we can accommodate that amount. Anything placed in Fort Knox will remain secure. Our nation's gold reserve is housed in a bombproof structure. Your treasures, if need be, could also be stored there. Of this I'm absolutely certain we can handle whatever you bring here."

"Thank you, Mr. President. Wonderful. That eases my concerns."

A moment of silence descended upon the room as both men savored their soup, each lost in the intricacy of their own thoughts. Their minds, both powerhouses of intellect, found solace in the quiet companionship of each other.

Pacelli finally broke the silence, his voice echoing softly in the grand dining room. "Where does the United States stand on foreign policy? Do you continue to embrace your isolationist ideals?"

"The Great Depression deeply scarred the U.S. economy," Roosevelt replied, his gaze distant as he contemplated the state of his nation. "After the devastation of World War I, we find ourselves quite content to remain on the sidelines of any brewing conflicts in Europe or Asia."

"Thank you for your candor," Pacelli responded, nodding in understanding.

"We prefer to steer clear of international politics at this juncture, Archbishop. If turmoil *were* to erupt in Europe, I would be extremely reluctant to involve us again."

"I understand, Mr. President."

"My primary focus for the next four years is my New Deal program. I aim to provide relief for the unemployed and impoverished, restore the economy to its former glory, and reform our financial system to prevent another crippling depression from ever occurring again."

"Those are commendable plans, Mr. President. It is noble of you to prioritize your country's recovery. You can't help someone else until you've first taken care yourself."

"Exactly my point. We cannot afford another setback like the ones we suffered in recent times."

"Your dedication to your country is truly admirable, Mr. President. It is no wonder you won the election by such a wide margin."

FDR's face lit up with a smile at the high-ranking Vatican official's compliment. "Now, am I to understand you may have had some influence over how the Catholic community voted, Archbishop?" FDR asked, recalling snippets of conversations he'd had with Kennedy regarding Pacelli's strategic visits across the USA.

"I try to sway everyone within my reach," Pacelli confessed, a hint of a smile playing on his lips.

"I've heard your influence extended beyond mere 'sway', Archbishop," FDR countered, his eyes twinkling with a knowing look.

"Ah. I did meet with cardinals and archbishops in key voting areas to encourage the parishioners to vote for you. However, I don't want to detract from your achievement, Mr. President.

Your dedication to the American public is the reason they voted for you so overwhelmingly."

"Thank you. I appreciated the Vatican's endorsement during this critical election."

For the next hour, Pacelli and FDR engaged in a lively discussion about their shared passion for treasure hunting, politics, and learning. As their conversation drew to a close, Pacelli provided guidance to the president regarding issuing any public statements about their meeting.

"Officially, this meeting's agenda involved discussing topics considered important by the pope—that is, I came here to enlist your support for the anti-Communist campaign declared by Pope Pius XI. Secondly, to extend an invitation from the Vatican to establish a Papal Nuncio in the United States. And lastly, clarify that Reverend Coughlin's attacks over the airwaves are in no way endorsed by the Vatican."

"That Coughlin infuriates me," Roosevelt grumbled, clearly irritated by the two-faced reverend who had initially supported his New Deal program only to openly recant it later.

"We have spoken with the reverend. I can guarantee you his inflammatory rhetoric will cease." Pacelli's voice was resolute. He did not go into the details of the bone-chilling conversation he'd had with Reverend Coughlin in which he'd given a stark ultimatum: cease the onslaught directed at the President, or face fatal consequences.

"Thank you, Your Excellency. I appreciate your involvement with the reverend."

"My pleasure, Mr. President. May I say I am looking forward to further conversation with you in the future?"

"It would be my pleasure, Archbishop."

6 November 1936
New York City
Pier 59

On the brisk morning of November 6, 1936, in the bustling metropolis of New York City, Pier 59 was abuzz with activity. Vatican Secretary of State Pacelli was preparing for his return trip aboard the majestic SS Conte di Savoia cruise liner back to Rome.

Chapter 39

7 November 1936

The Art of War
#17 According as circumstances are favorable,
one should modify one's plans.

USA mission accomplished. My confidential discussions with the United States cardinals secured a second term for President Roosevelt. The election was a landslide victory.

President Roosevelt affirmed his isolationist stance and promised to keep America out of the conflict in Europe. He agreed to appoint a personal representative to the pope, thereby establishing a direct line of communication between the Vatican and the White House.

My whirlwind tour of America was a resounding success. The impact of my visit will be felt for generations to come. The United States of America is now yet another cog in the great mechanism we are creating that will secure the Vatican's financial stability for centuries to come.

Secretary of State,
Archbishop Eugenio Pacelli

March 9, 2000
10:48 a.m.
Vatican Secret Archives

Mario found himself rooted to the spot, his eyes wide with shock as he delved into the journal entries detailing Pacelli's meteoric rise to power within the hallowed halls of the Vatican. As he read about the Pacelli's cunning manipulations and how he laid low many an unsuspecting victim in his path, a biblical proverb by King Solomon resounded in his mind:

My Child, if sinners entice you, turn your
back on them! They may say:
"Come and join us.
Let's hide and kill someone!
Let's ambush the innocent!
Let's swallow them alive as the grave swallows its victims.
Though they are in the prime of life, they
will go down into the pit of death.
And the loot we'll get!
We'll fill our houses with all kinds of things!
Come on, throw in your lot with us,
we'll split our loot with you."
Don't go along with them, my child!
Stay far away from their paths.
They rush to commit crimes.
They hurry to commit murder.
When a bird sees a trap being set, it stays
away. But not these people!

> *They set an ambush for themselves;*
> *they booby-trap their own lives!*
> *Such is the fate of all who are greedy for*
> *gain. It ends up robbing them of life.*

Mario was haunted by the thought that FDR had unwittingly entrusted his fate to the archbishop; he had been taken in by his deceptive charm. How had a man as astute as Roosevelt fallen prey to Pacelli's web of lies?

With a mind swirling with questions, Mario turned the page and continued his journey through Pacelli's past life.

Chapter 40

8 November 1936

The Art of War
#2 Waging War
Thus it may be known that the leader of armies is the
arbiter of the people's fate,
the man on whom it depends whether the nation shall be
in peace or in peril.

I received word from my brother that the Rome-Berlin Axis has been formally declared, joining our two titan-nations together as allies. Francesco is pleased with this outcome, as am I.

Grandfather would be proud of our accomplishment. We have fulfilled the first step in the Council's grand mission.

Well done, brother. We have set in motion what past generations could not.

Secretary of State,
Archbishop Eugenio Pacelli

Chapter 41

17 November 1936
5:32 p.m.
The Vatican

"Here's to our victory, brother," Eugenio Pacelli said, raising his glass of exquisite fourteen-year-old Cognac. This was their first opportunity together to revel in their achievement following his whirlwind American tour.

"Indeed, a momentous occasion, brother," Francesco responded. The clink of their glasses filled the room, a testament to their dual triumph. "Our chosen ones have emerged victorious."

The Council's decision to back Hitler—a more formidable leader than Mussolini—had proven to be the better choice. The Rome-Berlin Axis, established on October 25, 1936, was a masterstroke of genius.

Francesco had always known Hitler would prove the superior choice to spearhead the Council's mission. The opportunity to work alongside the Führer, with managing Mussolini's command of Italy, was a privilege of immense significance.

"The formidable leaders providentially falling into our laps," Francesco mused, sinking into the plush sofa in Eugenio's office.

"We've achieved what our ancestors could only dream of," Eugenio affirmed, striding over to clink glasses once more with his elder brother, toasting to their victory.

"But our journey is far from over. There is so much more we have yet to accomplish."

"Indeed, Franco. We will conquer all that lies ahead."

Chapter 42

16 March 1938

The Art of War
#3 Planning Offensives
Preserving the enemy's state capital is best;
destroying their state capital is second best.
Preserving their army is best;
destroying their army is second best.
Preserving their battalions is best;
destroying their battalions is second best . . .

Germany's annexation of Austria is complete. Now that he owns both Germany and Austria, Hitler is convinced I am a prophet; everything I foretold two decades ago has come to pass.

The people of Austria welcomed the Anschluss. Not a single shot was fired. Fed up with the depression and ravages leftover from World War I, the Austrians welcomed Hitler with a parade as he entered Vienna. Rudolf Hess reported the jubilation of the Austrian crowd, 250,000 strong, almost deafened the Führer.

The Third Reich has begun its rise to power; soon all of Europe shall be engulfed in its shadow.

Secretary of State,
Archbishop Eugenio Pacelli

Chapter 43

11 March 1938
Munich, Germany

"Mein Führer." Rudolf Hess greeted Hitler with a crisp heil Hitler salute as he stepped into the leader's office. The room was heavy with the weight of decisions made and choices yet to come that would shape the world. Tens of millions of lives hung by a thread.

"What news do you bring of the Austrian invasion, Herr Hess?" Hitler barked, a storm brewing in his icy blue eyes.

"The Anschluss was a triumphant success. The Austrian people have embraced their annexation into the Nazi regime with unimaginable excitement, Mein Führer," Hess reported, his voice filled with pride.

"Exactly as the archbishop foretold," Hitler mused, a slow smile spreading across his face. Archbishop Pacelli's predictions were unfolding with uncanny accuracy. The plan to expand Germany's territory was exceeding even Hitler's own ambitious expectations. The Great Depression had left Europe in ruins, and the Nazi philosophy had proven a pillar of strength for the struggling nations. The promise of jobs and food had the Austrians welcoming the Nazi military with open arms, a sight Hitler had not anticipated.

"Austria has extended an invitation for your presence, Mein Führer. They wish to honor you with a grand parade. It promises to be a celebration that will echo through the annals of history."

Yet another surprise, and a distracting one. Hitler's orders from Cardinal Pacelli had been clear—confiscate Austria's gold upon gaining control of the country. This gold was to be Hitler's first payment to the Vatican in exchange for his ascension to the position of Führer of the Third Reich. Pacelli had kept his end of the bargain; Hitler intended to honor his.

The prospect of a parade in his honor was an unforeseen twist. The tales of prosperity enjoyed in Germany had spread like wildfire across Austria's citizenry, igniting a desire for the same in their country after years of depression and hardship. In a striking display of allegiance to the Nazi Party, an astounding 800,000 Austrians were drafted into the German army, with another 150,000 serving in the elite Nazi military unit.

Four days later, Hitler stood on the balcony of the Neue Hofburg, his gaze sweeping over the Heldenplatz Square. A vast ocean of over 250,000 exultant faces hailed their Führer, their cheers reverberating through the square like a thunderous applause. Overwhelmed by the Austrians' fervor, Hitler issued a decree to the crowd, his voice booming with authority: "As Führer and Chancellor of the German Nation and Reich, I announce before history the entry of my homeland into the German empire!"

Chapter 44

27 November 1938

The Art of War
#24 Keep him under strain and wear him down.

Pope Pius XI has proven to be a thorn in the Council's side. He is an obstinate man with a volatile temper. His defiance is not serving him well.

Under the direction of the Council, the Vatican assassin had to persuade His Holiness to cease and desist his aggressive onslaught against the Nazi regime. The pope's clandestine distribution of Mit brennender Sorge, which accuses the Nazis of racial anti-Semitism, was discovered in Germany's Catholic churches. The Council did not take kindly to this covert assault that went against their will.

There are consequences for defying the Council's agenda. Any act of disobedience is swiftly and ruthlessly dealt with.

I fear a grim fate looms for Pope Pius XI.

Secretary of State,
Archbishop Eugenio Pacelli

Chapter 45

25 November 1938
Pope Pius XI's Living Quarters
Vatican City

Pope Pius XI was slumped over, unconscious and bound to a Victorian spoon-back chair, his body leaning precariously over the ropes tied around his navel. His limbs had been securely fastened to the chair's armrests and legs. Across the room, the Vatican assassin, Dante, sat in anticipation, waiting for the pope to stir after rousing from the effects of the chloroform that had plunged the pope into unconsciousness.

Dante held no admiration for Pius XI. The recent revelation of the pope's covert distribution of his papal letter *Mit brennender Sorge* in churches across Germany was a blatant act of rebellion against the Council. In his decree, the pope had accused the Nazi government of breaching the 1933 Reichskonkordat, a treaty designed to shield the priests and clergy in Germany from persecution by the Nazi regime. This treaty, negotiated by Archbishop Eugenio Pacelli between the Vatican and the rising Nazi regime, had been directed into existence by the Council of Black Nobility itself. Defiance against the Council was not without severe repercussions.

Slowly, Pope Pius XI began to stir, his head lifting from the stupor induced by the injection. Upon realizing he'd been confined within his own quarters, the pope strained against the ropes holding him captive to the sturdy Victorian chair. His gaze fell upon his left arm, which was bound to the armrest—an IV tube was taped to the back of his hand where a needle had clearly fed him a dose of intravenous fluids.

"Your struggle is futile, Your Holiness," came the assassin's chilling voice.

"What's the meaning of this?" Pope Pius XI yelled. He hadn't noticed the figure cloaked in darkness sitting across the room.

"I am an envoy of the Council, here to discuss your recent *transgressions*, your Holiness." A sinister anticipation laced Dante's words.

The pope was no stranger to these confrontations; he refused to be cowed by the Council's henchman. He knew this man was part of the elite force cherry-picked from the Vatican's Swiss Guard. These were the Council's go-to men for matters requiring a more . . . delicate touch.

Only those popes who remained loyal to the Council of Black Nobility were spared these private "discussions". Pope Pius XI had forfeited this privilege with his recent defiance.

"You can't intimidate me. I'm the pope, the Vicar of Christ, for God's sake!"

"I was counting on such a response, your Holiness," Dante said, moving towards a table near the pope. He opened a black suitcase, revealing an array of tools that would not be out of place in a surgical theatre. He turned the suitcase towards the pope, revealing vials, syringes, scalpels, forceps, surgical tape, a stethoscope, and a thermometer. All the tools necessary for a thorough interrogation that was designed to extract the desired outcome from a victim.

The pope remained silent, refusing to give to this Black Nobility enforcer the satisfaction of his fear.

Dante selected a syringe and a vial from the case. Inverting the vial, he plunged the syringe into it, drawing out a small amount of fluid. "This should suffice for the next round, Your Holiness." He placed the loaded syringe on the table, a grim promise of the ordeal to come.

"What is that concoction?" Pope Pius XI was already suffering from a throbbing headache brought on by the initial injection. Was it a truth serum? He was prepared to confess his actions openly. He harbored no shame for his defiance against the Council. The anti-Semites populating Hitler's Nazi regime deserved exposure.

"That injection will help you gather your wits enough to change your mind."

A malevolent grin spread across Dante's face. The assassin reached for another syringe and vial. Holding the vial aloft, he pierced it with the needle, drawing up two-tenths of a milliliter of the ominous fluid.

"And this one will end your life. The decision lies with you, Your Holiness."

"What is it you want, assassin?"

Dante found himself satisfied by the pope's directness. No groveling or pleading like his usual victims at this stage. Pope Pius XI was renowned for his straightforward, no-nonsense demeanor. He was also infamous for his fiery temper. Dante was eager to see if Ambrogio Damiano Achille Ratti, the man beneath the papal vestments, would unleash his fury at any point during their confrontation.

"Firstly, you must withdraw your papal letter from every church in Germany."

"Never!"

"Wrong response, Your Holiness," Dante smirked, relishing the pope's growing anger. He was eager to put his tools of persuasion to work. Towering over the pope, he plunged the second syringe into the IV tube attached to the pope's hand.

A wave of agony surged up the pope's left arm. He tensed as the burning pain reached his heart, triggering a heart attack. After the pope endured five long seconds of unbearable pain, the assassin injected the first syringe into the IV tube, releasing adrenaline that halted the heart attack. The pope collapsed, unconscious.

Dante prepared two more syringes with the same amount of fluid for the next round of torture. Seeing the octogenarian pope was in no rush to wake up, Dante retreated, settling into the Victorian chair on the other side of the room.

After half an hour, the pope began to stir, this time remaining hunched over in his chair. "You are an evil man," he rasped in a hushed tone.

Dante crossed the room and loomed over the pope. Aware that the pope was already thoroughly sapped of his energy, the assassin hoisted the pope's head and rested it against the chair's backrest. The pope's visage was one of sheer exhaustion following the artificial heart attack. This was proving too effortless. Having heard tales of Ambrogio Ratti's resilience, Dante had anticipated more defiance.

Continuing where he left off, Dante said, "Secondly, you will halt your radio broadcasts denouncing the Nazi government's actions in Germany."

"Have you . . . no soul?" Pope Pius XI's voice was now barely a whisper.

"That question does not really matter, Your Holiness. I am merely here to fulfill my orders."

"The Nazis . . . are fostering animosity towards . . . Christ and His Church. . . ." The pope's voice was so faint that the assassin had to lean in to catch his words.

"Once again, that's not my place to judge, Your Holiness. Will you adhere to the Council's directives?"

"I will *not*." Pope Pius XI let his head droop forward, his eyes shut, unwavering in his mission to expose the Nazi government.

Dante seized the second syringe and plunged it into the IV tube. The pope remained hunched over as he convulsed in agony. After a mere three seconds, Dante administered the first syringe to prevent the man from succumbing to his heart attack. His objective was the pope's compliance, not a pointless lethal confrontation.

The pope remained hunched over, once more unconscious. Dante prepared two more syringes for the third round of persuasion. He then retreated to his chair to scrutinize the pope from a distance. He was taken aback by the pope's staunch resistance to his torture regimen. Most of his victims capitulated after the first dose, but this one was living up to his reputation. The pope's unwavering dedication to his ideals was commendable. Dante hadn't anticipated he would harbor respect for this pope.

An hour had passed when the pope began to rouse, emerging from the clutches of his second heart-stopping ordeal. His breaths came shallow and weak. " His lips cracked open and out came the ghost of a sound, the words barely reaching the assassin's ears from across the room.

"It . . . it shall be done."

Dante rose from his chair, satisfied. The clomp of his black polished leather shoes reverberated ominously as he crossed the room and stood before the old man. He meticulously untied the frail pontiff from the imprisoning Victorian chair, his actions calculated and devoid of warmth. With an unyielding grip, he hoisted the pope to his feet and steered him towards his bed—a sanctuary of respite following the harrowing sessions of torture.

The pope, his body wracked with exhaustion, curled up in a fetal position. He surrendered to sleep almost instantly.

Dante draped a blanket over the pope, a chilling contrast to the cruelty he had just inflicted. He then turned his attention to his instruments of persuasion, methodically placing them back into his suitcase.

With one last glance at the sleeping pope, the assassin exited the sleeping quarters, leaving behind a silence that was as ominous as the promise he had exacted.

Chapter 46

9 February 1939

The Art of War
#21 When he concentrates, prepare against him.

Pope Pius XI has summoned all of Italy's clergy to Rome to deliver a speech he has been relentlessly toiling over the past few months.

The two heart attacks he had in November ultimately only instilled in him a spirit of vengeance. His discussion with the Vatican assassin did not sway him—he has broken his promise to follow the Council's directives.

I fear this will not end well for the pontiff.

Secretary of State,
Archbishop Eugenio Pacelli

Chapter 47

10 February 1939
4 a.m.
Pope Pius XI's Living Quarters
Vatican City

Dante found himself once again in the pontiff's quarters sitting across the room from Pope Pius XI, who was bound anew to the very same Victorian chair that held him the prior year. "Déjà vu, Your Holiness," he taunted.

"Your threats hold no power over me. I have rallied all of Italy's clergy to Rome—I am ready to unveil this monstrous deceit," the pope retorted, his voice seething with defiance against the Black Nobility. He had no intention of bowing to the Council's outrageous demands. His objective was not theirs. His motto "The peace of Christ in the kingdom of Christ" stood in stark contrast to the pagan agenda dictated by the Black Nobility.

"That is precisely why I am here. You assembling the clergy is what alerted the Council's attention. Hence we find ourselves in conversation to change your mind yet again, Your Holiness."

"You will never sway me. I will deliver my speech tomorrow to the entirety of the Italian clergy. You cannot stop me."

"Obviously, your memory fails you, Your Holiness. You seem to have forgotten what was said during our previous encounter. Decisions were made."

Dante strode over to the table beside the pope. With the same calculated precision as before, he unlatched the briefcase, opened it, and swiveled it so the pope could clearly see its chilling contents. Reaching into the meticulously organized briefcase, the assassin selected a vial and syringe specifically intended for the pope. Holding the vial aloft, he inserted the syringe into the cap, drawing out exactly two-tenths milliliters of fluid. He placed the syringe onto the table and returned the vial to its designated slot. Turning towards the pope, he asked, "So I ask again, for the last time: *what is your decision*, Your Holiness?"

Pope Pius XI immediately noticed the absence of a second syringe and vial. There was no room for negotiation this time—only a choice between compliance or death. "If I accede, I'll be forever dead inside, as Judas was after his betrayal of Christ," the pope confessed, his head slumping forward in defeat. "If I don't, then I die at your hands." Taking a deep breath, he said, "I choose peace."

Dante's voice was a whisper as he seized the syringe. "As you wish, Your Holiness. Allow me to paint a picture of your imminent fate: upon injection of this serum, I will depart, stopping only to alert the waiting witnesses of your impending demise. These witnesses, incidentally, have already crafted your final words, which will be circulated among the press when the time is right."

The pontiff, bound to the Victorian chair, sat upright, his gaze locked on the assassin as he listened to the chilling narrative of how his final moments would play out. It was as if the assassin were relishing every horrifying detail. Searching the assassin's eyes, the pope sought any hint of mercy, a glimmer of hope—but all he found was an abyss of darkness. A soulless void. This man had already surrendered his soul and its rights to the Black Nobility.

"Later this morning , Archbishop Pacelli will announce your departure from this world, Your Holiness."

"Then make it swift, you soulless brute," Pope Pius XI retorted, sitting upright, his head held high as he faced his impending death with unyielding courage. There would be no swaying his opposition to the Council.

"I commend your resolve, Your Holiness," Dante noted, a hint of admiration in his voice. The pope would mark his first victim who hadn't wept, begged, or pleaded for his life. The assassin was somewhat surprised to find this diminished the satisfaction he derived from this final act.

He held the syringe aloft, expelling any air trapped within the tube—he didn't want an air bubble to enter the pope's veins and grant him an instant death. The purpose of this injection was a slow, agonizing death, defining the final moments of the pope's life.

Moving behind the chair, the assassin tilted the pope's head to one side and plunged the syringe into his neck.

The pope's reaction was immediate—the injection rendered him helpless incubating the slow death. Dante untied the frail figure from the chair and moved him to his bed before covering him with blankets. Returning to the table, he stowed away the syringe, closed the briefcase, and exited the room, leaving the pope to his fate.

Archbishop Pacelli entered the room, ready to oversee the final chapter of the pope's life. Crossing the room to check on the pontiff, he could see the pope was barely conscious.

"My soul parts from you in peace," the pope whispered weakly, his gaze meeting Pacelli's.

Dr. Francesco Petacci, the pope's chief physician and a pawn in the Black Nobility's grand scheme, entered the room mere moments later. His presence was no mere coincidence—

he was the father of Claretta Petacci, the infamous mistress of Benito Mussolini. The Black Nobility had strategically placed Dr. Petacci as the pope's primary physician to ensure they had a constant, watchful eye over the pope. The Council left no room for error, orchestrating every move, every interaction so that no single individual could ever disrupt their ultimate mission.

The doctor crossed the room to join Pacelli. Both men loomed over the pontiff. At precisely 5:31 a.m., the pope, his eyes flickering with the last vestiges of life, looked up at the two men before uttering his final words as he succumbed to cardiac arrest. "Peace. Peace."

Dr. Petacci, his duty done, crossed the room to open the doors, allowing the four chosen cardinals into the papal quarters to initiate the solemn proceedings that accompanied a pope's passing.

This included the prescence of the Camerlengo, a figure of authority chosen by the College of Cardinals who was tasked with the final confirmation of the reigning pope's death. This archaic procedure required the Camerlengo to call out the pope's Christian name thrice while gently tapping his forehead with a silver hammer. Upon receiving no response, the Camerlengo would declare the pope officially deceased. As it so happened, the Vatican's Secretary of State, Pacelli, had been appointed to this honorable position by the College of Cardinals to carry out these duties.

"Truly, the pope is dead," Pacelli announced, his voice reverberating with a chilling finality in the hallowed chamber. The select group of individuals chosen for this solemn occasion watched as the pope remained unresponsive to the soft, rhythmic taps of the silver hammer and the repeated calls of "Achille Ratti", the pope's baptismal name. The silence that followed each call was deafening, a grim reminder of the pope's mortality.

With a solemn expression, Pacelli reached out, his fingers gently wrapping around the pope's right hand. He carefully removed the Ring of the Fisherman from the pope's fourth finger, a custom-made symbol of authority that every pope wore to signify their succession of Saint Peter. This was the same ring the pope used to imprint the wax that sealed all official papal correspondence.

In the silent room, the only sound was the snipping of shears as Pacelli cut the ring off the pope's finger, a symbolic act witnessed by the select few marking the end of the pope's reign and authority. His era had come to an end.

In the absence of a pope, the Camerlengo was to ascend to the highest role, temporarily serving as the Acting Sovereign of Vatican City. Pacelli, in his capacity as Vatican Secretary of State and the Executive Director of Vatican Operations, would now make all decisions during this interim period until a new pope was elected.

The weight of the Vatican now rested squarely on his shoulders.

Chapter 48

3 March 1939

The Art of War
The greatest victory is that which requires no battle.

I Am Pope.

On my sixty-third birthday yesterday, the Council fulfilled my ascension to the papacy. My confirmation was the fastest in history, requiring a mere three ballots. Thanks to the Council's influence, all sixty-two cardinals took part in the voting, helping to push through my landslide victory.

The Council instructed I take the name Pope Pius XII in honor of both my predecessor and the founder of the Vatican Secret Archives. An honor, indeed.

I am grateful to you, Grandfather, for this honor. It was your hand that guided me to the papacy. Now I am positioned to fulfill the Council's mission. I will not disappoint you.

Pius pp. XII

Chapter 49

March 9, 2000
11:55 a.m.
Vatican Secret Archives

In the dimly lit aisle, Mario cast a furtive glance at his
wristwatch and realized with a start he had been utterly
consumed reading the pope's cryptic journal—over three
hours had passed without him noticing. The clock was ticking
towards noon and now here he was, grappling with the daunting
task of creating a convincing forgery that might deceive the
cardinal overseeing him. The question that gnawed at him was
how he could execute this audacious swap without arousing
Cardinal Borelli's suspicion.

His eyes darted back to the journal as if seeking divine
inspiration from its ancient pages. Suddenly, a sinister idea
began to take shape in his mind. "Bait and switch," he murmured,
his voice barely above a whisper, addressing the journal as if it
were a sentient being he was plotting to abduct from the Secret
Archives' hallowed confines.

With a newfound determination, he swiveled towards the
towering bookshelves, his gaze sweeping over the countless
books that filled the cold steel shelves. He selected five books
whose size shared a striking resemblance with the journal.
With a sense of urgency, he carried them over to the worktable,
meticulously placing each one atop the journal to gauge if there
was a perfect match. The third book he tested fulfilled that

purpose. Gingerly opening the book, his eyes darted across the pages, scanning its contents to determine whether it would be intriguing enough to divert the cardinal's attention:

Pope Benedict XIII's reign was tarnished with double-dealing by one of his main administrators, Niccolo Corscia, who engaged in extraordinary levels of bribery and corruption. This resulted in distrust of the papal authority, which continued throughout the seventeenth and eighteenth centuries . . .

"That'll do," he murmured to the ancient book that appeared to hold its own cryptic secrets from the Vatican's scandalous past.

That revelation hit Mario like a freight train—there were *centuries* of corruption that had festered in the shadows of the Catholic Church long before Pope Pius XII took the helm. The Church—his Church—had a dark underbelly, that much was undeniable. It was as though a long-hidden facet of the Church had been unveiled, and it was almost like those with the power to do something about it had conveniently overlooked it, akin to having an alcoholic brother-in-law whose existence everyone quietly acknowledged but would never discuss. It was easier to turn a blind eye to such uncomfortable truths, bury them deep beneath layers of denial.

But now, Mario found himself face-to-face with a harsh reality that he could no longer ignore. The Church he had pledged his life to had been weaving a web of lies long before he was ever born. His faith, once unshakable, now trembled on the precipice of doubt. The trust he'd placed in the Catholic Church had shattered, leaving him with the daunting task of concealing this truth from the world. The thought of the devastation that truth would wreak on the hearts of the world's faithful—a quarter of the global population—felt unbearable. The revelation would be a blow too harsh for many to bear. What would ensue if those billions learned of the corruption wrought within the hallowed halls of their beloved Catholic Church?

His eyes, hardened by the shocking revelations gleaned the past three hours, bore into the cover of Pacelli's journal.

With a sense of grim determination, he opened Pacelli's journal and spread its pages out like a fan, his left hand clutching both front and back cover while his right gripped the paper. With a swift, decisive motion, he tore the pages free from the spine, then set both cover and pages back on the worktable. He repeated the process with the eighteenth-century book, his heart pounding in his chest all the while. A sudden thought struck him, and he reached into his backpack and pulled out the Bible that Roberto had gifted him on his seminary graduation. As if guided by some divine hand, his Bible turned out to be the exact same size as the two gutted books lying on the table.

Mario cradled the Bible, a cherished gift from Roberto. It was an anchor of his hope and faith in his daily life, its pages filled with highlighted passages, scribbled notes, and verses committed to memory. The Bible was more than just a book to Mario—it was a symbol of his faith and a testament to his unwavering belief in Roberto's potential for redemption. He had seen a glimmer of hope in Roberto's eyes when the man had presented the Bible to him, the front matter inscribed with words that tugged at his heartstrings. Mario had clung to the hope that Roberto, despite his worldly ways, might one day find solace in the teachings of Jesus Christ. He prayed that Roberto's harsh upbringing under the nuns and the mother superior at the orphanage hadn't completely extinguished the flame of the Holy Spirit within him. This Bible was not just a book; it was a symbol of Mario's faith and hope for his best friend's salvation.

With a dreadful heart, he took a deep breath and began the painful process of separating the pages from the cover of his beloved Bible. His head slumped forward and his eyes squeezed shut in a futile attempt to block out the reality of his actions.

What am I doing?

The realization that he was on the brink of stealing a priceless document from the Vatican Secret Archives crashed down on his conscience. This act was a stark contradiction to the vows he had taken, a betrayal of everything he held sacred. The gravity of his actions hung over him like a dark cloud, threatening to consume him in its shadow.

The question of the act's morality gnawed at him, a relentless tormentor in the silent, oppressive gloom of the Archives. He had to remind himself that the very institution he had pledged his life to had been weaving a web of deceit around him since time immemorial. "Perhaps Roberto has been seeing things clearly all along," Mario murmured into the suffocating silence, his voice barely a whisper.

"Did you say something?" Cardinal Borelli's voice sliced through the stillness, his figure emerging from around the corner to find Father Marino standing before his worktable.

"I—" Mario's words were abruptly cut off as he choked on his own spit, and a violent coughing fit seized him. The cardinal halted, maintaining a safe distance from the spluttering priest. "Are you certain you're feeling okay, Father?" The cardinal's voice was laced with concern.

Mario gestured to give him a moment, his hand raised as he fought to regain control over his breathing. "Swallow first, then speak," he muttered to himself, his voice raspy.

The cardinal observed Mario's struggle, his gaze unwavering.

"I apologize, Cardinal," Mario managed to croak out, clearing his throat once more. "You took me by surprise."

"I apologize for startling you, Father."

"I'll pay more attention next time, Cardinal," Mario promised, his voice still hoarse.

"Did you manage to locate the book I asked you about earlier?"

"I'm finishing the scanning process as we speak," Mario replied, subtly positioning himself to obstruct the cardinal's view of the mutilated books on the worktable. "I'll bring it to you in the next hour."

"I'll anticipate you having it in my hands by one o'clock, Father," the cardinal replied, craning his neck in an attempt to glimpse the worktable Mario was shielding.

"Yes. One o'clock sharp," Mario assured him.

The cardinal turned on his heel, his suspicion of Mario's illness prompting him to make a mental note to handle the book with gloves. He didn't want to risk contracting whatever disgusting ailment the young priest seemed to be suffering from.

Mario raced to the end of the aisle and watched the cardinal's retreating figure disappear behind the heavy metal door of the Secret Archives. A dull thud echoed ominously throughout the vast tomb.

His gaze lingered on the sole entryway to the Archives, his mind racing. He had to complete the scanning of the entire journal and save it on a microSD chip before one o'clock. With no time to waste, he hurried back to the worktable to continue scanning the pages from Pacelli's journal. Securing those pages inside the eighteenth-century book cover would have to wait.

Chapter 50

March 9, 2000
12:45 p.m.
Vatican Secret Archives

The scanner hummed its final note as it processed the concluding page to Pacelli's journal. Mario's eyes darted to his watch—the hands indicated a quarter to one. With a sense of urgency, he carefully nestled the pages from Pacelli's journal within the cover of his favorite Bible Roberto had gifted him. The pages from the eighteenth-century book were then artfully inserted into the vibrant cover of Pacelli's journal, creating a convincing decoy. Finally, the contents of Roberto's Bible found a new home within the cover of the eighteenth-century book, which Mario now returned to its original place on the shelf. The intricate shell game of swapping contents and covers was now complete.

Retrieving his iPod from his backpack, he deftly ejected the microSD card from the Vatican's scanner and inserted it into his laptop's SD card reader. His fingers danced over the keyboard as he navigated through the files, transferring the scanned pages of the journal onto the storage card. The transfer of 16 Gb of data crawled along at a snail's pace, but after a painstaking five minutes, he removed the microSD chip and reinserted it into his iPod. A glance at his watch revealed he had a mere four minutes to reach the cardinal's office on time, a journey that typically took six minutes.

With the journal securely hidden in his backpack, he hoisted the pack onto one shoulder and began to jog down the aisle towards the exit. Once he emerged from the Archives, he was forced to adjust his pace to a brisk walk—the hallowed halls of the Vatican were no place for running. This was a sanctuary of worship, tranquility, and harmony. Any disruption to the serene atmosphere would be seen as a sign of disrespect.

As he turned into the corridor of offices, he checked his watch again. He had arrived at Cardinal Borelli's office at 1:02 p.m. Two minutes late. He entered the office to find Borelli reclining in his leather chair, feet propped up on the desk, engrossed in *L'Osservatore Romano*, Vatican City's official newspaper. Borelli folded the newspaper onto his lap and glanced up at Mario, then at the clock on the wall. His silence and piercing gaze conveyed his disappointment at Mario's tardiness. This was not acceptable.

Mario lingered in the doorway, his hand gripping the doorknob, a sheen of perspiration on his forehead. "I'm sorry I am late, Cardinal. I have that book you requested," he said, his voice hushed in the confines of the revered cardinal's office.

"Thank you," Borelli responded, his tone icy as the winter chill. He lowered his feet from the desk and placed the newspaper aside. "Bring it here. I want to look at it."

With a sense of dread gnawing at his gut, Mario approached Borelli's desk and placed the fabricated journal before him.

The cardinal opened the cover, his eyes narrowing at the sight of the spine separated from the rest of the book. "Is this the condition you found it in, Father?" His gaze pierced through Mario.

Mario hadn't had the time to properly affix the eighteenth-century book's contents to the journal's cover. Scanning the journal and saving it to his microSD card had consumed every precious second he had. He hadn't anticipated this level of scrutiny and was unprepared for questions. Lies didn't come easily to Mario, and his discomfort was noticeable. Sweat trickled down his forehead as he managed to stammer out a single word: "Yes."

Cardinal Borelli's eyes flicked to the beads of sweat on Mario's forehead. "Are you sure you are feeling alright, Father?" he asked, pushing his chair back to create more distance between them. "You've seemed unwell the past couple of days."

Mario hastily pulled a handkerchief from his pocket and dabbed at his forehead. "I'm feeling a bit under the weather, Cardinal. Perhaps I should take the rest of the day off to avoid spreading any potential illness."

"An excellent idea," Borelli agreed, pulling out his own handkerchief and placing it over his mouth. With a dismissive wave of his hand, he signaled for Mario to leave immediately.

With a sense of relief washing over him, Mario turned and swiftly exited the cardinal's office. He was eager to escape the cardinal's scrutinizing gaze and secure the copied journal in the safety of his home where he could privately study its secrets.

With Mario's hasty departure, Cardinal Borelli reached into the recesses of his desk drawer, his fingers closing around the familiar bulk of an oversized can of Lysol spray. With a grim determination, he aimed it at the space Mario had just vacated and unleashed a ten-second barrage of disinfectant against the unseen enemy he perceived to be lingering in the room. He was a man of faith—but he also had faith in the bold claim emblazoned on the can, "Kills 99.9% of Viruses and Bacteria".

Rising from his seat, he embarked on a thorough sanitization mission, dousing the entire office with a generous dose of the virus-and-bacteria killer. Satisfied that he had eradicated the potential threat, he returned to his seat, tucking the Lysol back inside its drawer. Leaning forward, he reached for his phone to dial a seldom-used internal Vatican number, his heart pounding with a sense of foreboding.

"Housekeeping," came the gruff response on the other end of the line.

"This is Cardinal Borelli from the Vatican Secret Archives," he began, his voice steady despite the chill creeping up his spine. "We may have an issue with the new priest assigned to archiving duties. He's acting suspiciously."

"Consider it handled," the voice on the other end promised, the tone as frosty and detached as the stark black attire his clandestine department was reputed to wear.

The cardinal hung up the phone, a shiver running through him. He had always found interactions with "housekeeping" unsettling, but as Cardinal of the Secret Archives, it was his duty to report any irregularities, no matter how insignificant they might seem. The Vatican was a place of strict protocol, and any deviation from the norm was treated with utmost seriousness. The recent unfortunate incident involving Father Benedetti was a stark reminder of this. Now, Cardinal Borelli found himself in a similar predicament with Father Mario Marino. The priest's recent change in behavior had left the cardinal with no choice but to alert "housekeeping".

Picking up the folded *L'Osservatore Romano*, he leaned back in his leather chair, propping his feet up on his desk with a sense of grim satisfaction. He had done his duty for the sake of the Archives and the Vatican. Now he could return to the day's news to let his mind ease its worries.

Chapter 51

March 9, 2000
2:14 p.m.
Roberto's Mansion

After making a couple of unusual detours, Mario finally found himself standing before the imposing double doors to Roberto's mansion. He rapped sharply on the grand entrance before pushing it open slightly to call out, "Berto, you home?"

The response came from the depths of the mansion. "Mario, is that you? What are you doing here so early?"

Stepping inside and shutting the massive door behind him, Mario made a beeline for Roberto's office. Roberto was already at his office door when Mario reached him, a look of concern etched on his face. "What's the matter?"

"You won't believe what I've done."

"You look like you're hyperventilating. Take a seat and tell me about it." Roberto directed Mario to the chair poised in the middle of the room.

Mario plopped into the plush leather club chair. "You can't breathe a word of this to anyone."

"You know I won't."

"Promise?"

"I promise. Now, what's got you so spooked?"

Lowering his voice to a hushed whisper, Mario confessed, "I stole the journal from the Archives."

"No way."

"Keep it down, will you? I'm not proud of this." Mario squirmed in his seat uncomfortably, the guilt of his transgression gnawing at him.

"Let me see it."

"I don't have it."

"Where is it?"

"Remember that old locker at the train station we used to stash our stuff inside when we'd sneak out of the orphanage?"

"Whoa. I haven't thought about that thing in years."

"I hid it there," Mario whispered, his gaze meeting Roberto's. "I'm really scared, Berto."

"I can see that. What's going on?"

Mario unzipped his backpack and pulled out his iPod. He pressed the microSD card into Roberto's palm. "Insert this into your computer. I'll show you what I'm talking about."

Roberto took the storage device to his desk and plugged it in. Mario set his backpack down then moved to stand behind Roberto. As his friend clicked on the folder, a multitude of JPEG files filled the screen.

Roberto's eyes scanned through the hundreds of JPEG files contained in the folder. "Damn, you've been busy, dude."

Mario, recalling where he had stopped reading, pointed on the monitor. "Click on that one."

Roberto clicked on the indicated JPEG file.

3 March 1939

The Art of War
The greatest victory is that which requires no battle.

I Am Pope.

On my sixty-third birthday yesterday, the Council fulfilled my ascension to the papacy. My confirmation was the fastest in history, requiring a mere three ballots. Thanks to the Council's influence, all sixty-two cardinals took part in the voting, helping to push through my landslide victory.

The Council instructed I take the name Pope Pius XII in honor of both my predecessor and the founder of the Vatican Secret Archives. An honor, indeed.

I am grateful to you, Grandfather, for this honor. It was your hand that guided me to the papacy. Now I am positioned to fulfill the Council's mission. I will not disappoint you.

Pius pp. XII

Roberto's eyes scanned the journal entry, his brow furrowing in confusion. "So, he ascended to the papacy. What's the significance of that?" he questioned, his tone laced with skepticism.

"It's more than that, Berto," Mario said, his voice trembling. "They had Pope Pius XI *killed* so Pacelli could become pope."

Roberto's eyes widened, his gaze flicking back to the monitor as he digested the revelation. "Alright, slow down," he said, his fingers tracing the lines of text on the screen. "What's this reference to *The Art of War* about?"

Mario's eyes gleamed with a mix of fear and trepidation. "Pacelli liked to cite strategies from *The Art of War* to show off how he manipulated Hitler into becoming the Führer of the Third Reich. His grandfather gifted him a translated version of that ancient text when he was just twelve. He must have studied it more than his Bible."

"Seriously?" Roberto's voice contained a mixture of disbelief and intrigue. He closed the JPEG file, his hand hovering over the mouse in trepidation before clicking on the next.

2 September 1939

> *The Art of War*
> *#26 Attack where he is unprepared.*
> *Sally out when he does not expect you.*

Hitler invaded Poland as instructed. Nazi ground forces breached the Polish army's defenses at the border between Germany and Poland. They are now en route to take possession of the capital. The Luftwaffe already destroyed the Polish Air Force, leaving the skies clear for the ground forces' unchallenged dominance. Their Panzer tanks have cut through Polish defenses with precision. The expansion of Nazi-occupied territory is proceeding as planned.

We have coerced the Soviet Union into signing the German-Soviet Nonaggression Pact in exchange for two-thirds of Polish lands. This arrangement will keep them out of the war.

The Council's mission is proceeding exceedingly well.

Pius pp. XII

"Holy shit," Roberto blurted out. "Are you sure this thing is real?"

"From what I've read, it's the real deal. Seems like Pacelli's actual journal," Mario replied. He hesitated. "I need you to do something."

Roberto's gaze shot up to meet Mario's, a flicker of surprise in his eyes. He had never heard his friend speak with such a tone of voice.

Mario handed Roberto a new microSD card he'd purchased before coming over. "Make a copy and *keep it hidden.*"

Roberto promptly plugged it into another port, closed the JPEG and the file folder, then copied the files onto the new microSD Card. "Done."

Mario extended his hand. "Give me my SD card."

Roberto complied, removing Mario's original and placing it in his waiting palm. Mario then walked over to the plush leather sofa where he delved into his backpack to retrieve a bag from the local pharmacy.

Roberto's brow furrowed in confusion. "What's with the first aid kit?"

Mario's gaze pierced into Roberto with an intensity that was hard to ignore. "I've been thinking about this all the way over here. I need you to implant this into my flesh to ensure it never falls into the wrong hands."

"What the . . . *What?*"

"You took some pre-med courses in college, didn't you?"

"Are you out of your mind?"

"Maybe it's that your conspiracy theories have seeped into my brain or something, but I'm convinced this needs to be hidden. The safest hiding place I could think of was inside my body. This way I'll always know where it is. Will you do it?"

Roberto glanced from his friend to the first aid kit. "You're serious, aren't you?"

"Dead serious. There's something not right about this journal and it terrifies the bejeebies out of me."

"Alright, alright, I'll do it," Roberto conceded, joining Mario by the couch and peering into the bag. "Did you get everything we'll need?"

"I think so," Mario replied.

Roberto saw the first aid kit was filled with Band-Aids, gauze, tape, needle, thread, antiseptic, and burn lotion. "What are we supposed to use for local anesthesia?"

"I couldn't find anything that would do. Do you think drinking alcohol really works, like they do in the old western films?"

"We can try. Or I could knock you out," Roberto suggested, holding up his fist and smiling.

"No, no. Let's try the alcohol first."

Roberto rose, making his way to his personal bar that was tastefully integrated into his office wall to choose a suitable libation. His gaze was drawn to the crystal decanter of brandy elegantly poised on the rich mahogany surface of the bar. He handed the glass to Mario, his gaze never wavering from his best friend's face. Without a moment's hesitation, Mario tilted his head back. The brandy disappeared down his throat in a single audacious gulp. A few droplets escaped, staining his black shirt with dark wet splotches.

Roberto watched in surprise, his eyebrows arching at the spectacle. "I suppose being a priest who partakes in daily sacraments of wine has honed your drinking skills."

"Easy to do when you have a purpose. Let's do this." Mario rose to his feet, unbuckled his belt and lowered his black trousers. "I was thinking of this area, within the fatty tissue. What do you think?" caressing his right thigh.

"As good a place as any." Roberto tore open the antiseptic wipes from the kit.

Mario settled onto the sofa, starting to experience the effects of the alcohol he had quickly consumed.

"Whoa. It's been a while since I've felt this."

Roberto looked up at his friend, a smile playing on his lips as he watched Mario succumb to the alcohol. "You want another round, just to be sure? This is going to hurt."

"Good idea. One more. You know I'm a wimp."

Roberto retrieved the empty glass and refilled it with a generous serving of brandy before handing it back to his friend. He then left the room to retrieve his scalpel, a relic from a pre-med biology course he'd taken at the university. His intellectual curiosity had led him to explore fields outside his own, providing him with unique perspectives that had proven invaluable throughout his career. The synthesis of unconventional approaches had produced a revolutionary idea for his startup, and the rest was history. Five years later, Microsoft had handed him a check to the tune of two hundred million dollars.

Upon returning to his office, he found Mario unconscious, the empty brandy glass lying on the couch beside him. *Perfect. I didn't think you could handle this even with the brandy.*

After thoroughly sterilizing the scalpel, needle and SD card, he made a one-inch incision along Mario's thigh. Twenty minutes later, the microSD card was securely sown beneath Mario's skin. Mario had thankfully slept through the entire procedure, even when Roberto stitched the wound.

"Alright, buddy, you're good to go," Roberto whispered gently to his courageous friend. Mario's only response was a soft snore.

After washing his hands, Roberto returned to his computer to delve deeper into the journal. He randomly selected another JPEG, revealing yet another page from Pacelli's journal.

Chapter 52

9 *August 1941*

The Art of War
IV: Tactical Dispositions
#11 What the ancients called a clever fighter
is one who not only wins,
but excels in winning with ease.

A young maiden came to visit me today. She claims to have escaped from the Treblinka extermination camp. Hard to believe. She utilized her legal authority to sign over her family's estate to the Vatican in exchange for assurances that her parents would be released from prison.

The added property will be a nice addition to our portfolio. Thank you for your contribution.

Pius pp. XII

Chapter 53

26 July 1941
5:30 p.m.
Treblinka Extermination Camp
Poland

In the heart of the Treblinka extermination camp, a group of ten female prisoners bustled with a sense of urgency inside the camp kitchen. They had been tasked with the preparation of food and drink for the evening's festivities. The first Saturday of the month had arrived, a day that stirred a discernible sense of anticipation among the soldiers—it was their one night out of the month they were allowed to indulge in revelry. Their eagerness was only heightened by the expected arrival of a dozen "ladies of the night" from the local brothel.

The soldiers' pent-up testosterone had made them particularly aggressive towards the camp's male prisoners throughout the day. Earlier, a guard had brutally bludgeoned a man with the butt of his rifle for not moving swiftly enough, sending him to the infirmary with eyes swollen shut from the savage beating. The male prisoners found solace in the prostitutes' monthly visit, as it seemed to pacify the soldiers' aggression for a few days, sparing many an unnecessary trip to the infirmary.

"Hannah, you must do this," implored Nedivah, one of the older ladies in the kitchen. A young girl of only sixteen years, Hannah's youthful features had been hardened by the harsh realities of the camp, making her appear much older than she was. Her body, mature for her age, could easily pass for a woman in her twenties.

Hannah's voice trembled with fear as she replied, "But what if they catch me? They'll execute me."

"You bear a striking resemblance to her. Just remember what we've taught you and you'll escape. We'll cover for you," Nedivah reassured Hannah, her voice firm yet gentle.

"But my parents . . ." Hannah's voice trailed off, her concern for her imprisoned parents evident.

"If you don't do this, we're all doomed," Nedivah stated bluntly. Her name, meaning "giving" in Hebrew, reflected her selfless desire for Hannah to escape the horrors of the camp and live a full life. She was willing to risk everything for the young girl's freedom.

"But what about the prostitute?" Hannah asked, her voice barely a whisper.

"That woman chose to sin against our God," Nedivah replied, her tone hardened.

"But . . ." Hannah's voice wavered, her body trembling with fear.

Nedivah's patience was wearing thin. Her hands gripped Hannah's shoulders tightly."We don't have time for this, Hannah. It's your life or hers. What's your decision?"

Hannah knew she had no choice. They had been meticulously planning her escape for months. This might be the only chance she got to save herself, and potentially her parents as well. It was a matter of life and death. "I'll do it," she finally said, her voice filled with determination.

In a separate chamber within the same building, the prostitutes were busily adorning themselves for a night of forced pleasure with the Nazi guards. Nedivah, with a tray of champagne in her hands, stepped into the room, her eyes scanning the dozen ladies of the night. Locating the young woman that bore a striking resemblance to Hannah, Nedivah ensured she received the first glass of alcohol, which was laced with a potent drug designed to plunge her into unconsciousness. Once all the women had been given their glasses, Nedivah approached her target, who was already succumbing to the drug's effects.

"Pardon me," the prostitute slurred, reaching out to grasp Nedivah's arm, "Is there a restroom here? I'm not feeling well."

"Of course. Let me help you there." Nedivah set down her tray and got the young woman onto her feet. "What's your name?"

"Olga," the prostitute managed to utter, leaning heavily on Nedivah. Together, they staggered towards the bathroom where Hannah was already waiting, ready for the swift swap into the prostitute's attire.

"Help me get her into the stall out of sight," Nedivah said. They stripped the unconscious Olga, replacing her clothes with Hannah's prisoner garb. Hannah then slipped into the prostitute's outfit, which surprisingly accentuated her youthful curves. The guards would be none the wiser that Hannah was not the original lady of the night.

"We need to get her back to the kitchen so we can monitor her. We'll give her more of the drug if need be, to ensure she remains unconscious. If anyone asks, your name is Olga," Nedivah instructed.

With Olga's arms draped over their shoulders, they maneuvered her back to the kitchen where another female prisoner, Alma, came over to assist. They gently laid her down in a secluded corner and covered her with a white tablecloth.

"You can do this," Nedivah said, gripping Hannah's hands and looking her directly in the eye. "I believe in you."

These were the last words Hannah would ever hear from her friend in the death camp. Nedivah would never again see the world beyond the barbed wire of the Treblinka extermination camp.

Once Hannah had departed to join the group of prostitutes, Alma kneeled beside Olga to etch a six-digit number into the unconscious prostitute's left forearm. Hannah's number.

Hannah was trembling as she entered the room where the remaining prostitutes were preparing for the evening. It would be less than an hour before they were ushered into the ballroom to entertain the guards. Three of the prostitutes turned their heads towards Hannah, recognizing the change but remaining silent. They understood the dire consequences that would follow should they report anything unusual to the Nazis. Instead, they kept their mouths shut, choosing to avoid becoming another statistic in the Nazi's grim record books.

Fifteen minutes later, the door swung open with a chilling creak. A Nazi guard filled the frame, his grating voice filling the room. "Ladies, the men are growing restless. Ensure you're ready to entertain in a quarter of an hour."

A cold shiver of dread slithered down Hannah's spine at this announcement. She mustered her courage, donning a mask of feigned excitement and giggling in unison with the other women. They all maintained a cautious distance from Hannah, wary of being entangled in her dangerous charade.

Olga. I must remember I am Olga now, Hannah repeated to herself, adopting the identity of the unconscious prostitute.

Once amidst the throng of guards, Hannah proved adept at keeping them entertained. Her quick wit was her shield, her flirty remarks her weapon. She danced from one guard to another, never lingering long enough to raise suspicion. Each interaction was a calculated risk, a delicate balance between blending in and not getting so familiar as to accidentally reveal her true identity. Discovery would mean certain death.

A guard, his eyes clouded with lust, grabbed at Hannah's dress, pulling her close. "What's your name, sweetheart?"

"Olga," she replied, her voice a playful giggle as she tugged at her dress, feigning coyness.

"Why don't we slip away into one of these rooms and have a little fun?" he suggested, his pent-up desire evident in his leering gaze.

"That's reserved for dessert time, gut aussehend," she retorted, keeping up the charade.

The guard elbowed his companion, a smirk spreading across his face, "Did you hear that? She thinks I'm handsome."

His companion rolled his eyes. "Of course she called you handsome. We're *paying them* to flatter us, you idiot," he said, delivering a hard punch to his fellow guard's arm. Their ensuing brawl, a contest of strength and bravado, provided the perfect distraction for Hannah to slip away from the lecherous pair.

As the evening wore on, she fluttered around the room like a butterfly, skillfully avoiding any sordid encounters in the backrooms. As the clock's hands crept towards the stroke of midnight, the girls were herded back into the confines of the dressing room, a sanctuary where they could finally stop their act after the night's draining exploits. But not Hannah—there would be no reprieve for her. Fresh cold waves of fear washed over her at the thought of being discovered. Even so, she was a mere quarter of an hour away from the sweet taste of freedom.

"Alright ladies, your services have been appreciated, but it's time for you to depart," a guard announced.

One by one, the women rose, their bodies weary but their spirits unbroken. They followed the guard down the dimly lit corridor towards the German Wehrmacht military truck they had arrived in. The truck was a hulking beast, its green canvas top flapping in the night breeze. This was their chariot, destined to transport them back to the brothel nestled in the heart of Treblinka. Each woman took turns reaching out to grasp the hand of the escort assisting them up into the back of the transport. A shiver of dread coursed through Hannah as she took the soldier's hand, his grip firm and unyielding.

Once inside, she found a spot next to a young woman who promptly shifted away, creating a chasm of distance between them. After the last of the prostitutes had been loaded onto the truck, the soldier hopped up onto the back and pulled down a tarp, securing it to the tailgate with a swift, practiced motion. He rapped on the back of the six-wheeled behemoth, signaling to the driver that they were ready to depart.

The truck rumbled to life, pulling away from the barracks and making its way towards the front gate. Just as the gate began to creak open, a shrill whistle pierced the night air. A soldier was frantically blasting his whistle from the kitchen window in a desperate bid to halt the departing truck. Hannah's heart plummeted into her stomach. She lowered her head, tears welling up in her eyes as she braced herself for the inevitable.

Her escape had been thwarted, and she was ready to face her fate—execution on the spot.

* * *

In the aftermath of a night filled with the intoxicating allure of German beer and the company of seductive women, the captain of the guard found himself meandering towards the kitchen seeking a late-night snack. As he pushed open the heavy kitchen door and flicked on the harsh overhead lights, his

251

eyes were drawn to the colossal refrigerator and its promise of sustenance.

The remnants of the evening's feast were predictably scant, his soldiers having ravaged the generous provisions supplied by the Nazi government as part of their monthly reward; however, a solitary turkey leg, untouched and inviting, caught his eye. Claiming it as his own, the captain settled onto a stool at the cold, metallic island in the center of the kitchen, ready to savor his meal in solitude.

A subtle movement caught his attention. From the corner of his eye, he noticed the white tablecloth piled in the corner shift, accompanied by a low, grumbling noise. As he turned his gaze, a stranger emerged from beneath the cloth, her face appearing as she groggily pulled the sheet down around her.

Reacting swiftly to the unexpected intruder, the captain dashed to the window, blowing his whistle in sharp, urgent bursts towards the front gate, signaling them to halt the departing truck. Swiveling back to face the young woman, he demanded, "Who are you?"

The woman, her eyes wide with fear, raised her arms in surrender and stammered, "Don't shoot! I'm not a prisoner."

The captain's eyes were drawn to the damning evidence inked into her left forearm—a prisoner number. His annoyance flared at this unwelcome interruption to his tranquil midnight feast. Without a second thought, he drew his revolver and fired a single, fatal shot into her forehead. Her body slumped forward, a crimson river of blood staining the pristine white tablecloth.

With a grim satisfaction, the captain returned to the window to blow his whistle twice, signaling "all clear" to the front gate so the truck could resume its journey. He returned to his meal, sinking his teeth into the succulent smoked turkey leg, its smoky flavor mingling well with the gunpowder odor from his discharged revolver.

* * *

The shrill sound of the whistle echoed twice, a chilling signal that sliced through the frigid night air like a knife. The gate guard, an imposing figure silhouetted against the harsh glare of floodlights, gave the Wehrmacht truck driver a stern nod, granting him permission to depart from the grim confines of the death camp. With a sudden lurch, the truck roared to life, its heavy wheels crunching gravel as it trudged through the camp's imposing double gates into the night. The truck was destined to return in a month's time, its cargo of pleasure providing a fleeting distraction for the guards once again. But when it did return, one woman would be conspicuously absent.

Hannah, her body curled into a protective hunch, kept her head buried in her knees, her tears falling silently onto the rough canvas floor of the truck. Hers were tears of relief, of joy, of the overwhelming realization she was finally escaping the specter of extermination. Freedom, a concept long so distant and elusive she had almost forgotten what it was, was now within her grasp.

The young woman beside her shifted closer, her hand gently stroking Hannah's hair in a comforting gesture. Despite their circumstances, this call-girl found a well of compassion swelling up within her for the young escapee. Now that the women were all safely beyond the camp's barbed-and-razor-wired fences, headed back to the relative safety of the brothel, a sense of relief had washed over them. Tonight, no one else would die—except for the unfortunate young woman whose fate had already been sealed thanks to her bearing a striking resemblance to Hannah.

Chapter 54

9 August 1941
Castel Gandolfo, Italy

Nestled just south of Rome, an enchanting hamlet lay perched on the edge of the serene Lake Albano. Cradled within the lush grassy embrace of the Alban Hills, the majestic Apostolic Palace of Castel Gandolfo had served as a tranquil sanctuary for the pope for centuries. This sprawling estate, spanning a breathtaking one hundred thirty-five acres, boasted a grand seventeenth-century villa as its crown jewel—the papal palace. A symbol of divine opulence, it had come into the papacy's possession in 1596, a result of the previous owners' unfortunate inability to settle their debts with the Vatican. As pope, Eugenio Pacelli often sought solace in Castel Gandolfo's splendid seclusion, basking in the splendor of the magnificent summer retreat.

In the palace's bustling kitchen, a trio of dedicated staff were meticulously crafting the pope's meal, their hands deftly moving with practiced ease. The newest addition to the team, a young woman with a spark of determination in her eyes, had proven her culinary competency, and today had been granted the honor of delivering the pope's lunch.

Meanwhile, in the solitude of his private quarters, Pacelli sat in tranquil meditation, patiently awaiting his midday meal. His lunch was to be a study in simplicity and elegance: a vibrant Caprese salad, featuring heirloom tomatoes, fresh basil, and creamy mozzarella, accompanied by crusty ciabatta bread, a drizzle of locally sourced olive oil, and a glass of rich, full-bodied Chianti. This was his preferred meal, a humble yet satisfying feast that reflected his modest tastes.

A soft summer breeze danced through the curtains, whispering the tale of a door that had been gently pushed open. Pacelli, nestled in his chair, sat with his eyes closed, lost in silent prayer as the staff member delicately positioned the plate laden with the local harvest's succulent bounty before him. He counted the rhythmic ticking of the clock, anticipating the thirty seconds or so it would take to hear the sound of the door closing, signaling the staff member's departure from his presence. With his eyes still veiled, he drew in a deep breath, savoring the vibrant aroma of basil and tomato intertwining with the robust scent of the Chianti wine. He waited with saintly patience, ready to relish his meal in solitude once the staff made their discreet exit.

The tantalizing fragrances given off by his humble feast were practically intoxicating, pulling him into a trancelike state. Pacelli, absorbed by the heavenly bouquet, took some time before he finally noticed the customary creak of the door signaling the departure of his staff had not come.

A chilling sense of being observed crept over him. The pope opened his eyes and gazed at the entry door; there he found the staff member staring back at him apprehensively, disregarding all established protocols.

Suppressing his irritation at this blatant disregard for his privacy, he growled, "You must be new."

"I am, Your Holiness."

"Did your supervisor neglect to inform you about the specific demands I have regarding the delivery of my meals?"

"He did, Your Holiness," the striking young woman replied, her figure accentuated by the snug fit of her waitstaff uniform.

"Then why are we engaging in this conversation? Please *leave*." Pope Pius XII concluded his directive by reaching for the goblet of Chianti to cleanse his palate before indulging in his meal. As he lifted the cup to his lips, savoring the scent of tannins, he realized he still didn't hear the expected sound of the door opening and closing.

"Woman, what is your purpose here?"

"I need to speak with you, Your Holiness."

"Who are you?"

"My name is Hannah Goldstein. I escaped from a Nazi extermination camp. You are my last resort to save my parents."

"You escaped from an extermination camp?" The pope found his initial annoyance replaced by a spark of interest.

"I switched places with a prostitute brought to camp to entertain the Nazi soldiers," Hannah confessed, tugging at the hem of her skirt that was a size too small. Having infiltrated the palace, she'd had to make do with whatever uniform she could find to secure an audience with the pope.

"Come closer, my child," Pius XII beckoned, wanting the young woman to approach so he could get a better look at her.

Hannah moved closer to his dining table. "I'm very sorry to interrupt your meal. I understand this is a sacred time for you, but I am desperate."

"What is it you believe I can do for you?"

"My parents are still prisoners in the concentration camp. They were still alive when I escaped. I'm hoping you could use your influence to secure their release. They have substantial wealth and property that could be used to help grease the negotiations."

The pope reclined in his chair, his gaze cool and calculating as he assessed this girl and the intriguing mention of her family's property and wealth. He maintained a strategic silence, his mind whirring as he evaluated the situation. Hannah had demonstrated cunning in her escape from a Nazi concentration camp and in securing an audience with him. He knew he could turn her apparent desperation to his advantage.

"And what lengths would you . . . go to, to secure your parents' release?" he asked, his voice a low murmur.

"I would do *anything* to get my parents back, Your Holiness," she replied, her voice trembling with determination.

He remained silent, contemplating Hannah's complete surrender to whatever he desired. Gazing her body up and down, he appreciated the way she fit inside the tighter-than-normal uniform. She was a very attractive young lady, likely no more than twenty years old. She could prove a very satisfying delicacy for his sexual desires.

"Remove that uniform. It doesn't suit you."

The command hung in the air, heavy and unexpected. Hannah's eyes widened, her gaze locked onto the Vicar of Jesus Christ, searching for any signs of jest. But the pope's expression remained unyielding, his demand met only by silence.

With trembling fingers, Hannah began to unfasten her dress, the fabric whispering to the floor. Now clad only in her undergarments and black shoes, she stood vulnerable before the Supreme Pontiff.

"The rest."

With a swift, deliberate motion, Hannah reached behind her and unclasped her bra, allowing it to tumble to the ground. She bent forward, her fingers deftly unbuckling her shoes. She stepped out of them, her bare feet making contact with the cold marble floor. With a final act of surrender, she slid her panties down, unveiling her slender alabaster body in its entirety.

"Stay there," Pope Pius XII commanded as he rose and strode past Hannah towards the door. A glint of a key in the keyhole was followed by a loud metallic click that echoed ominously throughout the chamber. Turning around, his gaze fell upon the exquisite silhouette of the young woman standing bare in the room. She remained motionless. Her earlier words, 'I would do anything to get my parents back, Your Holiness', sounded in his mind like a haunting melody.

With a calculated stride, he bridged the gap between them, his hand descending gently to rest upon her shoulder. His touch was an unspoken command, steering her towards the luxurious couch nestled in the room's farthest corner.

A shiver ran down Hannah's spine at the icy touch, yet she complied with the silent directive. Pope Pius XII guided Hannah, bending her over the back of the couch, positioning her in a way that left her vulnerable to him. Lifting his cassock to reveal his arousal, he breached the boundary of this supplicant young woman.

Hannah was utterly devastated by this shocking twist of fate. She found it inconceivable that she was bartering her own flesh and blood to the Holy See.

Each individual has their own demons, she mused.

She tried to detach her mind from the sacrilegious act being committed by her Supreme Pontiff, who was now becoming increasingly forceful. Even the pope, she realized, was not immune to the carnal cravings of the human body. His breaths were becoming more labored now; Hannah's thoughts shifted to the imminent liberation of her parents from the concentration camp. The thought of their reunion filled her with a sense of joy that was almost overwhelming. Her mind flooded with memories of a time not so long ago when the Nazi regime plunged Europe into chaos with their radical ideologies. She vividly recalled the heart-wrenching moment she'd been torn away from her parents upon entering the Treblinka extermination camp. She was herded with the other attractive females in one direction while her parents were led away to the labor camp.

Engulfed in her own mental fortress, distanced from physical reality, she barely heard the pope release his long guttural groan, a clear indication he had climaxed within her. She remained still, a statue frozen in time, until the Supreme Pontiff's spasms subsided. Using her hips for support, he retreated from Hannah, his cassock falling back into place, concealing any trace of their illicit encounter.

Still bent over, her fingers white-knuckled as they gripped the back of the couch, Hannah remained statuelike, her mind racing with thoughts of what to do next. She dared to glance sideways, catching a glimpse of the pope in her peripheral vision. He stood there motionless, his gaze fixed on her.

"Turn around," he commanded.

Summoning the strength to push away from the back of the couch, Hannah straightened, turning to face the pope. Overwhelmed by humiliation, she didn't even attempt to shield her exposed body, instead locking her gaze with the man who had just violated her.

"You will ensure this matter remains our secret, my child."

The words "my child" rolling off the Supreme Pontiff's tongue broke her—a wave of revulsion swept through Hannah. After their encounter, she was far from the innocent girl she had once was. Driven by the desperate need to free her parents from their prison, she had been willing to do whatever it took. She just hadn't anticipated it would come to this.

"Of course, Your . . . Holiness."

"I will see what I can do to get your parents freed from prison," Pius XII declared, then retreated to his table by the window to indulge in his meal.

Hannah swiftly comprehended that their clandestine rendezvous had reached its conclusion. She darted over to her discarded garments and dressed with a haste born of desperation. Tying off her ribbons, she snatched up her shoes and made a beeline for the door, eager to escape the pope's private chambers. She turned the key and slipped out the door, praying she could avoid any unwanted encounters with the other staff of the castel.

The meal Hannah had brought was now a quarter of an hour past its prime. Pope Pius XII reached for the glass of Chianti, indulging in a customary sip before commencing his midday repast. As he gazed out at the serene expanse of Lake Albano, a sense of relaxation washed over him, a postcoital tranquility. A gentle breeze played with the sleeves of his cassock, and the pontiff found himself contemplating a leisurely siesta.

Chapter 55

21 August 1941
Castel Gandolfo, Italy

Hannah received a sealed letter from the hands of a palace servant, a missive from the pope himself. She held her breath, waiting until the servant had retreated from her room before she dared break the official wax seal. Her heart pounded with anticipation and dread for the news the missive might contain about her parents.

August 21, 1941

My beloved child Hannah,

It is with a heavy heart that I must relay to you the tragic news that your parents have perished in the Treblinka extermination camp. They were taken from this world before I could reach out to the camp Kommandant.

Know that I share in your sorrow.

Plans have been set in motion to secret you off to the United States of America. The archdiocese there will offer you a sanctuary that we, amidst this horrific war, cannot provide. The USA remains a neutral entity. They will offer you safety and the promise of a brighter future.

My assistant has coordinated your departure from a secluded airfield south of Rome. You will take flight under the cloak of the new moon tomorrow night.

With deepest condolences,

Pius pp. XII

Tears welled up in Hannah's eyes as she absorbed the pope's somber words, his stillborn attempt to save her parents. Her emotions were a whirlwind, a tumultuous mix of grief over her lost parents and hope for a better future in a far-off land. The anti-Semitism of the United States, she had heard, was a far lesser evil compared to the horrors she had witnessed in Europe. At least the Americans had the decency not to round up Jews for execution.

She closed her eyes, offering a silent prayer for her parents' souls in Heaven. She took three deep, shuddering breaths, attempting to steady herself in the face of this devastating news, but it was to no avail. She collapsed onto her side sobbing uncontrollably, her face buried in a pillow, the crumpled letter clutched in her trembling hands.

There was no comfort for Hannah in her loss. She was now utterly alone in the world. As far as she knew, all her relatives had met the same cruel fate as her parents in the Treblinka extermination camp. How could she possibly carry on?

Chapter 56

22 August 1941
Rome, Italy

Hannah Goldstein, along with a band of Jewish refugees who had miraculously evaded the Gestapo's clutches, were guided to the verdant expanse of a secluded airfield. Each of these persecuted souls had entrusted their properties and estates to the Vatican's safekeeping, a desperate gamble in the face of the Nazi onslaught. The Vatican, in turn, pledged to restore these assets once the monstrous tide of war had receded.

The night was a cloak of impenetrable darkness, the absence of the moon amplifying the cold that seeped into Hannah's bones, stirring a wave of nausea. She steeled herself against the discomfort, refusing to let her physical state jeopardize her chance to escape the war-torn continent.

Two Vatican staff, their flashlights dimmed to mere pinpricks of light, shepherded the Jewish group towards the silhouette of a DLH Junkers Ju, its formidable dual propellers a promise of salvation. The Vatican had managed to secure this air transport from Deutsche Luft Hansa airlines, who had secretly contracted to ferry the Jews hidden in Castel Gandolfo to the relative safety of the United States. Despite the chaos engulfing Europe, the pope and the Vatican still wielded powerful influence over factions sympathetic to the Catholic Church, thereby aiding Jews in their desperate flight.

The group ascended the aircraft's stairs one by one, each step a leap towards an uncertain future. Hannah was the last to enter the aircraft, her heart pounding in her chest.

As she disappeared into the belly of the plane, the Vatican staff, shrouded in black, retreated, leaving the pilot to prepare for the long journey. The engines roared to life, the grass beneath trembling under the force of their power.

The DLH airplane taxied down to one end of the private airstrip, the grassy runway stretching out before it. With a surge of power, the brakes were released, and the DLH Junkers Ju hurtled forward before lifting off into the inky abyss.

The moment it reached a thousand feet, a sudden explosion ripped through the hull in a blinding flash that lit up the fields below. The plane had been sabotaged, a deadly trap set by the pope's assassin to ensure no one ever bore witness to the pope's indiscretions.

Chapter 57

9 May 1941

The Art of War
#17 All warfare is based on deception

The Council has orchestrated a daring mission for Rudolf Hess to penetrate the heart of England. He will meet with the British Government's highest officials and convince them to become spectators in our European war.

Hess will negotiate the terms of the peace proposal with the British Government, which includes relief from the Luftwaffe air raids. The peace proposal promises Hitler will withdraw the Nazi military from Western Europe and cease all war operations in the West. Hitler demands that no country will be burdened with reparations from the war.

With the British cowed into complacency, Hitler can then unleash the full might of the Nazi military upon the Soviet Union. It shall be the Third Reich's crowning glory in the expansion of its territory. The Tzar's treasure will soon belong to the Vatican.

Pius pp. XII

Chapter 58

6 May 1941
Rome, Italy

"I wish for you to fly to England to negotiate a peace proposal with the Duke of Hamilton," Pope Pius XII commanded Rudolph Hess over a secure phone line, his voice full of authority.

"Yes, Your Holiness. I am your loyal servant."

"Bohle, despite his position, lacks the necessary prominence within the Nazi ranks to effectively communicate our peace proposal. We need to dispatch someone whose stature mirrors that of Hitler himself."

"What about Adolf?"

The removal of Rudolf Hess from Hitler's side would sever the pope's direct line of communication with the Führer. The Council had stressed the importance of keeping Britain out of the war so that the German war machine could focus all its efforts on the Soviet Union front. Pacifying Britain at this juncture was crucial. The Third Reich needed to capture more territory to project ultimate power over Western and Eastern Europe. In Hess's absence, the pope would have to resort to slower coded messages to communicate with Hitler.

"You will meet with Hitler tomorrow. I will call on a secure phone line to explain the details of your mission to England. Convincing Hitler to temporarily release you from service for this critical mission will be a task in itself."

7 May 1941
Berlin, Germany

"Outrageous!" the Führer's voice thundered through the room, his fury inescapable over the pope's audacious demand. "Wilhelm Bohle is already en route to negotiate with the British." He could hardly believe the pope would dare alter his plans without first consulting with him. Ernst Wilhelm Bohle, the Foreign Minister of the Nazi Party, was Hitler's chosen envoy.

Pacelli chose his words carefully, a blend of flattery and logic designed to sway Hitler. "Mein Führer, the British are not biting," he countered, his voice steady in contrast to Hitler's heavy breathing. "Bohle has failed to make the progress we need. We must send a figure of greater prominence, someone who commands your level of respect and authority. Who better than your deputy to convince the British to accept this proposal? It is by divine providence that your loyal assistant is a man who truly understands your vision for a thousand-year Reich. His presence alone will command the attention of the British and ensure the ratification of this peace proposal."

Sensing Hitler's hesitation, the pope delivered his final argument. "To expand the empire's territory, you cannot afford a war on two fronts," he stated, invoking the wisdom of *The Art of War*. "It is absolutely crucial we pacify Britain so you can focus on expanding into Soviet territory, Mein Führer." The Council would not risk stretching the Nazi army thin across two fronts. The attacks needed to remain consolidated on one military front, and that front was the Soviet Union.

Hitler fell silent, his mind whirling with the pope's words. His mentor had been a steadfast ally in his rise to power, guiding him to become the Führer of the Nazi Party then all of Germany.

Surely, the pope would not propose something that could jeopardize the fate of the Third Reich?

The problem was, Hitler knew the pope was correct—Hitler's chosen foreign affairs representative *wasn't* the right man for this mission. He was weak. It would take someone of Hitler's own stature to convince the British to accept this peace proposal. The British needed to believe in the sincerity of Germany's peace offering, and who better than Rudolf Hess to convince them?

Hess sat in the dimly lit Führerbunker near Hitler, his gaze fixed on his master. The Führer's face was a canvas of emotion, shifting from stubborn defiance to reluctant acceptance as he absorbed the pope's words. It was becoming clear to Hitler that the pope's argument was irrefutable—Hess was the only man capable of executing this critical mission.

As the line went dead, Hitler turned to Hess, his face a mask of resignation, haunted by the realization that he might be bidding his closest ally a final farewell. "This mission could very well be a one-way journey for you, my friend."

"I will persuade the British that I am an emissary, and they will ensure my safe return to Germany," Hess responded, his voice brimming with confidence. He had faith in the pope's wisdom, even if it meant severing the pontiff's direct line of communication with Hitler.

As they moved into the anteroom, Hitler draped his arm around Hess in a rare display of affection. "Hess, you really are stubborn. I will miss you."

10 May 1941
Augsburg, Germany

Rudolf Hess, in a daring act, commandeered a Messerschmitt Bf 110D from Augsburg, Germany, taking off a mere thirty-one miles west of Munich. His target was the Grand Dungavel House, the Scottish stronghold of the Duke of Hamilton. Their acquaintance traced back to the 1936 Olympic Games in Berlin. Hess was banking on leveraging this connection to secure a meeting with Prime Minister Winston Churchill. He remained devout in his mission to secure the strategic peace proposal with the British government on behalf of Germany.

Fate, however, had other plans. Hess, flying over the rugged Scottish landscape, missed his intended landing site by a staggering twelve miles. With his fuel reserves dwindling, he was forced to parachute from his plane, landing in the pastoral fields of a farmer named David McLean in Eaglesham, Scotland. The sight of the flaming Messerschmitt with its Nazi insignia was enough to send McLean out into the field, pitchfork in hand.

"Are ye alright?" McLean asked, his pitchfork pointed menacingly at Hess.

"I need to reach the Duke of Hamilton. Can you assist me?" Hess replied in his best English.

"Ye look in no shape to meet anyone, lad," McLean retorted, his thick Scottish accent braying into the quiet night. Seeing the German's injured state, he took pity on him and helped him to his feet. The pair made their way to the farmer's humble cottage where his wife served Hess a comforting cup of tea by the fireside and tended to his injured ankle.

As word of the crash spread, curious neighbors gathered at McLean's doorstep, peppering him with questions about the mysterious pilot.

"Who is he?"

"Says his name is Captain Alfred Horn," McLean said, repeating the clandestine name Hess had given him.

"What does he want?"

"He's pigheaded. Wants to meet the Duke of Hamilton."

"Why?"

"Won't say."

When the Home Guard arrived to apprehend Hess, the farmers were reluctant to hand him over, believing his plea for peace to be sincere.

However, the unexpected turn of events forced a change in plans. The covert attempt at an exchange between England and Nazi Germany was exposed, forcing the British government to deny the accusations of double-dealing with the enemy. Hess's mission to meet Churchill was thwarted, and he was imprisoned in the Tower of London for the remainder of World War II.

Chapter 59

30 July 1941
Secure Phone Call

Pope Pius XII: Burn all the evidence!

Adolf Hitler: We are working on that as we speak, Your Holiness.

Pope Pius XII: What's taking so long?

Adolf Hitler: My commanders are trying out methods of elimination.

Pope Pius XII: Adolf, if there are any survivors, they will retain legal right to their artwork, property, possessions, and money—including the gold meant for the Vatican!

Adolf Hitler: You are instructing me to eliminate millions of Jews?

Pope Pius XII: I am instructing you to protect all the artwork and gold you have confiscated. Do you want your Führermuseum or not?

Adolf Hitler: It's all I've been dreaming of since you first put the idea in my head.

Pope Pius XII: Burn all the evidence.

Adolf Hitler: I will, Your Holiness.

Chapter 60

The Art of War
Laying Plans
#15 If a general heeds my strategy he is certain to win.
Retain him.
When one refuses to listen to my strategy,
he is certain to be defeated. Dismiss him.

These imbeciles are testing my patience. Their fluctuating allegiance to our cause is exhausting. I have instructed Hitler to devise an efficient method of annihilating his enemies. The Nazis are without a vision.

Without a vision, the people will perish.

I have furnished Hitler with a detailed plan for the Final Solution, the methodical extermination of the Jews. The meeting to set this Final Solution into motion is scheduled for the forthcoming month—with the initiation of the plan set for January. Nothing shall obstruct the Council's mission.

Pius pp. XII

Chapter 61

Honolulu Star-Bulletin

Sunday, December 7, 1941   Price: 5¢

WAR!
OAHU BOMBED BY JAPANESE PLANES

At 7 a.m. local time, Japanese Zeros attacked Pearl Harbor killing over 2,000 service members.

The following American ships were lost during the attack:

- USS Arizona
- USS Oklahoma
- USS Nevada
- USS California
- USS West Virginia
- USS Cassin
- USS Downes
- USS Oglala

Chapter 62

8 December 1941
Congressional Floor, U.S. Capitol Building
Washington, DC

President Franklin D. Roosevelt, a figure of unwavering resolve, ascended to the podium before the joint session of the United States Congress, ready to deliver a speech that would echo through the annals of history.

"Mr. Vice President, Mr. Speaker, members of the Senate and House of Representatives.

"Yesterday, December 7, 1941—a date which will live in infamy—the United States of America was suddenly and deliberately attacked by naval and air forces of the Empire of Japan. The United States was at peace with that Nation and, at the solicitation of Japan, was still in conversation with its Government and its Emperor looking toward the maintenance of peace in the Pacific." FDR's voice continued to resonate throughout the chamber as he recounted the treacherous actions of the Japanese Empire.

"I believe that I interpret the will of the Congress and of the people when I assert that we will not only defend ourselves to the uttermost but will make it very certain that this form of treachery shall never again endanger us."

Roosevelt paused, his gaze sweeping over the sea of faces in the Chamber of the House of Representatives. "Hostilities exist. There is no blinking at the fact that our people, our territory, and our interests are in grave danger. With confidence in our armed forces—with the unbounding determination of our people—we will gain the inevitable triumph—so help us God."

The president's grip tightened on the podium as he prepared to make his monumental declaration. "I ask that the Congress declare that since the unprovoked and dastardly attack by Japan on Sunday, December 7, 1941, a state of war has existed between the United States and the Empire of Japan."

With a unanimous vote from every Congressman in the room, the United States took decisive action, entering the tumultuous waters of World War II.

Chapter 63

The Art of War
Waging War
#3 Victory is the main object of war.
If this is long delayed, weapons are blunted,
and morale depressed.
When troops attack cities, their strength will be
exhausted.

Damn! The Japanese brazenly attacked the United States of America—they blatantly disregarded the Council's commands!

President Roosevelt has thundered forth a declaration of war against Japan. It's only a matter of time before those Yankee fools set their crosshairs on the Nazis as well and bring this war to its cataclysmic end.

The Final Solution must be enacted and executed without delay. The Vatican must have its future secured. The clock is ticking.

Pius pp. XII

Chapter 64

20 January 1942
Wannsee Conference
Berlin, Germany

Reinhard Heydrich, the formidable director of the Reich Security Main Office, summoned the crème de la crème of the Nazi Party to a clandestine meeting in the tranquil suburb of Wannsee, Berlin. Lieutenant General Hermann Göring had bestowed upon Heydrich the authority to rally these influential leaders, all with the aim of executing the Council's genocidal mission.

"Another possible solution to the Jewish problem has now taken the place of emigration—that is, evacuation of the Jews to the east . . ." Heydrich's grumbles rolled across the room, his words piercing the silence. His audience, the Reich elite—more than half of them distinguished with doctorate degrees from prestigious German universities—listened in rapt attention. These men, representatives of various government ministries and members of the SS, were about to be entrusted with a grave task. The SS—the Schutzstaffel Protection Squads—were ready to execute any duty, no matter how morally reprehensible. The Final Solution to the Jewish Question was about to become one of those duties, aided by the Gestapo's efforts.

Heinrich Himmler, the Reichsführer of the SS handpicked by Hitler himself, rose to his feet. His voice was blanketed in a candid fervor, echoing Heydrich's sentiments. "It is imperative this mission—this Final Solution—be carried out to its conclusion."

Himmler, a man whose anti-Semitism ran deep, was eager to see the Jewish population eradicated. His hatred for the Jews was unfathomable, his desire to see them exterminated insatiable.

After hours of intense discussion and probing questions, the fifteen men in the room reached a chilling consensus: the Final Solution to the Jewish Question was to be implemented without delay. Europe's Jews would be rounded up like cattle and transported by train to one of the 457 extermination camp complexes scattered across Eastern Europe and exterminated.

Chapter 65

24 February 1945

The Art of War
Laying Plans
#20 Hold out baits to entice the enemy.
Feign disorder and crush him.

Adolf Hitler has become an overbearing tyrant that blatantly defies my every command. I have been compelled to renounce our alliance and sever ties with this rebellious despot. Cast adrift from the Vatican's support, the Third Reich now teeters on the brink of collapse.

The Council graciously accepted my plea to extricate us from any further dealings with Hitler. There is no choice but to put the mission on hold. It shall be resurrected at a more opportune time.

Pius pp. XII

Chapter 66

28 February 1945
Führerbunker
Berlin, Germany

"Destroy it ALL!" Hitler roared, his voice shaking the halls as readily as the bombs that now fell on Germany.

"Every single piece, Mein Führer?" Lieutenant Müller dared to ask.

"Every last one! Leave NO trace behind!"

"Understood, Mein Führer." The lieutenant departed to carry out the command to annihilate all artwork seized from the Jews, leaving the leader of the Third Reich alone in the depths of the Führerbunker.

The mere thought of the pope betrayal ignited an uncontrollable fury within him. The realization that he had been manipulated all along, positioned as the ultimate fall guy, the sacrificial lamb for this global catastrophe, sent him spiraling. The world had banded together to paint him and his Nazis as tyrants. The grand promises of the Thousand-Year Reich were evaporating before his very eyes.

Where had he faltered? For so long, everything had unfolded just as the pope had foreseen. Hitler's ascension through the ranks of the Nazi Party. His appointment as Chancellor by President von Hindenburg. His rise to the position of the Führer of Germany. The expansion of the Nazi empire. The conquest of all of Europe. He had been faithful in following every instruction from his mentor. He had dutifully shipped all the gold seized from the Jews to Rome as tribute. What had shifted? What had gone awry?

The horrifying truth was becoming glaringly evident: Hitler was saddled with irrefutable evidence that he and his monstrous regime had ruthlessly looted the Jews of their wealth, their priceless art, and had orchestrated the systematic genocide of an entire race. Unquestionable proof that his Nazis were nothing more than glorified thieves and savages, a far cry from the sophisticated Aryan nation of superior beings he had deluded himself into believing would reign supreme over the world for a millennium. These Nazis, these cold-hearted beings, were numb to the atrocities they committed, their humanity extinguished in the face of their heinous acts.

The Führermuseum, his Holy Grail, had been nothing but bait, the golden ticket the pope had used to lure Hitler into this irreversible endeavor. In the end, it was all a ruse. Hitler was merely a pawn, a marionette in the grand scheme of things. The 'Thousand-Year Reich' was just a grandiose tale designed to cloud Hitler's judgment.

"Really? The pope did all this for gold?" Hitler seethed. The thought of the pope nestled safely behind his Vatican fortress, safe from ever having to answer for his role in masterminding this world war, was too much to handle. "I'll kill him!"

Their agreement from the beginning had been for the Nazis to ship all the gold seized from the Jews to the Vatican, while Hitler got to keep all the valuable artwork so he could fill his Führermuseum with priceless artwork, statues, and tapestries after war's end. Gold watches, rings, necklaces, even the fillings in the Jews' teeth—all went as payment to the pope. What use did Hitler have for a bit of gold when he commanded the mightiest empire the world had ever seen? He'd considered the deal a bargain, almost too good to be true. Besides, the enormous amount of priceless artwork in Nazi possession far exceeded the value of the gold collected from the Jews. Hitler thought Pacelli a fool for granting such a great deal. *What's the catch?* he'd wondered in the early days.

Slowly, over many years, he became aware that all the gold he shipped to the Vatican was being rendered untraceable. Melted down into gold bars, its origin wiped from history. On its own, gold left no provenance. The same could not be said of the artwork confiscated from the Jews.

Running out of options, Hitler finally gave in and executed a plan to rid all that evidence from his lands, creating an alibi that he'd never been involved in the strategic plundering of the Jews and their priceless treasures.

Burn it all. He'd learned this lesson in his early meetings with Pacelli. *Burn all paper communications, leaving no evidence of our meetings.* Hitler would apply the pope's instruction to his current situation, burning every piece of artwork no matter how priceless it was. He might have been the pope's puppet, but he refused to be his scapegoat.

Chapter 67

2 June 1945
Munich, Germany

In the shadowy aftermath of World War II, the Vatican ratlines emerged, clandestine escape routes for Nazi war criminals seeking refuge from the ruins of Europe. The process of conversion was a simple one—the Nazi war criminal would confess their heinous sins to a Catholic priest, who would then absolve them of their sins with a blessing. The priest would assign them a new Christian name, a fresh identity, and the newly reborn Christian would then embark on a dangerous journey to South America.

This clandestine operation, repeated in hushed whispers in Catholic churches across Europe was orchestrated by none other than Jesuit priest Robert Leiber.

* * *

"Ah, you must be the infamous Franz Stangl. We've been eagerly awaiting your arrival." Leiber greeted the notorious Nazi commander with a chilling calmness, guiding him through the Vatican's clandestine entrance. Stangl, once the commanding officer of the Sobibor and Treblinka extermination camps, was directly responsible for nearly a million Jewish lives extinguished in the gas chambers and furnaces. The Jesuit, with an air of solemnity, led Stangl down a dimly lit corridor to his private quarters where the process of absolution and assigning a new Christian identity would commence. Once the ritual was complete, Leiber orchestrated safe passage for this harbinger of death to the distant shores of Brazil.

"But what about my family?" Stangl's voice wavered, his mind filled with images of his loved ones caught in the crosshairs of the Allies' relentless hunt for Nazi collaborators across Europe.

"Rest assured, arrangements for their safe passage to Brazil have already been set in motion."

"Thank you. I am eternally indebted to you, Father."

Chapter 68

The Art of War
Weaknesses and Strengths
#9 Subtle and insubstantial, the expert leaves no trace;
divinely mysterious, he is inaudible.
Thus, he is master of his enemy's fate.

Robert Leiber has been a phantom, expertly smuggling away the Nazi elite to a haven in Argentina. His mission to safeguard the architects of the Final Solution has been nothing short of extraordinary. I salute his audacity in seizing the reins of this operation.

Leiber is a faithful and reliable sentinel. His work guiding the Nazi hierarchy to sanctuary will in turn prevent the world from ever learning of the Vatican's involvement.

Pius pp. XII

Chapter 69

March 10, 2000
1:25 p.m.
Roberto's Mansion

"What are you reading?" Mario asked. The priest had woken late in the morning following his amateur surgery to find Roberto intensely focused on the computer screen. He'd let him be, at least until his curiosity couldn't take it anymore.

"Check this out," Roberto replied, his eyes still glued to the screen. He'd been poring over Pope Pius XII's journal notes all night and had just unearthed secrets about Leiber and his infamous ratlines.

From 1924 to 1929, Robert Leiber served as a key advisor to Eugenio Pacelli during his tenure as Nuncio in Munich and Berlin. Leiber's advisory role extended through Pacelli's time as Cardinal Secretary of State. Following Pacelli's election as Pope Pius XII in 1939, Leiber continued to provide counsel and support until the pope's death.

Never a Vatican official, Leiber was respected and feared as the "unofficial official." Hushed whispers within the halls of the Vatican revealed, "I do not fear the pope, but I do fear his secretary."

"This Leiber character had a deep-rooted connection with the pope. Look at this." Roberto pointed at the screen.

Mario rubbed his eyes, still groggy from his hangover, slowly rose from the office couch, and walked over to the computer. "Slow down. Who's Leiber?"

"Robert Leiber, the mastermind behind the Nazi exodus from Germany via the ratlines."

Leiber breathed new life into Bishop Hudal's plan, setting up a "ratline"—a secret escape route for Nazis fleeing Europe. Around the time of Operation Barbarossa, Leiber had written to the Austrian bishop, urging him to view the ratline mission as a crusade. As one of Pius XII's closest confidants, Leiber had the authority to act as the pope's intermediary and messenger.

Despite his historical training, Leiber destroyed all personal papers before his death, leaving no trace of his actions for future generations to study. Before he died he confessed that he did so out of fear the papers would cast his pope in an unfavorable light.

"Seems like Leiber followed the same playbook as the Nazis, eradicating all traces of his paper trail," Roberto mused, noticing the parallels between this man's actions and the orders Pacelli gave Hitler to incinerate all correspondence.

"What exactly is a ratline?" Mario asked, his curiosity piqued.

With a swift click, Roberto opened a new tab and searched for information on the term.

Ratlines were clandestine escape networks for Nazis seeking refuge from the ruins of post-World War II Europe. These covert routes primarily led to safe havens in Latin America, with Argentina, Brazil, and Peru acting as primary destinations. One route snaked its way from Germany to Rome to Genoa before reaching South America. The **ratlines** were backed by the clergy of the Catholic Church.

"This is incriminating evidence," Roberto said, leaning back to better absorb the information.

Spain, rather than Rome, acted as the initial hub for the covert ratline operation that aided the Nazi/Fascists' escape, though the master plan was hatched within the Vatican's walls. A key orchestrator included Charles Lescat, a Frenchman from the Action Française—a group once suppressed by Pope Pius XI but later reinstated by Pope Pius XII.

By 1946, Spain itself was a safe haven for hundreds of war criminals and thousands of ex-Nazis and Fascists. The Vatican's cooperation in handing over these fugitives was deemed "negligible" by the United States Secretary of State; Pope Pius XII, however, went on record imploring for Christ's mercy, stating he would rather see these Fascist war criminals exiled to the New World than languishing in POW camps in Germany.

"Backed by the Vatican, eh? So, these ratlines were essentially endorsed by Pope Pius XII himself. That's a damning revelation, isn't it?"

"Unreal," Mario muttered, limping back to the couch and flipping open his laptop, eager to join his friend in delving deeper into the mystery.

"You know that saying, 'A picture is worth a thousand words'? In this case, it's reversed, and it seems those thousand words paints a picture sinister beyond belief. Your 'Christian' pope was no saint," Roberto said, his hands flashing air quotes.

"We need to dig deeper. There's more to this than meets the eye."

"I'm all in, brother. This conspiracy stuff is my jam."

Roberto's fingers danced over the keyboard, clicking on the next entry in his search. As he sifted through it, his mind indeed began weaving a conspiracy theory.

Mario, laptop balanced on his knees, was unearthing more about the Nazi war criminals' escape. He hoped ignoring Roberto would deter him from launching into another one of his monologues. Mario was just as keen to uncover the Vatican's hidden secrets but didn't want Roberto's crazy theories sidetracking him. Alas, he knew Roberto was bound to share any theory that popped into his head regardless. His friend's mind was a breeding ground for suspicion, especially towards those in power. The only difference now was that there was solid evidence backing up those paranoid thoughts.

"Here's a wild thought." Roberto reclined, hands clasped behind his head, his gaze distant as he pondered the Vatican's future. "Given Pope John Paul II's advancing age, I wouldn't be surprised if the next pope came from Argentina."

"Ha!" Mario scoffed at his best friend's outrageous prediction. "Now you've lost it. You clearly don't know your papal history. No pope has ever been elected from the Americas."

"Look at all this evidence. Those connections. Don't you think it's plausible?"

"There's no clear lineage from the Americas to Saint Peter. It's never going to happen."

"But consider all this *evidence*," Roberto said, waving his hands towards his computer monitor. "After digesting all this, don't you think a pope would eventually have to come from Argentina? An Argentinian cardinal would have insider knowledge about the war criminals the Vatican sent to his country post-World War II. This future pope, being from Argentina, would be perfectly suited to deflect any suspicion that might lead to an investigation."

"Your intelligence sometimes borders on arrogance. *There has never been a pope from the Americas*, got it?"

"Alright, alright." Roberto paused, recalibrating his theory. "Then how about this: if not from Argentina, then the next pope will have to be from Germany to make sure this mess stays hidden. If this information leaks, someone will have *lots of splainin to do, Lucy*," Roberto said, mimicking Ricky Ricardo from the American TV show *I Love Lucy*.

"I see your point," Mario conceded, though he still kept shaking his head in disagreement. "But the Vatican has its protocols for when the College of Cardinals convenes to vote for the next pope."

"Do you really believe the Vatican isn't aware of this ticking time bomb within its walls? Consider the scandals they're already grappling with—the child-abuse allegations that are shaking the Church to its core. And yet, this . . . this is a whole new level of cover-up." Roberto was grappling with the mountain of undeniable evidence of the Vatican's decades-long deception. Who could say if this holy autocracy was still pulling the world's strings?

"But . . . this information stays buried. You gave your word."

"Unbelievable." Roberto was astounded at his best friend's unwavering loyalty to the Vatican.

"I can't be the one to shatter the faith of millions worldwide with this revelation, do you understand?"

Mario could see the frustration etched on his best friend's face. He had to carefully plan his next move with the journal. How was he going to justify removing it from the Vatican Secret Archives?

"You know what?" Roberto rose abruptly, his patience with his friend wearing thin, "I need a break. I'm going to take a shower and clear my head." He'd decided to hit his favorite bar since it was Friday night. He needed a distraction after all this intense research involving the pope and the Nazis. His irritation was further fueled by his best friend's insistence on keeping the conspiracy a secret.

"Okay, I guess I'm going to head home and change," Mario said as he watched Roberto stride towards the office door. "Can I come back tomorrow and stay for the weekend?"

"Whatever," Roberto replied curtly, exiting the room. "Just don't show up too early. I might have company over."

"Got it. No need to explain." Mario heard Roberto's bedroom door slam shut down the hall, signaling the end of their discussion.

Mario logged into his Vatican email, hoping there would be a message from Cardinal Borelli waiting for him. Perhaps the cardinal, paranoid about getting sick by Mario, would grant him a day off on Monday too? He could use the extra day for research.

But there were no new emails from the cardinal. Mario knew he would have to face his duties on Monday: scanning the Archive documents, while doing his best to avoid Cardinal Borelli. Any questions about the decoy journal could send him into a panic, arousing the cardinal's suspicion. If questioned, Mario knew he would eventually crack and confess to stealing the journal from the Vatican Secret Archives. He was a terrible liar. Ultimately, he would lose his esteemed position in the Vatican.

Closing his laptop, he decided it would be safer in Roberto's mansion than in his own apartment and left it on the couch. He grabbed his backpack and departed Roberto's mansion, heading back to his apartment for the night.

Chapter 70

March 10, 2000
Friday Evening, 11:30 p.m.
Rome, Italy

Roberto roared up to the swanky Roman nightclub, La Dolce Vita, in his gleaming, brand-new sunflower-yellow Lamborghini Murciélago. The intoxicating growl of its 6.2-liter six-speed V-12 engine, boasting a staggering 575 horsepower, rattled the Roman streets as he drove, turning heads and drawing attention. He made sure to rev the engine just before pulling up to the nightclub, a siren call to the valet.

Giuseppe, the valet, always looked forward to Roberto's arrival. He was like a signal flare to the city's most stunning women. Word would spread like wildfire through the female network in Rome of his presence, and soon the nightclub would be awash with women in figure-hugging dresses and vibrant colors. Giuseppe would offer his hand to each as they stepped from their limousines and cabs, each one a vision of beauty, each one hoping to be chosen to accompany Roberto home that night.

Giuseppe recalled a quote he'd read in *Car & Driver* that seemed to encapsulate Roberto's lifestyle perfectly:

"A Ferrari," the owner of both sports cars explained, "is the nice girl you take home to Mom and Dad. The Lamborghini is the wild slut you sleep around with on the side."

Roberto, with his newfound wealth from the Microsoft windfall, had no interest in settling down or discovering his roots, no need for a nice girl. His Lamborghini and insatiable lust for pleasure suited his chosen lifestyle to a tee. With his money, his Lamborghini, and his reputation, he had his pick of the stunning women inside the nightclub. The possibilities were endless.

This is going to be a wild night, Giuseppe mused to himself, striding towards the Lamborghini.

"Buona sera, signore," the sleek-tuxedo-clad Giuseppe called out over the Lamborghini's engine, greeting his favorite patron.

"Buona sera, Giuseppe. What's the atmosphere like inside?"

"You'll want to have a word with Romeo," the valet suggested, taking Roberto's keys and shaking his hand, accepting the generous tip. "He's got a real catch for you tonight."

Slipping into the driver's seat, Giuseppe maneuvered the powerful supercar a mere twenty feet to its prime parking spot right in front of the elite establishment. The owner had a clear strategy: showcase the most luxurious cars right at the entrance. This was free publicity, luring people to queue up and pay the cover charge for the privilege of rubbing shoulders with the nightclub's elite guests. Displaying Roberto's car was a particular favorite, as it attracted the crème de la crème of female clientele. With Roberto in the house, the presence of these high-end beauties drew in wealthy hangers-on eager to impress, hoping to escort one of the remaining ladies home for the evening. On such nights, the upscale nightclub reaped handsome profits thanks to Roberto's presence. He was always a welcome guest, and in return, Roberto enjoyed unparalleled service during his visits.

"Buona sera, Romeo. I hear you have some news for me."

Romeo, having already prepared Roberto's drink as soon as he spotted his high-tipping regular, slid it across the bar.

Leaning in for a discreet conversation, Romeo subtly nodded to the left. "The lady in red at the end of the bar might pique your interest."

"Mille grazie." Roberto placed a $100 bill on the bar, picked up his drink, and began to saunter towards the lady in red.

"Hold on, signore," Romeo called out, stopping Roberto in his tracks. "She's drinking *this*." Romeo slid a martini with two olives across the bar towards Roberto.

Roberto grinned at Romeo. "You're a lifesaver. You always know how to take care of me. Grazie." He slid another $100 bill across the bar, picked up both drinks, and resumed his journey towards the woman in the red dress.

"Buona sera, bellissima," Roberto greeted.

The blonde swiveled, her smile a dazzling display of pearly whites framed by ruby red lips, her flawless skin barely concealed by expertly applied makeup. Her golden tresses cascaded around her shoulders, partially veiling her ample bosom as she turned to face Roberto. "Buona sera."

Roberto's usually smooth facade faltered at her radiant beauty. This woman was in a league of her own. Despite his wealth and status, Roberto was fundamentally a geeky programmer. He tried to emulate the suave James Bond with his designer clothes, luxury cars, and opulent mansion, but at his core, he was a lucky nerd who had struck gold by selling his software company. It was his millions that made him attractive to women. But this woman was different. She was sophisticated.

"I'm Roberto," he managed to say, regaining some of his composure. "The bartender said you're drinking one of these." He raised the martini towards her, his confidence returning.

"How thoughtful of you," the blonde responded flirtatiously, tilting her head to the side and grinning. "I'm Paola."

Paola's warm response eased Roberto's nerves. He might even stand a chance with this goddess. "Care to dance?" He extended his hand, attempting to appear confident. This was his usual tactic to progress to the next stage of his pickup routine— lead the woman to the dance floor.

Placing the cocktail on the bar, Paola delicately took his hand and followed Roberto's lead. They took to the floor and began swaying to the rhythm of the music, cutting loose. The song soon transitioned to a slow dance, and without hesitation, Paola draped her arms over Roberto's shoulders, her hands clasped behind his neck, indicating she wanted to continue dancing. He reciprocated, his arms encircling her slender waist, their bodies swaying in sync. The woman moved closer, resting her head on Roberto's shoulder.

He was thoroughly enjoying this intimate moment with the stunning blonde. *This is going better than I could have ever imagined*, he thought. The woman he had deemed out of his league was now melting into his arms. *How did I get so lucky?*

Paola lifted her head to whisper into Roberto's ear, "Why don't we go back to your place."

Without a moment's hesitation, he took her hand and led her towards the exit, the blonde following his lead.

Giuseppe, spotting Roberto heading for the door, grabbed the keys to the Murciélago, sprinted to the sports car, and positioned it at the entrance, where Roberto and Paola were presently engaged in a passionate kiss.

"Your chariot awaits, Sir Roberto," Giuseppe said, elevating his language and likening Roberto to a prince with his princess.

Breaking away from his kiss, Roberto responded, "Grazie, my good man."

Roberto helped the stunning blonde into the front seat of his Lamborghini. Despite her tight red dress, she slid gracefully into the low-slung leather seat. Roberto closed the scissor door and quickly moved to the driver's side. Giuseppe held the door open for Roberto. After shaking the valet's hand to slip him one last $100 bill, Roberto winked as he slid into the car. The pair of lovebirds sped off into the cool night.

Chapter 71

March 10, 2000
Earlier that Afternoon
4:30 p.m.
Rome, Italy

Exiting Roberto's opulent mansion, Mario journeyed across the city via metro to his modest apartment. Roberto's residence was luxurious, but it was too extravagant for Mario's simple tastes. He preferred his humble abode provided by the Catholic Church, a testament to his vow of celibacy.

His apartment was situated across the street from his former Catholic church, a place he no longer directly served ever since his promotion to his esteemed position within the Vatican Secret Archives. Upon seeing his old church, the doubts that had crept into Mario's mind intensified. Had he been fortunate to obtain this prestigious role, or was he merely a disposable pawn like Father Benedetti, who had stumbled upon the same forbidden knowledge? Mario knew he had to tread carefully, his conspiracy radar now on high alert. Was it that Roberto's influence was making him paranoid? Could all this truly be happening?

"Excuse me, Father?" A woman, slightly older than Mario, approached him from behind. Lost in his thoughts, he hadn't noticed her approaching.

He shook off his thoughts, ready to perform his priestly duties regardless of the turmoil brought on by the Vatican Secret Archives. "Yes. How may I assist you?"

"May I confess to you in private, Father?"

"Of course."

"Can we go inside your place? I don't want anyone to overhear."

Mario glanced at the church across the street, knowing that the confessional was the appropriate place for such matters. However, seeing the woman's distress, he made an exception.

"Alright, I'll make an exception for you. Please, come in." He unlocked the front door and stepped inside, the woman trailing behind him. He flicked on the light and placed his backpack on the couch. Something seemed amiss here, but he couldn't quite identify it. "Would you like something to drink?"

"Do you have a coke? I could really use one."

She found herself unexpectedly taken aback by the striking good looks of this priest. Her recollections from her formative years were filled with images of grizzled, old men, their skeletal fingers wagging in her direction, prophesying that if she didn't mend her ways, she was destined to walk the path of a lady of the night.

After a couple of minutes, he returned to the living room and handed her the drink.

"What is your confession?" he asked, moving a coaster in front of her so the soda wouldn't stain his coffee table, before settling into his club chair.

"I am a prostitute, Father, and I'm ashamed of my sins."

Mario remained unfazed. He had taken confessions from many ladies of the night. However, a prostitute's confession paled in comparison to the dark, hidden secrets he had heard from the seemingly innocent and devout members of his congregation, those who paraded their holiness in public while concealing their darkest sins.

"I'm so sorry I have to do this, but I couldn't pass up the money." The prostitute felt a pang of remorse as she looked into the eyes of the handsome priest.

"Money makes us do things—" Mario was cut off by a sudden, sharp sting on his neck. His hand flew up instinctively, fingers brushing against the foreign object - a syringe embedded in his skin. He looked at the prostitute, her lips forming the words "I'm so sorry" but couldn't hear her—his world faded into darkness.

The man in the all-black suit standing behind Mario removed the syringe from his neck and guided the priest's slumping form sideways, draping him across the armrest. Luca, the Vatican assassin, placed the empty syringe back inside his Vatican-issued briefcase filled with his other tools of persuasion. He turned to the prostitute. "Go to the bedroom and get ready."

Two other men in black suits emerged from the shadows and carried Mario into the bedroom. There they undressed him and placed him on the bed. They opened two large black cases filled with equipment for a photo shoot. They set up the lampstands and shades, transforming the room into a stage for an incriminating photo session.

The scantily clad prostitute crawled into bed beside the unconscious priest. She felt a pang of guilt, but the man's offer of two months' rent was too tempting to refuse.

"Make it look like you're kissing but keep out of the way. I want to see his face clearly," Luca instructed the prostitute as the other assassins began to take photos of the compromising scene.

Chapter 72

March 11, 2000
1:33 a.m.
Rome, Italy

Roberto eased his sports car into the central spot of his expansive five-car garage, the engine's purr rebounding off the walls. He exited the car and strode over to the passenger side to assist his stunning companion for the evening. "Welcome to my palace, princess," he theatrically bowed, arms spread wide.

"It's quite the spectacle," Paola replied, closing the distance between them, wrapping her arms around Roberto's neck and pulling him into a passionate kiss. He was lost in the softness of her lips, the intoxicating scent of her perfume. Was she a nice girl? He could see himself settling down with this one— beautiful, intelligent, seductive . . . and *blonde*—his ultimate weakness.

He closed his eyes, savoring the slow, sensual kiss, pulling her closer. He didn't want the moment to end. . . .

Ow! A sharp sting interrupted his blissful reverie.

He pulled out of the kiss to clutch at his neck where he'd felt the sharp pain. *What the hell?* He felt the syringe there, and his gaze locked with Paola's before he slowly crumpled to the cold cement floor of his garage.

When he regained consciousness, he found himself bound to his bed, his hands and feet tied to the bedposts. His eyes fluttered open to find a striking man with slicked-back dark hair and dressed in an all-black suit standing at the foot of his bed.

"Who the hell are you?" Roberto demanded, straining against the ropes that held him captive in his own bed.

"I'll be the one asking the questions, Roberto," the man, Mateo, responded coolly.

"You can go to hell," Roberto spat, his anger flaring at being held prisoner in his own home. "And how do you know my name? You want money? Is that it?" His mind raced, trying to make sense of the situation. These men weren't your typical thugs. They were too well-dressed, too organized. They were after something else.

"Are you done?" Mateo asked, his patience with Roberto's incessant rambling wearing thin.

"Yes." Roberto fell silent.

"Where did you get this?" Mateo held up the microSD card they'd found while searching Roberto's office.

"I don't know what that is," Roberto lied, playing dumb.

"You're going to make this difficult, I see." Mateo signaled to one of his men, who brought over a black briefcase. He opened it, revealing an array of vials, syringes, scalpels, and other ominous-looking tools.

Roberto's heart pounded in his chest as he took in the contents of the briefcase. "What's that for?"

"Either you tell me where you got this chip"—Mateo held up the microSD chip again—"or we'll have to persuade you."

"You don't scare me," Roberto bluffed, trying to maintain a brave front.

"I'm going to ask you one more time: *where* did you get this chip?"

"I told you, I don't know," Roberto insisted, recognizing that these men were Vatican assassins. They weren't after money; they were after information.

"I see you do recall where this chip came from," Mateo observed, noting Roberto's eyes flicking to the upper left, a telltale sign of a lie being told.

Roberto remained silent, trying to figure out how he could get out of this situation. Unfortunately, he had nothing to bargain with.

"We have a policy at the Vatican: nothing ever leaves the secure halls of the Vatican Secret Archives. Nothing. And yet, you somehow violated our protocol, Roberto."

"It wasn't me—" Roberto began before Mateo cut him off.

"Ah. Now we're getting somewhere." The assassin smiled. "Who *did* remove this information from the Vatican? Confess."

Roberto clamped his mouth shut, his mind racing. He'd sooner meet his maker than betray Mario.

Mateo, realizing mere words wouldn't break Roberto, reached into his briefcase. He withdrew two vials and two syringes, placing them ominously on the table. He methodically filled each syringe with two-tenths milliliters of two separate mysterious fluids, then signaled for one of his men to pin down Roberto's arm.

Roberto's heart pounded in his chest as he watched the scene unfolding. "What are you doing? What is that?" he stammered, his eyes wide with terror.

"This, Roberto, is going to be quite painful," Mateo warned, then plunged the first needle into Roberto's left arm. He swiftly withdrew it, reaching for the second syringe.

A searing pain shot up Roberto's arm, making its way towards his heart. It was unbearable. He could feel his heart shuddering, struggling to pump blood through his veins. He tried to scream, but no sound came out. He convulsed, his heart seizing under the intense pain. He barely registered the second injection—adrenaline coursed through his veins, counteracting the induced heart attack. He collapsed back onto the pillow, gasping for breath as his heart resumed its normal rhythm.

"What the . . . fuck was that?" Roberto managed to croak out, his voice barely a whisper.

"That, Roberto, was an induced myocardial infarction. A heart attack, if you will," Mateo replied coolly.

Roberto lay there, eyes closed, trying to gather his strength. His mind was a whirlwind of fear and confusion.

"Now, I'll ask again. Where did you get the chip?" Mateo pressed.

Summoning the last of his strength, Roberto motioned for Mateo to lean in closer. As the assassin did so, Roberto gathered a mouthful of saliva and spat in Mateo's face. "Fuck you," he hissed.

Mateo recoiled, wiping the spit off his face. He turned away and in a rage filled a syringe with a lethal dose of fluid. Swiveling back to Roberto, a cruel smile played on his lips. "I'm going to relish this, you piece of shit." With a swift, brutal motion, he plunged the syringe into Roberto's arm, emptying its deadly contents.

Roberto's body jerked violently for a moment before going eerily still. His heart ceased to beat. The interrogation had reached its grim conclusion.

Mateo methodically returned the vials and syringes to the black briefcase before snapping it shut with a finality that echoed dully in the deadness of the room. He surveyed his team, his gaze landing on Paola. "Make it look like an overdose," he ordered, his voice cold and detached. "The rest of you, comb the entire house. Ensure that chip's the only one. And wipe his computer clean."

Chapter 73

March 11, 2000
Saturday, 8:30 a.m.
Rome, Italy

Mario awoke, his head pounding as if a drummer had taken residence inside his skull. He was half-covered by sheets, his body bare. He tried to piece together the fragments of the previous night through the relentless throb of his headache. He sat up, his head heavy in his hands, his mind a whirlpool of confusion. He hadn't been drinking at Roberto's, had he?

Staggering to the bathroom, he reached for the Advil, downing four instead of his usual two. He leaned heavily on the sink, his reflection staring back at him. His eyes were squeezed shut against the pain, but when he opened them, he saw a smear of rose-colored lipstick on his cheek. His heart pounded harder.

The prostitute. The confession. The pieces were slowly falling into place.

After a few minutes, the Advil began to dull the pain. He splashed water on his face, running a comb through his hair to tame the unruly strands. He dressed quickly in his usual black attire and white collar. He needed to get to Roberto's. He needed to know if anything unusual had happened there too.

He hailed a cab and gave the driver Roberto's address. As they pulled up to the mansion, the flashing red lights of emergency vehicles filled his vision. He instructed the driver to wait and rushed towards a paramedic standing in the doorway.

"What happened?" he asked, his heart pounding in his chest.

"Overdose," the paramedic replied.

"Can I go in? I'm his brother," Mario lied, desperate for answers.

Mario bolted through the grand foyer, his heart pounding in his chest as he navigated the throng of emergency personnel. His eyes locked onto the grim sight of six firemen and two EMTs. They were all standing in solemn silence around a medical examiner, who was halfway through zipping up a black body bag.

That's when Mario saw him.

"No!" he screamed, a raw, guttural sound of pure anguish. His eyes remained glued to Roberto's pale, lifeless face as it disappeared behind the zipper.

Every head in the room was staring at Mario, their expressions a mix of sympathy and shock. A nearby fireman, his face etched with empathy, gently guided Mario into the living room.

Mario allowed himself to be led, his legs feeling like jelly beneath him. He collapsed onto the plush couch, his body wracked with sobs. "No, no, no, no, no," he repeated, his voice a broken whisper. His hands cradled his head as he shook, tears splattering onto the expensive rug beneath him. The reality of his loss was a crushing weight suffocating him.

"Was he your brother?" The fireman's voice was gentle, his eyes filled with understanding.

Mario could only nod, his throat too tight to form words.

"I'm sorry for your loss, Father," the fireman said, his voice filled with the practiced sympathy of someone who had delivered this sort of news far too many times.

"Why?" Mario managed to choke out, sitting up and wiping at his tear-streaked face.

"We suspect he died of an overdose. The lab will need to confirm, but he shows all the signs. I'm sorry. These things happen."

"Wait, but . . . he doesn't do drugs." Mario's tears had stopped, replaced by a chilling resolve. His headache was receding, his mind clearing. He stood, moving past the fireman into Roberto's office. His eyes scanned the room, looking for anything out of place.

His laptop was open on Roberto's desk, but the microSD card was missing. A quick search of the desk revealed nothing. Booting up the laptop, Mario was met with a blank screen— all his files had been erased. Roberto's computer had suffered the same fate. The Vatican had discovered his transgression and were meticulously erasing the evidence he'd collected. His hand instinctively grazed his right thigh, feeling the stitches and the concealed microSD chip within.

They hadn't found this copy. But if they'd silenced Roberto for knowing too much, then Mario was undoubtedly next on their hit list.

With a newfound sense of urgency pulsing through his veins, he exited the office and strode out the front door to his waiting cab.

"Do you know where the red-light district is?"

"Sì, padre." The cab executed a swift U-turn in Roberto's driveway, setting course for the infamous locale. Twenty minutes later, Mario found himself deposited in the heart of Rome's seedy underbelly.

"I'm sorry about your brother, padre."

"Thank you. God bless you."

Even in this part of town, a row of newspaper vending machines lined the sidewalk, offering up Rome's newspapers, real estate papers, rental guides, and tourist guides. Mario wasn't one for headlines, but the bold print and catchy phrases designed to lure in passersby managed to catch his attention. Among them was the *L'Osservatore Romano*, Vatican City's daily newspaper that reported on the Holy See's activities as well as international events impacting the Church worldwide.

Mario's heart skipped a beat as he saw his own face plastered on the front page.

L'OSSERVATORE ROMANO

GIORNALE QUOTIDIANO   POLITICO RELIGIOSO
Unicuique suum   *Non praevalebunt*

PRIEST FEAST

A local priest, recently elevated to a prestigious position within the Vatican, was found in bed with a prostitute . . .

Father Mario Marino has served in the Vatican Secret Archives since February. It is a heartbreaking sight to witness such a revered clergyman's rapid fall from grace . . .

The image was damning—a snapshot of him naked in bed, his modesty obscured by a blur. The woman from the previous day—the one who had claimed a need to confess her sins—was nestled beside him, her arm draped over his chest, her lips pressed to his skin. This scandalous image would be impossible to justify to Mario's superiors. A picture spoke a thousand words, regardless of the fact that he'd clearly been unconscious when it was taken.

"How did this happen?" Mario muttered to the newspaper stand. He fed coins into the slot, pulled open the door, and snatched a copy. Unfolding it, he began to read.

"Father? Is that you?" A female passerby who had paused to buy a copy of the same newspaper was glancing from its cover to Mario and noting the striking similarity.

"No, no," Mario stammered, his words tumbling over each other as he turned tail and hurried away.

The woman watched as he disappeared down the street towards the red-light district. "Such a shame," she murmured, shaking her head at the sight of the fallen priest.

Mario rounded the corner then paused to read more of the article. A shiver ran down his spine as he absorbed the damning evidence laid out before him. Whatever drug they had administered had completely incapacitated him. He had no memory of the previous day's events. With his photo splashed across the front page of every Vatican newspaper, there would be no explaining his side of the story to the cardinal—how could he explain something he couldn't even remember? His body may have been present, as the photos clearly showed, but his mind had been absent. He was at a loss to explain what had happened, or how his image had ended up on the cover of the Vatican newspaper so swiftly.

Despite the historical tales he'd read about Pope Pius XII and World War II, Mario had never imagined the Vatican could operate with such corrupt ruthlessness in the modern era. Yet, who else could have orchestrated the rapid dissemination of such a damning image using the Vatican's own newspaper as the vehicle?

As he pondered the murder of his best friend, it dawned on him that the Vatican was rapidly tying up loose ends. He was next. His only hope was to find the woman in the scandalous photograph. She was the only potential eyewitness who could explain what had really happened.

He navigated the streets, a shadowy jungle even in the morning that pulsated with the undercurrents of the previous night's illicit activities, its stench thick with a mix of cheap perfume and lingering desperation. Mario spotted two women, their attire revealing their profession. Approaching them, he interrupted their hushed conversation. "Pardon me, ladies," he began, holding up the newspaper while strategically concealing his own image. "Do you recognize this woman?"

One of them gasped, her eyes welling up with tears. "Oh my God!"

"What did I say?" Mario asked, taken aback.

"The paramedics . . . they just took her away," the other woman managed to say, her arms wrapped protectively around her sobbing friend. "They said she OD'd, but we know she's been clean. Gina was seven-months sober."

Mario shuddered. The news of another death just hours after his friend's sent a wave of terror through him. "I'm sorry for your loss."

"Thank you, Father," the woman replied, her friend still weeping in her arms.

"Could you direct me to Gina's apartment?" he asked, hoping to find any clues that might help explain this tragedy.

"It's a few blocks down this street, on the left. Ask around when you get close. Someone will guide you."

"Thank you. And again, I'm truly sorry for your loss," Mario said, offering a comforting touch on the woman's shoulder before he ventured down the street in the direction she'd indicated.

As he walked, a figure in black caught his eye. A man, dressed head to toe in black, was walking away from the direction of Gina's apartment. Mario's blood ran cold. He recognized the all-black uniform of the Vatican's assassins. The cleanup crew was already here.

Mario whirled around, his heart pounding like a drum as he sprinted back the way he'd come.

"Call 1-1-2!" he bellowed at the two women as he dashed past them. One of them fumbled for her phone, her fingers trembling as she dialed the emergency number. The assassin, hearing the command, drew his silenced handgun, his aim deadly accurate. With a single muted shot, he pierced both phone and skull—the hollow point bullet exploded out the other side of the woman's head in a gruesome spray of blood. Her crying companion screamed, her voice echoing off the buildings before she too fell victim to the assassin's lethal precision. Their bodies crumpled to the ground, blood pooling around them.

The assassin's gaze never left the priest, watching as he darted into a dead-end alley. He slowed his pace, a predatory grin spreading across his face. He knew the priest was trapped in there with nowhere to go. The assassin stopped about fifty feet from the entrance to the alley and waited for the inevitable moment when the man's panic became too much—he'd run for it, try to escape. That was the moment he would end the traitorous priest's life.

Just as the assassin predicted, the priest burst out of the alley, skidding to a halt before spinning around and sprinting in the opposite direction of the assassin. The assassin raised his gun, his steady aim trained on the back of the priest's head.

He squeezed the trigger.

The hollow point bullet entered the back of the priest's skull and exited through his face in a gruesome display of violence. He fell limp to the ground.

The assassin approached the lifeless body. His gloved hand reached into the priest's back pocket to retrieve his wallet. Identifying the body had indeed once belonged to a certain Mario Marino, the assassin slipped the wallet back into the corpse's pocket. He dragged the body into the alley and up to a pile of trash bags stacked against the alley wall, where he stuffed it in amongst the refuse. It would later be discovered by the polizia following an anonymous phone call.

In the depths of the dead-end alley, the assassin's ears pricked up at a sound emanating from a dumpster some fifty yards down the way. With a swift glance to ensure no prying eyes were present, he smoothly drew his handgun from its shoulder holster and advanced down the alley.

As he neared the dumpster, a sudden movement alerted him—a feral cat leaping out. His reflexes, honed to a razor's edge, responded instantly—he fired, extinguishing the cat's life in a gruesome display against the dumpster.

"Fucking cat," the assassin muttered, his gaze assessing the smear against the dumpster. He sheathed his weapon and pulled out his phone. His fingers deftly typed out a message on an encrypted line to the Vatican:

Package Destroyed

He sent the message. With that, the assassin melted away, his path leading him back to the Vatican, ready for his next assignment. This loose end had been neatly tied up.

PART II

Chapter 74

March 11, 2000
Rome, Italy
Five minutes earlier

With a surge of adrenaline, Mario sprinted towards the two women, screaming, "Call 1-1-2!" One of the women turned her head sharply, her eyes scanning for the source of the priest's terror. She spotted the pursuing figure dressed in all black and pulled out her phone, her fingers trembling as she punched in the emergency number. Before the phone could connect, a chilling crack pierced both the phone and the woman's skull. She crumpled to the cold pavement, a crimson river flowing from her temple. Her companion let out a shrill truncated scream before she too collapsed lifelessly beside her.

With his heart hammering in his chest, Mario dared not risk a backward glance at the gruesome execution. Terror was his fuel, the icy realization he was next on the executioner's list propelling him forward. He swerved abruptly into a nearby alleyway and crashed into a figure whose attire mirrored his own.

"Please, you must help me!" Mario implored the stranger, his eyes wide with terror. As he scrutinized the man, he was taken aback by the striking similarity of his face. It was as if he was gazing into a mirror.

"Come with me," the man ordered, his grip ironclad on Mario's arm as he steered him deeper into the dead-end alley.

They ducked behind a grimy dumpster and the stench of rotting garbage filled Mario's nostrils. The stranger, who introduced himself as Benoit, locked eyes with Mario, his gaze intense as he relayed crucial instructions. "The man chasing you is an assassin from the Vatican," he explained in a hushed whisper. "I'm here to take your place. Stay silent, stay hidden, and you might just survive. Do you understand, Mario?" His fingers dug into Mario's shoulders, his viselike grip ensuring the priest remained in the present and absorbed every word.

"Who are you?" Mario stammered, his mind reeling from the sudden, bizarre encounter.

"Mario! We don't have time for questions," Benoit snapped, his grip tightening. "Hand me your wallet. Now."

Without protest, Mario complied, handing over his wallet.

"Take this," Benoit commanded, extracting a card from his shirt pocket and thrusting it into Mario's hands. "It's your survival guide. For the next quarter of an hour, you must be a statue, a ghost. Understand?"

"Yes. Be still and silent for fifteen minutes."

Benoit stood, his gaze drilling into Mario's eyes. "Not a sound."

Mario bobbed his head in affirmation, his eyes glued to the stranger garbed in priestly attire as he sprinted down the alleyway towards the street where the assassin lay in wait. Mario watched as his "twin" glanced at the assassin, then pivoted left to flee. Mario's breath hitched as his twin's face erupted, his body crumpling to the ground. He watched in abject horror as blood spurted from his head, staining the pavement fifty yards away.

Fourteen agonizing seconds later, the assassin sauntered up to the lifeless body. His hands coldly rifled through the twin's back pocket and retrieved Mario's wallet. After confirming the identity of the corpse, he slid the wallet back into the lifeless man's pocket. Then, with a chilling nonchalance, he dragged the body behind a mound of garbage bags just inside the alley.

A stray cat emerged from the shadows behind the dumpster and brushed past Mario, causing a bottle to topple. The assassin's head snapped towards the sound. Drawing his gun, he stalked down the alley towards the dumpster. As he neared it, gun raised, the startled cat bolted.

Pffff. The silenced gun whispered its deadly secret as it discharged; the bullet tore through the cat, splattering its innards across the dumpster.

"Fucking cat," Alistar spat, his voice laced with annoyance. He holstered his weapon and pulled out his cell phone. His fingers danced across the buttons for a moment, followed by a definitive tap.

With a final glance at the crime scene, Alistar slid the cell phone into the inside pocket of his suit and left the alley.

Mario exhaled slowly, his heart still pounding like a drum as he watched the assassin disappear around the corner. A sense of familiarity about the malevolent hitman stirred in the depths of his memory, like a ghostly echo. He closed his eyes, his head dropping forward weighed down by the storm of thoughts swirling in his mind.

Who was he? Mario wrestling with the mystery of the double who had just sacrificed his life for him. The memory of the card the doppelganger handed him flashed in his mind. With a sense of urgency, he pulled it out, his eyes scanning the instructions.

**Your life is in danger. They are looking for you.
Do not trust anyone until you get to this address.**

His twin had given him clear instructions: stay put for fifteen minutes. Mario would wait, then make his way to the address on the card. His mind was a battlefield, thinking of the innocent lives lost the past few hours: Roberto murdered and made to look like he'd overdosed; the prostitute who had set him up, also supposedly overdosed; two innocent women gunned down for being in the wrong place at the wrong time; this mysterious stranger, the body double, who had sacrificed his life to save Mario's. Why was all this happening?

"It's that damn journal," Mario cursed quietly.

He huddled behind the dumpster, legs drawn up to his chest, his chin resting on his knees, waiting for the agonizing fifteen minutes to pass. Glancing at his watch, he realized he had been lost in thought for more than eighteen minutes. Fear gripped him, making him hesitant to leave the safety of this makeshift haven. What would he find at that address? More death?

Taking a deep, steadying breath, he rose to his feet and peeked out around the dumpster to make sure that it was safe. Slowly, he began his cautious journey down the alleyway. As he reached the end of the alley, he couldn't help but glance at the lifeless body of his "twin", the pool of blood around him a grim reminder of his fate. Stepping out further, Mario looked both ways to ensure the coast was clear. Turning left, he set off in the direction of the address on the card.

Chapter 75

March 11, 2000
Saturday, 10:14 a.m.
Rome, Italy

With a sense of trepidation, Mario approached the address inscribed on the card: the Trinity Bank of Italy. He double-checked the address on the card, then lifted his gaze up to the bank's imposing edifice. *This must be it*, he thought. He ventured inside, his eyes meeting the greeter stationed in the grand lobby.

"May I assist you, Father?" asked the man clad in a meticulously tailored double-breasted blue Italian suit, crisp white shirt, and vibrant red tie. His name tag read: Xavier, Greeter.

"I'm not entirely sure. I was given this card with instructions to come here." Mario presented the card to the impeccably dressed greeter.

Xavier scrutinized the card. "Ah, yes. We've been eagerly awaiting your arrival." He returned the card to Mario and said with a voice laced with intrigue, "Please, accompany me." With a swift pivot, he began to navigate towards the bank vault, bypassing the tellers with an air of authority.

Mario hesitated, his feet cemented to the polished marble floor. The cryptic card had cautioned him to trust no one until he reached this destination. Was he expected to place his trust in the hands of the individuals at this bank?

Observing Mario's hesitation, Xavier retraced his steps. He leaned in, his voice barely above a whisper. "We're privy to the incident involving your *twin*." His gaze was unflinching, piercing into Mario's soul. "Please, allow me to guide you to a secure location."

Mario was taken aback by Xavier's revelation. How was he aware of the events that had unfolded merely an hour ago? Who could have even witnessed them? The assassin had gunned down the only other souls around.

With his options dwindling and his twin's sacrifice still fresh on his mind, Mario decided to follow his instincts and trust this individual. Xavier again gestured for him to follow, so he did. Mario was led through a gated area into a restricted zone. As they approached the vault, Xavier swung open the imposing steel door, ushering Mario inside. Once within the confines of the vault, Xavier secured the door, effectively locking them in. He turned to face Mario. "Mario, our primary objective is your safety."

"How do you know my name?"

"We've had you under surveillance for several weeks now. I'm here to escort you to a more secure location where you'll be safe."

Xavier's gaze shifted to the safe deposit boxes that lined the room from floor to ceiling. He reached for a box at eye level, numbered 1013, and pressed the two keyholes. Suddenly, the room began to descend. The bank vault, adorned with genuine safe deposit boxes, was in fact an elevator.

Mario's heart pounded in his chest as the vault continued its descent. "Where are you taking me?"

"To our secure subterranean facility."

When the vault-elevator came to a halt, Xavier swung open the door to reveal an underground area that resembled a professional office space. It was akin to a floor in a high-rise building, minus the windows. Mario stepped out, taking in the expansive area. A man in a finely tailored brown suit strode past with folder in hand, heading towards a meeting down the hall. Another man, also in a suit, moved in the opposite direction to a boardroom meeting. Inside the boardroom, Mario could see four men huddled over a large blueprint, engaged in a heated discussion. They glanced up as Mario exited the elevator; their expressions suggested they were familiar with his identity.

A man of impeccable taste approached Mario. He was exquisitely dressed in his single-breasted dark grey suit, crisp white shirt, and red tie, a testament to the Templar's refined dress code. His hair was slicked back, and his Italian shoes gleamed under the office lights. "Mario, we've been eagerly awaiting your arrival," the man said, extending his hand in a welcoming gesture. The bold red letters on his white nametag identified him as Dominic.

Eyeing the nametag, Mario replied, "Why am I here?"

Dominic nodded to Xavier, silently signaling that he would take over from here. Xavier retreated into the vault, closing the door behind him before it began its ascent back to street level.

"Follow me, I'll explain everything," Dominic gestured, his arm sweeping down the hallway towards his office. Mario, his curiosity piqued, followed Dominic's lead. Stepping into the office, Mario was greeted by a visual feast of thirteenth-and-fourteenth-century battle scenes. Knights in full regalia atop their steeds, swords drawn, dominated the paintings. A flag bearing a red cross on a white background fluttered in the breeze, held aloft by another knight. Dark-brown bookcases filled to the brim with tomes lined an entire wall.

Dominic circled his desk and sank into his high-backed leather chair. "Please, take a seat."

Mario complied, settling into the leather chair opposite Dominic's.

"Mario, I understand you must have a myriad of questions. This morning has been quite eventful for you."

"That's putting it mildly," Mario retorted, Roberto's sarcasm echoing in his voice.

"We've had our eyes on you for several weeks now."

"Xavier mentioned that. But why? What have I done?" Mario leaned forward, his anticipation palpable.

"Perhaps it would be best if I start by explaining who we are."

Mario listened, his mind a whirl of confusion and curiosity.

"We are the Poor Fellow-Soldiers of Christ. You may know us as the Knights Templar."

Mario's eyes bulged in disbelief. Lore had it that the Templars had been annihilated in 1307 by King Philip IV. "I was under the impression you were all extinct."

"Quite the contrary. As you can witness, we are very much alive."

"But how is that possible?"

"King Philip IV orchestrated a mass execution of our brethren. Under the most gruesome torture, our forefathers confessed to heinous acts they never committed." Dominic's voice dipped into a mournful tone as he recalled the dreadful day King Philip IV seized his ancestors. They were subjected to brutal torture and forced to confess to fabricated charges of heresy, homosexuality, devil worship, spitting on the cross, fraud, and more. After that fateful day, the surviving Templars seemingly fled Europe, disappearing into obscurity.

"I came across a scroll in the Archives stating the pope absolved the Knights of their crimes."

"The Chinon Parchment," said Dominic, well-versed in his history.

"That's the one."

"Despite that written absolution, the so-called fair King Philip continued his brutal torture and execution of our brothers."

"Why would he do that?"

"Despite our title as the Poor Fellow-Soldiers of Christ, our ancestors amassed a fortune thanks to the numerous donations and gifts they received from those they safeguarded. We became incredibly wealthy, enabling us to lend money to those in need."

Mario leaned forward engrossed in Dominic's narration of his people's history.

"King Philip IV was heavily indebted to our ancestors. Seeing their immense power and wealth, the king schemed to have them arrested, confess to false charges, and executed, thereby erasing his debts forever."

"That's horrific."

"King Philip also aimed to seize our wealth, long ago. The rumor about us finding Solomon's treasure is indeed true. We did find King Solomon's treasure."

Mario's eyes widened in astonishment upon hearing this revelation. "That treasure would be worth billions today."

"Trillions, to be precise—which is why we swore an oath to protect it from people like King Philip and the Vatican."

"Why the Vatican?"

"The pope and his Vatican believe they are the rightful heirs to Solomon's treasure. You must remember the Bible verse where Jesus tells Peter, 'Now I say to you that you are Peter, and upon this rock I will build my church, and all the powers of hell will not conquer it. And I will give you the keys of the Kingdom of Heaven.'" The Templar recited Matthew 16. "You see, the Vatican believes *they* are that church."

"I understand the verse, but it speaks of Heaven, not King Solomon's treasure."

"Mario, the magnitude of Solomon's treasure is beyond comprehension. We're talking about centuries of treasures unearthed from Solomon's Temple. As I mentioned, it would be worth trillions in today's currency. In the wrong hands, it could alter the course of history. That's why we must keep it from the pope and the Vatican."

"I'm still puzzled about the Knights Templars. The legends suggest you've been extinct for centuries."

"Allow me to enlighten you with a history lesson from the inside." Dominic rose and began to pace around the office. "Our original moniker was the Poor Fellow-Soldiers of Christ. The world recognizes us as the Knights Templar, or Temple Knights. The Knights Templar were established around 1119 AD."

Mario listened, engrossed in the Templar's history as narrated by a Templar himself.

"The original eight Christian Knights approached the Patriarchy of Jerusalem, seeking permission to defend the Kingdom of Jerusalem. We took on the duty of safeguarding pilgrims journeying to the Holy Land to worship at the sacred shrines." Dominic paced across the carpet, his gaze distant. "These pilgrims traversed through Muslim-controlled territories, and many were robbed or killed. With the King of Jerusalem's approval, we set up our headquarters at Solomon's Temple. King Solomon, by today's standards, would probably be a trillionaire. Kings and queens would present him with tons of gold and treasure."

"The Old Testament declared King Solomon as the wealthiest and wisest man who ever lived," Mario added.

"Correct. In 1128 AD, the Vatican acknowledged us as God's army. The pope's decree granted us our military name, as you now know it: the Knights Templar." Dominic returned to his seat.

"What about all the treasure?"

"When my forefathers were stationed at Solomon's Temple, they began digging and excavating the temple grounds. That's when they stumbled upon Solomon's treasure, hidden deep in a vault beneath the temple."

"Wow." Mario's eyes widened at the revelation of how Solomon's treasure had truly been found.

"Wow, indeed. But they realized the treasure was too vast for any single nation or entity to possess. As the saying goes, 'absolute power corrupts absolutely'. Our forefathers vowed to prevent the treasure from falling into the wrong hands." Dominic then recited the vow every Templar took to protect the secrecy of King Solomon's great treasure.

"Where is it?" Mario was on the edge of his seat now, eager to hear the secret of the treasure.

"Ah, there's only one person who knows the answer to that question."

Mario waited in anticipation. "And?"

"Only the Grand Master ever knows the location of Solomon's treasure. And when he passes on the 'crown', so to speak, he reveals it to the next Grand Master, and so forth."

"Only one person in the entire world knows where Solomon's treasure is at any given time? You're joking, right?"

"No, my friend. The Grand Master Templar Knight is the only one in the world who knows the location of Solomon's treasure."

"Unbelievable." Mario slumped back into his chair, the anticlimactic end to the tale leaving him deflated.

"Believe it, Mario. The Grand Master took an oath. As I've reiterated, the treasure is too formidable for any single entity to command." Dominic observed Mario, whose countenance was etched with defeat. The whereabouts of the treasure would remain an enigma to him. It was akin to faith: trusting in something unseen yet acknowledging its existence. As an ordained priest, Mario knew he ought to grasp this concept better than most. This was a doctrine from his seminary education. Why was it so challenging for him to accept the existence of Solomon's treasure without seeing it? If it were a mere myth, why would the Vatican be so resolute over seizing it?

Sensing Mario was saturated with history lessons, Dominic concluded his tale. "On October 13, 1307, King Philip IV of France rounded up many Templars, accused them of heresy, and had them burned at the stake after extracting confessions through torture. Those who escaped capture vanished into obscurity creating satellites around the world like the one you are hiding in now."

Mario stared at Dominic, the history lesson concluded. The idea of a single man possessing the knowledge of Solomon's treasure was hard to digest. "That's it?"

"That's the long and short of it. I regret there's no more to share." Dominic noted the disappointment etched on the priest's face.

Like a spell breaking, Mario came back to the real world, realizing he was still a target for the Vatican's assassins. Who was that doppelgänger they had killed? "What does all this have to do with me?"

"Do you possess something the Vatican desires?"

Mario scrutinized Dominic, wondering if he could trust this man who claimed to be a Knights Templar. "I found a journal from Pope Pius XII detailing his involvement with Hitler during World War II."

"Do you have this journal?"

"It's, um . . ." Mario hesitated, debating whether to reveal his secret to this organization. "It's hidden."

"Hidden where?"

"I can't tell you that." Mario immediately thought about the journal he'd left hidden in the Rome train station locker.

Dominic leaned back in his chair, baffled the young priest was unwilling to trust the people who had just saved his life.

After a tense silence, Mario shifted the conversation. "What happened in the alley an hour ago?"

"We've been tracking unusual activity inside the Vatican, particularly following the funeral of your predecessor, Father Benedetti," Dominic revealed.

Mario absorbed Dominic's words. The Templars had been vigilantly monitoring the Vatican? How could they possibly possess detailed knowledge of Father Benedetti's untimely demise months ago?

"A young priest succumbing to a heart attack seemed suspicious to us. We increased our surveillance, deploying our insiders to watch for any anomalies. Recently, we noticed an uptick in activity among the Vatican assassins. We trailed them, but . . ." Dominic's voice faltered, grappling with the next revelation. "We couldn't save your friend. My deepest condolences."

"You're aware of Roberto's death?"

"That was the catalyst that put us on high alert—we were able to move into position just in time to protect you."

"The man in the alley, who was he?"

"One of our brethren. We had four decoys in the vicinity, each prepared to sacrifice their life for you." Dominic detailed the intricate operation to safeguard Mario from the relentless Vatican assassin.

"But why?"

"You must possess something of such significance that the powers-that-be want you eliminated."

"Why does the Vatican employ assassins?" Mario was vexed that the holiest of institutions engaged in assassination. He was familiar with the one hundred thirty-five Swiss Guard safeguarding Vatican City and the pope, but that was benign, expected; assassins, on the other hand, should have no place there.

"They are a covert division within the Vatican, tasked with eliminating those who pose a threat to the pope or the Vatican's reputation."

"I've never heard of them."

"Few have. This isn't public knowledge, Mario. Can you fathom the fallout if the Catholic faithful discovered the Vatican orchestrated mafia-style operations to neutralize potential threats to its existence?"

"They would abandon the Church."

"That's precisely why their existence remains a secret. They operate under the radar, leaving no trace of their actions."

Mario rubbed his thigh, feeling the microSD card embedded under his skin. The weight of this information was overwhelming.

Dominic noticed Mario's subtle gesture. Perhaps just a nervous twitch? "Let me escort you to your quarters so you can freshen up and rest."

"Thank you." Mario rose, appreciating the hospitality. "I could use some sleep."

Chapter 76

March 12, 2000
Sunday, 5:55 a.m.
Rome, Italy

Mario awoke drenched in sweat, haunted by the nightmare of Roberto's brutal murder. The image of the man in black—with eyes as demonic as the night, teeth sharp as razors, horns and skin as red as blood—jolted him from his sleep. Was this the same assassin that had hunted him yesterday? His lifelong dream of serving the Vatican had morphed into a terrifying nightmare. In less than a day, he had lost his best friend, been scandalized in the Vatican newspaper, pursued by a Vatican assassin, witnessed the execution of his doppelgänger, discovered the legendary Knights Templars, and was now taking refuge in their subterranean headquarters. How had his life spiraled into this chaos?

He ambled over to the room's dresser to find it half-filled with clean clothes. As he pulled out a shirt and underwear that seemed to be his size. How did they know? He slipped into the bathroom and changed into the fresh clothes. Emerging, he noticed the small table in the center of the room was now laden with juice, a carafe of coffee, and a pastry. The Templars really had thought of everything. He settled into the comfortable chair, savoring the juice and pastry while admiring the simple yet thoughtful accommodations provided by the Templars for his indefinite stay.

Having finished his meal, he ventured out of his room to explore the underground network. This area resembled a hotel corridor more than the bustling office space he'd entered from the vault elevator the previous day. Peering into one of the rooms, he saw rows of bookshelves reminiscent of the Vatican Secret Archives. Intrigued, he pushed the door fully open and stepped inside.

The volumes and records were meticulously sequenced in chronological order. He sauntered down the aisle watching the years recede until he arrived at the 1940s. Identifying a registry for the year 1941, he pulled it down and flipped it open. His gaze skimmed over the names until it anchored on "Hannah Goldstein"—*the* Hannah Goldstein from the journal, he was certain—who made her appearance in August 1941.

"How strange. The pope's journal claimed she died on the plane," he murmured to the journal.

"I see you've discovered our archives," Dominic's voice rumbled through the room, causing Mario to jump.

"You startled me."

"My apologies. That wasn't my intention." Dominic's eyes flicked to the registry in Mario's grasp. "Which name piqued your interest?"

"Hannah Goldstein."

"Ah, yes. She was a remarkably shrewd young girl. Managed to evade the clutches of the Treblinka death camp," Dominic said with a hint of admiration. "Her pregnancy proved an unexpected lifeline."

"She was pregnant?"

"Yes, she was suffering from morning sickness as she boarded the plane. Her severe nausea prompted the crew to remove her from the flight, which took off without her. When the plane met its tragic end, she took refuge in the forest for an hour before making her way to Rome. That's when we found her."

"She stayed here?"

"In the very room you're occupying now," Dominic admitted.

"What became of her?"

"She found sanctuary with us for a few months, after which we arranged for her to move to America—ironically, we fulfilled the pope's promise to her. There, we connected her with a welcoming family with whom she could raise her newborn son."

"Is she still alive?"

"Indeed, she and her son are thriving in America. He's a successful author, penning books on World War II. Quite the twist of fate, wouldn't you say?"

"Does the son know about the Templars?" Mario wondered about the extent of their secrecy.

"As far as we know, Hannah has kept our existence a secret from him. She's only told him that they escaped Europe during World War II."

"Do you keep in touch with her?"

"We check in occasionally. But as I mentioned, they're doing quite well. The old gal's getting on in years, but her cunning and intelligence have served them well. Their success doesn't surprise me."

Mario fell silent, contemplating his own situation, which mirrored Hannah's in many ways. He realized his knowledge of the Templars was limited to what he'd read in books and what Dominic had already shared with him.

"This is all so overwhelming. It's like a condensed version of the Vatican Secret Archives," Mario said, his gaze sweeping over the aisle of towering shelves. "What other secrets does this place hold?"

"We've been amassing knowledge for centuries. This is merely a fraction of our entire collection. The primary collection is housed at our headquarters, the location of which I cannot disclose. You understand."

"Absolutely," Mario acknowledged. The Templars obviously had to maintain their veil of secrecy.

"How long has this . . ." Mario paused, searching for the right term. "What do you call this place?"

"We refer to it as a 'Satellite'. We've been stationed in Rome since the late 1890s, vigilantly monitoring the Vatican and all its activities."

"What other Vatican-related information is stored here?"

"We have meticulously documented all our interactions with the Vatican. I believe you'll find it quite intriguing. Before Hannah's arrival, we were keeping a close eye on Father Eugenio Pacelli. . . . You're familiar with him, aren't you?"

"He ascended to the papacy as Pope Pius XII."

"Correct. Pacelli, in conjunction with the Black Nobility, was meticulously orchestrating their ultimate confrontation against us. Upon his ascension to the papacy in '39, he set in motion Hitler's initiation of World War II with the invasion of Poland later that year. Pacelli then directed Hitler to round up the Jews and seize all their possessions—their artwork, homes, real estate, gold, cash. Everything. Pacelli essentially held the Jews hostage for ransom."

"Ransom for what?"

"Solomon's treasure."

Mario remained silent, stunned by Dominic's revelation, eagerly awaiting further elucidation.

"With Pacelli manipulating Hitler like a marionette, the Nazis swelled in numbers and power. We were vastly outnumbered. Pacelli was convinced they were the rightful inheritors of Solomon's treasure and used the Jews as leverage to try and force our hand."

"This is a lot of information. Is there some place to sit down?"

"Certainly. Let's move to the reading area." The Templar guided Mario down the aisle to an open space furnished with four leather chairs arranged in a circle. As Mario settled into a chair, he encouraged Dominic to continue with the account of the covert war between the Templars and the Vatican.

"As I mentioned, we were significantly outnumbered by the Nazis and Mussolini's Fascists. The Vatican had their puppet strings attached to Germany, Italy, and the United States. The pope pulled Hitler's strings in Germany, his brother manipulated Mussolini in Italy, and FDR was under the influence of Catholic cardinals and the archbishop in the United States. We were at a stark disadvantage during the initial years of World War II."

"You're suggesting that World War II was a grandiose game of chess between the Vatican and the Templars, vying for control of Solomon's treasure?" Mario was struggling to digest this revelation. He had been raised on the teachings of the Catholic Church. Now he was hearing that the Vatican was essentially a bully, fighting to reclaim their 'toy'—the invaluable treasure of King Solomon that the Templars had discovered and sworn to protect. It felt as though the Vatican and the pope were merely a facade, an elaborate ruse in their pursuit of the world's most precious treasure.

"Yes, I suppose that's a succinct summary of World War II."

Mario stared at Dominic. This contradicted everything taught in history classes worldwide, everything taught in Catholic schools. What was the truth? What was a lie?

Seeing Mario struggling to comprehend, Dominic continued his explanation. "That's when we manipulated the Japanese into bombing Pearl Harbor in December 1941."

"Wait! You provoked them into bombing Pearl Harbor?"

"Yes, to draw the United States into the war. We had heard the Nazis were planning a meeting in December 1941 to intensify their extermination of the Jews."

Mario fell silent again, absorbing this shocking information. He still couldn't believe that World War II was essentially an elaborate chess match between two competing shadow powers.

"Regrettably, the bombing only postponed the meeting by a month. The senior government leaders of the Nazi Party convened in Wannsee, Germany."

"The Wannsee Conference," Mario interjected. "That's where the Nazis formulated their plans for the Final Solution to the Jewish Problem."

"Correct."

"Reinhard Heydrich and Adolf Eichmann spearheaded the effort," Mario added, using his newfound knowledge regarding the Final Solution.

"Indeed. It was at the Wannsee Conference that the pope escalated the extermination the Jews. The ball, metaphorically speaking, was back in our court."

"What did you do?"

"We were limited in power. The United States was now in the war, but they were moving too slowly. We recruited volunteers across Europe to hide Jews or assist them in escaping the Nazis. I'm sure you've heard some of those stories."

"You mean like Anne Frank?"

"Indeed. Tragically, Anne and her family were discovered and transported to a death camp where they succumbed to the horrors of the gas chambers."

"Your volunteers couldn't stem the tide."

"Indeed. The Nazis were systematically exterminating tens of thousands of Jews daily across Eastern Europe in their death camps."

"So what could you do?"

"We formulated a more extensive plan. Bear in mind, the pope had a significant head start in planning this war. The Grand Master Templar Knight and his lieutenants responded by developing our own Templar Final Solution to terminate the war."

Mario leaned in, captivated by this untold piece of intelligence. "What was the Templar Final Solution?"

Dominic glanced at his watch, realizing he needed to return upstairs. "Rather than me narrating, let me fetch you the archival journal from the Master Templar himself, detailing their grand scheme." Dominic rose and retraced their steps down the aisle. Returning with a book, he handed it to Mario. "This will provide you with the specifics of the Templar Final Solution of 1945." As Mario examined the book's cover, Dominic added, "I must return upstairs. I'll come back down in a few hours to see how you're doing."

"Thank you for all the explanations. And thank you"— Mario met Dominic's gaze—"you saved my life. I am eternally grateful."

Dominic nodded, turned, and exited the sitting area.

Mario reclined in the leather club chair, ready to delve into the journal the Templar had given him.

Chapter 77

1 April 1945
Sunday Morning
Rome, Italy

Five desperate Templar Knights huddled around a circular conference table, their minds whirring with strategies to halt the war. The Vatican held the reins of power, controlling the Axis forces with an iron grip.

"The Nazis are systematically eradicating millions of Jews in their extermination camps," the Templar Lord declared with a grave tone. "Their brutality towards the Jewish hostages knows no bounds. The pope will not cease this war until we surrender the ransom." He paused, his gaze sweeping over each of his lieutenants, a steely determination etched on his face. "We cannot allow him to take possession of Solomon's Treasure. What's our countermove?"

"The Allies are unable to penetrate the Eastern Bloc cities with aircraft to obliterate the camps. The pope has strategically scattered hundreds of camps throughout Eastern Europe to prevent an effective response," a knight replied.

"I'm not interested in their limitations. What resources do *we* have at our disposal?" the Templar Lord thundered, his fist crashing down on the conference table, demanding solutions.

"What if we eliminate the top leaders?" another knight proposed. The daring solution hung in the air.

"What are you suggesting?"

"Assassinate Hitler, Mussolini . . . and Roosevelt, to provoke the Americans out of their complacency. Sever the head, and the body will perish."

"Germany, Italy, and the United States," the Templar Lord mused, considering the audacious idea. "All three are vital cogs in the pope's war machine. This could be our game-changer."

The four Templars sat in silence, watching their Templar Lord as he mulled over this new strategy.

"Include Joseph Goebbels on the hit list. He's the natural successor to Hitler. His elimination is crucial," the Templar Lord decided, crafting a comprehensive plan to dismantle the pope's top leaders.

"Mobilize the teams immediately. Code names: Alpha, Beta, Gamma, and Delta," the Templar Lord directed his four Templar Lieutenants. "As a last-ditch effort, add Epsilon—for Eugenio Pacelli." The inclusion of the pope was a desperate move by the Templar Lord, a drastic measure to end World War II. He was aware that targeting the pope would incite the Vatican to full-scale retaliation against the Knights Templar. Taking out the pope would be a measure of last resort if all else failed.

"The primary targets must be eliminated by May first. Is my directive clear?"

"Yes, my lord," the four echoed in unison.

"Alert your teams."

12 April 1945
Thursday, 12:53 p.m.
Washington, DC

Elizabeth Shoumatoff, the renowned portrait artist, was poised in front of her easel, meticulously crafting a likeness of Franklin Delano Roosevelt. FDR sat opposite her, playing the willing subject for his portrait. The day before Friday the 13th was devoid of any significant events for the president. FDR, a man of superstition, never scheduled any important journeys on Fridays, and he held a particular aversion for Friday the 13th—he always ensured he was safely ensconced within the White House on such calendar days. The president of the United States of America was indeed a man haunted by superstitions, with Friday the 13th warranting the most suspicion of all.

So it was that Delta Team, employing a sense of poetic justice, had deliberately chosen the day before Friday the 13th to execute President Roosevelt. FDR, who was in constant communication with Pope Pius XII throughout the war, was deemed unworthy to die on a day that held significance for the Templar's ancestors when their brethren were executed in 1307. The president's fears led him to isolate in the White House, unwittingly setting the stage for Delta Team to execute their lethal mission.

A White House servant with a subtle French accent entered the Oval Office to serve the president his lunch. "Mr. President, it's time for your polio medication," he instructed, his voice carrying a hint of authority.

"You must be new," Roosevelt observed, his tone amiable, as he was known to be kind to all his staff.

"Thank you for noticing, Mr. President," responded the Delta Team leader masquerading as a member of the White House kitchen staff.

Franklin Roosevelt popped the two pills into his mouth and washed them down with a glass of water. He placed the glass on the table beside him then resumed his pose for Ms. Shoumatoff.

The Delta Team leader retreated towards the door, positioning himself out of the artist's and the president's line of sight. His eyes remained fixed on Roosevelt. He waited.

"I have a terrific pain in the back of my head," Roosevelt declared moments later. He suddenly slumped forward in his chair, unconscious.

"I'll fetch the doctor," the Templar announced, swiftly exiting the room.

"The president has suffered a massive cerebral hemorrhage," said Lt. Commander, Dr. Howard Bruenn, the president's cardiologist, delivering his grim diagnosis of the president of the United States of America.

Roosevelt never regained consciousness and passed away at 3:35p.m. on April 12, 1945.

Delta Mission Accomplished.

Δ *Team*

28 April 1945
Saturday
Dongo, Italy, Near Lake Como

"The road is blocked. We will have to take a detour, Il Duce," the driver informed Benito Mussolini and his mistress, Clara Petacci, who were both nestled in the backseat of the sleek 1939 Alfa Romeo 6C 2500 Sport Berlinetta. Disguised as a Spanish diplomatic vehicle, this car led a four-vehicle motorcade, a desperate attempt by Mussolini's loyalists to flee Italy.

"Just ensure we reach Switzerland and connect with the air transport," Mussolini retorted, his voice laced with tension.

They veered off the main road and journeyed another twenty kilometers into a desolate area just outside the quaint village of Giulino di Mezzegra.

"Il Duce, there's a military roadblock ahead. They don't appear to be Nazis, but Italian military. What's our course of action?"

"Proceed. I doubt they're searching for us," Mussolini commanded, his voice steady.

As they approached the roadblock, the driver rolled down his window, his heart pounding.

"State your purpose," the military officer, the Beta Team leader in disguise, demanded.

"We're en route to Switzerland," the driver responded, struggling to keep his voice steady.

"Exit the vehicle," the Beta Team leader ordered.

Suddenly, twenty Templar assassins masquerading as Italian officers of the 52nd Garibaldi Brigade emerged from the roadside brandishing machine guns. They swiftly surrounded the vehicles, ordering all passengers out.

The fifteen Fascists were corralled towards a stone wall. Mussolini and Petacci's faces were etched with terror as they faced the officers, who aimed their machine guns at them with deadly precision.

With a subtle nod from the Beta Team leader, a hail of bullets erupted, mowing down Mussolini, his mistress, and the entourage of the Italian Social Republic party. The Beta Team leader approached the lifeless bodies and delivered a final kick to Mussolini's head to confirm his demise. He turned to his second-in-command. "Make an anonymous call to Colonel Audisio. Inform him of Il Duce's location."

Colonel Walter Audisio arrived half an hour later and walked up to the stone wall where the fifteen Fascist Party members' bodies lay in a gruesome tableau. Audisio claimed the execution of Mussolini and his party as his own work. He then had the bodies loaded into a van and transported to the Piazzale Loreto in Milan. There, the bodies were subjected to the wrath of the local villagers before being hung upside down on meat hooks from the roof of a gas station.

Beta Mission Accomplished.

β *Team*

30 April 1945
Führerbunker, Berlin

I n the chilling depths of the Führerbunker, three members of
the Alpha Team successfully restrained Hitler, Goebbels, Eva
Braun, Stumpfegger (Hitler's personal physician), and three
Nazi officers. Joseph Goebbel's wife and children were bound
and confined in a room of the Vorbunker, which was situated on
the first floor of the Führerbunker.

"I will rip you to shreds!" the Führer screamed, spewing
venomous threats. "Goebbels, do something!"

But the Minister of Propaganda had been rendered
powerless to follow his leader's commands; he was bound to the
chair adjacent to the Führer and his newly wedded wife. Hitler
and Braun had exchanged vows the previous day, sensing the
impending doom of the war.

The Alpha Team's leader, a figure of authority and control,
sat at the table, meticulously drafting Hitler's last will and
testament as per the Templar Lord's directives. Hitler's last will
and testament distinctly outlined the following appointments:

- Goebbels as the Reich Chancellor.
- Karl Dönitz as the Reich President.
- Martin Bormann as the Nazi Party Minister.
- And most crucially, Hitler named no successor as
  Führer or leader of the Nazi Party.

The Alpha Team leader then composed a second document,
demanding Hitler openly confess his allegiance to Pope Pius
XII. With Hitler's hands untied and the cold barrel of a Walther
P38 Ruger pressed against his temple, the Alpha Team leader
commanded, "Sign both of these documents."

Hitler bent over the first document, his eyes scanning the words. He picked up the pen and signed his last will and testament. The Templar swiftly seized the signed document and passed it to his second-in-command. Hitler perused the second document, a confession of his instructions and guidance from Pope Pius XII.

Hitler spat at the Alpha Team leader, his face contorted in disgust. "I refuse to sign this! This is heresy!"

The Alpha Team leader walked behind Eva Braun and placed the pistol to her temple. "You will sign the document, or your bride will die."

Eva Braun's eyes flared with terror, fully aware that her beloved "wolf" would never succumb to the terrorists' demands. She shut her eyes tightly, inhaled deeply, and steeled herself for her inevitable end.

"I will never sign!"

The Templar swiftly reached into his pocket, extracting a cyanide capsule. With a swift, calculated movement, he cracked the capsule, a puff of deadly cyanide powder escaping. He seized Braun's head, forced her mouth open, and ruthlessly shoved the cyanide capsule inside. The acrid scent of bitter almonds filled the air as the powder spilled into her mouth. Before she could react, the Templar clamped her mouth shut, ensuring the lethal poison was ingested. Her body jerked once, then slumped forward, her life extinguished.

"You animal! What have you done?"

"SIGN THE DOCUMENT!"

"NEVER!"

At the Alpha Team leader's signal, two Templars lunged at Hitler, wrestling him back into his chair and binding him with ruthless efficiency. The second-in-command glanced at the Alpha Team leader, seeking confirmation. Upon receiving a curt nod, he seized Hitler's head, forced his mouth open, and rammed in another partially cracked cyanide capsule. As he clamped his hand over the Führer's mouth, Hitler's body convulsed before slumping lifelessly in the chair.

Goebbels sat frozen, his eyes wide with horror as he took in the sight of his Führer and Eva Braun, their lives snuffed out. A chilling realization dawned on him—he was next.

"Get rid of these abominations," the Alpha Team leader commanded, his voice cold and devoid of emotion. "Take them upstairs and burn the bodies. I won't have this filth turned into martyrs."

The Alpha Team dragged Hitler and Eva Braun out of the bunker and shot them point-blank in the head to stage a murder-suicide, their bodies doused in petrol and burned.

The Alpha Team leader sent a coded message to the Templar headquarters:

Alpha Mission Accomplished.

A Team

1 May 1945 5:02 a.m.
Vorbunker, Berlin (First Floor of the Führerbunker.)

"Time for some answers, Herr Goebbels," the Gamma Team Leader growled as he began his relentless interrogation of the newly appointed Reich Chancellor at the break of dawn.

"I've told you, I know nothing of your claims. All my orders came directly from mein Führer."

"Lies!" the Gamma Team leader roared, his face mere inches from Goebbels's. "Tell us how you were getting instructions from the pope!"

Goebbels shut his eyes, attempting to block out the verbal onslaught.

"He needs some persuasion." The Gamma Team leader signaled his first lieutenant to release the former Minister of Propaganda from his restraints.

Handcuffed, Goebbels was led down the corridor to the room where his wife and children lay unconscious, sedated by a sleeping gas. As the door swung open and the lights flickered on, Goebbels was met with the sight of his family sprawled peacefully on the bunker cots, oblivious to their intrusion. Two Templars shoved him into the room, the Gamma Team leader stalking in behind him.

"Admit to your Vatican-orchestrated crimes against the Jews."

"I . . . I don't know what you're talking about."

With a curt nod from the Gamma Team leader, his first lieutenant stood over Joseph's wife, Magda Goebbels.

BANG!

A spray of blood painted the wall behind her head.

BANG! BANG! Two more shots pierced her heart.

"NO!" Goebbels howled, witnessing the brutal execution. "I swear, I don't know what you're talking about," he sobbed, watching his wife's blood staining the sheets.

Another nod from the Gamma Team leader and two Templar officers knelt before two of the children, placing cyanide capsules in their mouths. Their jaws were clamped down and the lethal power released. Their bodies slumped lifelessly. The remaining four children then suffered the same fate.

Goebbels crumpled, held up only by his captors, tears splashing onto the concrete floor as he watched his family be massacred.

The Gamma Team leader drew his pistol and pressed the cold barrel against Goebbels's temple. "Confess," he hissed, each word a deadly promise. "Or you'll *wish* we'd handed you over to the Soviets."

Goebbels had heard the rumors of the Soviet Union's torture methods—boiling victims alive, mutilation, even crucifixion. His head dropped, resignation etched on his face.

"He's worthless," the Gamma leader grunted, exasperated with the Nazi leader.

BANG!

Goebbels crumpled to the floor, a pool of blood spreading around him. The newly appointed Chancellor of the Nazi Party was no more.

"Take the bodies upstairs and burn them. And kill the rest of those Nazi bastards in the other room."

A transmission was sent to Templar headquarters:

Gamma Mission Accomplished.

Γ *Team*

Chapter 78

March 12, 2000
Sunday, 9:55 a.m.
Templar Satellite's Basement

Mario slammed the book shut, his heart pounding at the gruesome details of the executions carried out inside the Führerbunker. The Templar teams had been merciless, eliminating the pope's top four henchmen with chilling precision. He could see now that the Vatican had cornered the Templars, forcing them to take out the proxy leaders to prevent Solomon's treasure from falling into the wrong hands. But what other horrors awaited him in these pages?

Drawing a shaky breath, he steeled himself before delving deeper into the dark truth behind World War II.

Chapter 79

8 May 1945
Rome, Italy
Templar Headquarters

The Grand Master Templar Knight broke the seal of the letter, its wax imprint of the pope's signet ring a stark reminder of the power backing the words inside:

7 May 1945

Do you truly think you've won, simply because you've toppled a few of my pawns? Your audacity in eradicating some of my most crucial pieces is commendable, but do you dare believe I've exhausted all my moves?

This deadly chess game is far from mate.

There remains an unsettled score, a consequence of your hubris. You've dragged an innocent into this deadly dance, used them as a weapon against me. They shall pay the price.

Pius pp. XII

4 August 1945
Washington, DC

"Your Holiness, how should I proceed?" President Harry Truman's voice trembled slightly as he sought counsel from Pope Pius XII, wavering in his decision to unleash irreversible hellfire on the nation of Japan.

"Mr. President," said Pope Pius XII through the secure phone line, "you bear the weight of the presidency, the duty to safeguard as many American lives as you can. Yes, innocent lives will be caught in the crossfire, but should you falter in this mission, the toll of this horrific war could multiply exponentially." The pope's words were a beacon of encouragement for the late FDR'S successor. Such divine words guiding the newly sworn-in president of the United States could potentially bring this gruesome war to a halt.

"But how will the world judge us?" Truman's voice was barely a whisper.

"Mr. President, envision a Normandy-style invasion of Japan. The casualties would be in the millions." The pope's words hung in the air, a sober reminder of the potential cost. "The bomb, however, could spare those millions their lives."

A heavy sigh escaped Truman's lips. "I suppose you're right. Your wisdom and guidance are invaluable, Your Holiness." With a final click, President Truman disconnected the secure line, a sense of gratitude washing over him for receiving divine counsel from the most sacred figure on Earth.

6 August 1945
8:15 a.m. Japan Standard Time
Tinian Airbase
North Marianas Islands

The atomic bomb codenamed "Little Boy" was nestled ominously in the belly of the Boeing B-29 Superfortress bomber, affectionately dubbed the Enola Gay. The bomber soared at a staggering altitude of 31,000 feet, casting a small but menacing shadow over the unsuspecting city of Hiroshima, Japan, a mere 500 miles from the heart of Tokyo. With a deafening roar, the bomb-bay doors swung open, releasing the monstrous 9,000-pound uranium-235 A-Bomb.

2,000 feet above the city, it detonated with a blinding flash, instantly obliterating everything beneath it. An estimated 80,000 lives were extinguished in an instant, including 20,000 brave souls of the Imperial Japanese Army. A colossal mushroom cloud, the harbinger of devastation, ascended miles into the sky, a grim testament to the destructive power unleashed.

7 August 1945
Rome, Italy
Templar Headquarters

The Grand Master Templar Knight dispatched a missive of dire urgency to the pope, a plea to halt the cataclysmic world war. It bore a single, thunderous decree:

ENOUGH!

7 August 1945
Rome, Italy
Vatican City

U pon receiving the audacious demand from the Grand Master of the Templars, a wave of fury washed over Pope Pius XII. His heart pounded in his chest like a war drum, his blood boiling with righteous indignation.

Without a moment's hesitation, he reached for the secure phone, his fingers swirling the dial with a sense of urgency. The voice of Truman crackled through the phone line in greetings.

The pope, his voice resonating with an unyielding command, directed the president of the United States to execute the deployment of the second bomb.

9 August 1945
Tinian Airbase
North Marianas Islands

The atomic bomb codenamed "Fat Man" was secured within the belly of the modified B-29 christened Bockscar. The formidable aircraft sliced through the sky, its deadly cargo aimed at the unsuspecting city of Kokura. However, the remnants of the previous day's bombing had shrouded 70% of the city in a thick, impenetrable cloud cover, adding undue risk to the mission.

The B-29, thwarted by mankind's ravaging of nature, veered off course and set its sights on its secondary target, Nagasaki.

At precisely 11:02 a.m., the monstrous 10,300-pound plutonium bomb was unleashed, detonating a chilling 1,650 feet above the narrow valleys of Nagasaki. The resulting explosion was cataclysmic, instantly claiming the lives of 40,000 unsuspecting souls.

9 August 1945
Rome, Italy
Templar Headquarters

The Grand Master Templar Knight, his hands steady and unyielding, broke the wax seal emblazoned with the pope's signet ring to reveal the secrets inscribed on the parchment.

*I am the one
who decides when
it is ENOUGH!*

Pius pp.XII

The words echoed in the Grand Master's mind, a bitter reminder of the pope's unwavering resolve. He understood the pope held the final play in this high-stakes game.

Their two formidable forces were locked in stalemate. The global "chess match" had reached a nerve-wracking impasse.

The Templars, guardians of Solomon's treasure, remained steadfast in their refusal to surrender it, while the pope was hell-bent on claiming the treasure no matter how many lives it cost. The Grand Master knew this battle of wills was far from over. The contest was destined to reignite at some future date.

Chapter 80

March 12, 2000
Sunday 11:23 a.m.
Rome, Italy

Mario had been sent reeling—it was all too much for him. Could it really be that World War II had been nothing more than a clandestine duel between two unseen superpowers vying for world dominance? Was the horrific loss of millions of lives mere collateral damage in the pursuit of a mythical treasure that might not even exist?

Dominic reappeared, finding Mario visibly drained after his deep dive into the secret annals of World War II. "Were you able to decipher the Grand Master's cryptic notes?"

Mario shot Dominic a look of frustration, his mind struggling to process the high-stakes game of cat and mouse that had been playing out between the Vatican and the Templars. "Was this all for Solomon's treasure?" he demanded.

"Indeed. The pope manipulated Hitler and the Nazis using the Jews as pawns in his ruthless quest for Solomon's treasure."

"Was it worth the massacre of millions?" Mario spat out, repulsed by this revelation. Millions of Jews dead, all in the name of acquiring some stupid treasure. This didn't even account for the countless lives lost on the battlefields of Europe and the Pacific.

"We swore an oath to safeguard Solomon's treasure from corrupt leaders incapable of handling such overwhelming responsibility," Dominic retorted, reiterating his Templar vow to protect the treasure.

Mario shook his head in disbelief. The grief he felt over World War II's casualties was too much to handle. Dominic fell silent, allowing Mario time to process his shock.

"Is this *duel* still going on?" Mario said, his voice barely above a whisper.

"I regret to inform you that it is. The Vatican, under papal leadership, continues its relentless pursuit of Solomon's treasure to this very day."

Mario exhaled deeply and sank back into his chair. "If all this is true, why did you stand by and let millions of Jews be slaughtered by the Nazis? Weren't you supposed to be the protectors of Christ's followers, the Jews, God's chosen people?"

"We were left with no other option," Dominic defended, his voice rising in defiance.

"*No other option*?"

"Try to see it from our perspective. The Vatican had been gearing up for this war for decades. It took us six years to put an end to it."

"Then you failed spectacularly, allowing the Nazis to exterminate six million Jews."

"The Vatican exploited the Jews! They were our Achilles' heel, a means of blackmailing us for Solomon's treasure. Our only recourse was to end the war because surrendering the Treasure was unthinkable." Dominic crossed his arms, his glare unwavering on Mario.

Mario scrutinized Dominic, attempting to empathize with the Templar's predicament.

"Let me pose a question to you, Mario. Would you entrust an organization like the Vatican—a proxy organization led by the Black Nobility and their pet the pope, who, by the way, encouraged the abduction and murder of millions *for ransom*—with the stewardship of the most invaluable treasure on Earth? Do you think they would stop there?"

Mario sat in silence, wrestling with the difficult decision. The Templar allowed him to ponder these grave questions. Dominic felt incensed having to justify his forefathers' decision, especially after rescuing the young priest from the very entity that sought to assassinate him.

His gaze bore into the priest. "The Bible states, 'The love of money is the root of all evil', 1 Timothy 6:10. If the Vatican was complicit with King Philip IV in rounding up and executing our brotherhood on October 13, 1307, all to gain possession of Solomon's treasure, what makes you believe it would be a responsible custodian of Solomon's treasure? We're not the villains here, Father."

"Please, don't call me Father," Mario requested, his head bowed in shame at the title ceremoniously bestowed upon him by the Catholic Church. His faith had been shattered, all because he'd accidentally discovered Pope Pius XII's journal. Perhaps Father Benedetti had met a more merciful fate when he was executed by the very institution he trusted.

"I apologize if I insulted you," Mario said, leaning forward, his elbows resting on his knees, mortified by his outburst accusing the Templars of not doing everything in their power to prevent the Holocaust.

Both men fell silent for a few minutes, mulling over their words.

"Why don't you reveal this to the world?" Mario asked, still hunched over with his head bowed.

"If we expose the Vatican and all their malevolent deeds, then they expose us. If we get exposed, then we'll have to reveal the location of Solomon's treasure. We don't do this as a professional courtesy among adversaries—it's a necessity. Safeguarding the other's secrecy preserves a tenuous balance."

"But why? The cost of this treasure has been paid with millions of lives. Doesn't that hold any weight?" Mario's voice held a note of desperation.

"Believe me, Mario, it's for the best that Solomon's treasure remains a secret to the world." Dominic's own voice held firm. He would not waver in his conviction.

Mario fell silent.

"Look at me, Mario." Dominic's tone forced Mario to meet his gaze. "You must not reveal this secret to the world. The fallout could be catastrophic, costing yet many more millions of lives."

Mario said nothing.

"Do you comprehend the severity of this?" Dominic pressed.

"I understand," Mario responded, his voice barely a whisper.

"I need your absolute assurance, Mario. You *will not* expose us or this information to the world."

Mario held Dominic's gaze. "I promise."

With that, Dominic turned and left Mario alone with his tumultuous thoughts.

After half an hour, Mario rose and walked down the aisle to return the book Dominic had given him. As he scanned the ledgers on the shelves, a smaller book caught his eye. He pulled it out and opened it to find the handwriting inside had been signed by none other than Hannah Goldstein. With the book in hand, he returned to the sitting area to delve into its entries.

Chapter 81

21 September 1941

I've been stuck in this basement for a month now. I don't know if I can trust these men.

Everything I thought I knew, I'm doubting now.

The Templars' leader told me it was the pope who tried to kill me. The plane with the other Jewish refugees was rigged to get rid of "evidence" of his transgressions.

I was evidence? I don't get it.

Who can I trust? Mom and Dad are gone. I've got no one to trust but me. I've got to grow up fast because I've got another life depending on me now. But who is the father? I was careful with the guards when I escaped Treblinka. The pope? He's the only one I wasn't careful with, couldn't be careful with. He wasn't careful when we . . . .

Being pregnant saved my life. Saved our lives. You're like a miracle in disguise, my little one. I'm forever grateful to you—and for now, we're safe.

Hannah Goldstein

20 October 1941

Another new moon.

Tonight, Pope Pius XII is going to make another batch of people disappear. Their plane is going to have an "accident" after takeoff. He is evil. If it wasn't for my morning sickness, I would've been one of those "accidents" two months ago, all because of him.

My baby, you saved my life. You saved us both. I'm forever grateful to you, my little miracle.

Hannah Goldstein

30 October 1941

The Templar say there's no chance of getting me to the United States right now. They're saying maybe next month. I guess I'm safe here for the time being.

Hannah Goldstein

19 November 1941

Tomorrow is Thanksgiving Day in the United States. The Templar seem pretty sure now's the safest time for me to make my escape to America.

I've packed up the few things they've given me. They provided me a new passport, some money, and the guarantee that there will be a safe family there ready to take in me and my baby.

My baby's going to be born in America.

Hannah Goldstein

Chapter 82

March 12, 2000
Sunday, 12:27 p.m.
Rome, Italy

"She *was* here," Mario whispered, the revelation hitting him like a punch to the gut. The young girl who had miraculously escaped the pope's sinister "destruction of evidence" had stayed here. Dominic had said as much earlier, to which Mario had felt some skepticism, but seeing her words inked on the page, it was undeniable. Hannah Goldstein was real—meaning the rest of what the Templar had told him most likely was too.

"Did you mutter something?" asked Dominic as he rounded the corner, catching Mario in his private musings.

"Hannah Goldstein. She really was here," Mario affirmed, closing the journal in his hands with a sense of finality, his gaze meeting Dominic's.

"If it weren't for her pregnancy, we would've remained oblivious to her existence."

"As you mentioned before."

"We relocated her to America, a safe haven for her and her unborn child."

"But how did you know who to entrust her to?"

"We have a global network of protection programs. During the war, many were compromised. But in November of '41, the US was still neutral. The Templar leaders felt it was safe to move

Hannah there, to join a loving family who would help her raise her son."

"And she wasn't afraid of being found out by the Vatican?"

"We gave her a new identity. Anna Muldoon. Her son went by Trevor Muldoon. They've been living comfortably ever since." Dominic's voice held a note of pride, a testament to the Templar protection program's success in saving extermination camp escapees like Hannah.

"Smart move, keeping the names similar. Hannah to Anna."

"Well, we didn't want to disrupt her life any more than necessary. The similar names ensured she wouldn't be discovered if someone accidentally called her by her real name."

"Clever," Mario mused, his mind racing with thoughts regarding his own fate. "Will I be relocated to America too?"

"Yes. As soon as you're ready, we'll give you a new identity and relocate you to the United States."

"I'd like to delve deeper into your archives, if that's okay?" Mario was eager to absorb the wealth of knowledge hidden from the world.

"Take all the time you need."

"I assume once I leave, I won't have access to this information again?"

"That's correct, my friend. For the safety of the Templars and any future Vatican victims, we can't allow you to return."

"I understand," Mario nodded, his gaze sweeping over the endless shelves of historical records. Turning back to Dominic, he said, "I apologize for my earlier words. I'm truly grateful for everything you've done for me. You saved my life. Thank you."

The Templar clasped his hands over his heart and bowed, touched by Mario's gratitude. "It has been our pleasure, Mario Marino." With that, he left the priest to his studies inside the Templar archives.

Chapter 83

May 7, 2000
Sunday, 11:55 a.m.
Templar Satellite's Cellars

Mario cast a final lingering glance around the room that had been his sanctuary, safeguarding him the Vatican's reach for the past two months. He couldn't help but wonder how many more souls would seek refuge in this very room fleeing from the Vatican's wrath.

A knock on the door startled him. Dominic's low voice greeted him from the other side, and Mario rose to let him in. "Are you ready to depart?"

"Yes," Mario replied, his voice steady. "I was just making sure I haven't left anything behind. I can't thank you enough for all you've done."

"The honor is ours. As Templars, it's our sworn duty to shield the oppressed."

Mario took one last look around, acutely aware that this was a pivotal moment in his life. Once he stepped out of this sanctuary, he would be exposed to the world and the lurking threat of the Vatican's assassins. He was no longer a priest shielded by the Catholic Church. What would life as a civilian hold for him?

With a deep breath, he turned towards the door and followed Dominic down the corridor to a hidden stairwell. They ascended, leaving the safety of the underground behind.

The Templars never risked using the bank vault elevator for departures, instead always opting for the secret stairwell exit. After a strenuous climb up five flights of stairs, they emerged through a concealed door set inside a brick wall onto a quiet street. A car was waiting there, ready to whisk him away to a private jet bound for America.

The sunlight was blinding. "How long has it been since I've seen the sun?" Mario mused aloud.

"There are times when I don't see the sun for weeks," Dominic replied with a slight chuckle.

The Templar chauffeur took Mario's luggage and stowed it in the trunk of the Fiat 500 hatchback. Dominic extended his hand. "Mario Marino, it's been an honor. If you ever need anything, here's my card. You can reach me directly."

Mario accepted the card, scanning it quickly before shaking the Templar's hand. "Thank you, Dominic."

With a nod, the driver started the car and pulled away from the secret entrance. Mario settled into the front seat as the Fiat cruised through the cityscape.

Forty minutes later, he was boarding a Gulfstream G650ER. The unassuming Templar private jet was set to refuel in Portugal before heading to Tennessee where a safe house awaited him. Given Mario's past as a Vatican priest, Dominic had chosen Tennessee due to its low Catholic population. Their absence would provide a safe haven for the former priest to live out his days, far from the reach of the Catholic network.

Chapter 84

The Templar chauffeur hauled Mario's single suitcase up to the doorstep of his quaint new cottage nestled in the heart of Milan, Tennessee. Its name, a nod to the renowned Italian city, would be a small comfort as Mario settled into his new life. Dominic hadn't been joking—this small town held the honor of having the lowest Catholic membership out of any town in the entire United States.

"Your key, Marco." The driver handed over the house key, addressing Mario by his new alias.

"Um," Mario hesitated, adjusting to his new identity, "thank you."

The driver returned to his car and Mario watched the Lincoln Town Car drive away until it faded into the distance. He inhaled deeply, turned the key in the lock, and stepped into the desolation of his new existence. He placed his luggage in the kitchen, emptied his pockets onto the counter, and took a moment to absorb the reality of his new dwelling, a modest gift from Dominic. The Templars, with their vast real estate empire, had countless hideouts like this one in their portfolio that they could fold into their protection program. Dominic had also arranged a bank account for Mario, providing a monthly allowance for his basic survival.

His gaze fell upon his passport, scrutinizing his new identity. Marco Antonio. A mere one-letter difference in first name. "They didn't want to disrupt my life too much, I suppose," he muttered at his new ID.

The silence in the unfamiliar house was suffocating. Mario was alone, stripped of the protection of the Catholic Church, the Templar underground, his closest friend. He was truly isolated. Roberto, his lifelong companion, was gone, claimed by a Vatican assassin. The void was unbearable.

"Goddamnit!" he screamed, slamming his fist onto the counter in a rare explosion of raw fury. He had never taken the Lord's name in vain before. "Why?" His voice reverberated through the vacant kitchen as he collapsed onto the countertop, his body wracked with heart-wrenching sobs.

He was utterly alone. No Roberto. No refuge in the Catholic Church. No priests. No evil Mother Superior. No Templars. Just him, alone in his desolation.

He wiped away his tears, his mind wandering to Hannah Goldstein. She too had found herself in the same predicament six decades prior. What terror she must have felt, pregnant and alone in a foreign land, constantly looking over her shoulder for Vatican assassins. She'd been fortunate to have a loving family to support her and her child. The trauma of being on the pope's hit list must have been soul-crushing. To trust the most sacred man on Earth, only to be violated in his private chambers. If not for her pregnancy, she might not have survived.

She was pregnant. Why didn't she blow the whistle on the pope for impregnating her? Was it fear?

He started questioning his own devotion—why hadn't *he* acted? Why not expose the Vatican before everything went to pieces? Now Mario's faith in the Catholic Church was shattered. The institution that had shielded him all his life had turned around and murdered his best friend, robbing Mario of the only family he'd ever known.

The game had changed. The Vatican had to answer for their deadly deeds.

The Templars had warned him against seeking out "Anna" and her son. He knew that if Dominic discovered he had defied this order, he would be expelled from the Templar protection program and left to his own devices. But what if he could persuade Anna to join him in blowing the whistle on the Vatican? There was power in unity. If he went public alone, he might be dismissed as a lunatic, but with another witness, they might be able to sway public opinion. With their new identities, they could stay under the radar, evading the Vatican and its network.

He pocketed his passport, key, cellphone, and American money, and set out for the library to research Anna and her son. Half an hour later, he was seated at a computer terminal inside the Mildred G. Fields Memorial Library. He navigated to www. dogpile.com, Roberto's preferred search engine, and searched for information on the Muldoons.

The public library computer was a far cry from the state-of-the-art machines Roberto had owned, but Mario was nonetheless grateful for the access to the world wide web. He scanned the top search results:

Trevor Muldoon, American fiction author with more than 20 thriller novels.

Born in Naples, Florida on May 25, 1942.

Trevor Muldoon currently resides in Naples, Florida. His two-acre gated estate is situated

```
near the Gulf of Mexico. Trevor Muldoon is an avid
golfer with an 8 handicap.
    Anna Muldoon has been Trevor's business
manager for more than 35 years.
```

Driven by a newfound resolve and unwavering determination, Mario set course for Naples, Florida. It was obvious Hannah—Anna Muldoon—resided there with her son in a self-imposed exile. Mario believed that with her damning evidence and his own personal testimony, they could finally expose the Vatican's dark secrets, delivering justice to all those wronged by the institution.

With a sense of urgency, he scoured through travel websites before swiftly securing a seat on a Southwest Airlines flight to Naples, Florida. The printer hummed as it spat out his flight confirmation and the dossier on the Muldoons. Gathering his documents, he exited the library, his heart pounding with anticipation.

He was going into battle.

Chapter 85

May 9, 2000
Tuesday, 4:55 p.m.
Naples, Florida

A medical examiner by the name of Dr. Janet Doerr was engrossed in work on her computer, finalizing the autopsy notes she had just completed. The new $30 million facility her company had recently transitioned into was a marvel of modern technology—every record was digitally stored on a central mainframe, accessible from any of the strategically placed computer stations throughout the building. Dr. Doerr relished this efficiency. The new facility was a stark contrast to the old one, which had been riddled with human error, especially where paper files were concerned. Those had constantly been misplaced, misfiled, mistaken, or missing.

Miss Filed, Miss Placed, Miss Taken, and Miss Sing were dames of the old place. I'm so happy those old maids were taken out to pasture, Janet thought, chuckling to herself as she reminisced over outdated protocols and procedures.

She smiled, appreciating how smoothly her new computer workstation operated as she typed in the last notes. Oh, what smooth operation. A single click and there it was, her signature, perfectly legible. No more re-signing forms for the audit department who had frequently complained about her illegible handwriting.

The words "smooth operation" sparked an image in her mind of a tall, handsome brunette man, shirtless and barefoot in the sand, his tan abs and muscles on display. After a long day of dealing with the deceased, she would often fantasize about coming home to such a man, a welcome escape from her grim reality.

At thirty-one, Dr. Doerr was unmarried and without any potential suitors. The Naples area was not exactly teeming with prospects. Her daily routine consisted of leaving work, picking up healthy groceries, and spending half an hour on her NordicTrack, all the while gazing at posters of Halle Barry in her home gym. The posters featuring the actress as Jinx in the James Bond movie *Die Another Day* was a constant source of inspiration. Halle Barry, in her orange bikini and short-cropped hair, was the epitome of how Dr. Doerr aspired to look. Occasionally, people would even tell her she reminded them of Halle Barry, a compliment she attributed to her mixed heritage.

And what heritage was that, exactly? The truth was, she didn't know. Adopted at birth by a loving elderly German couple in Palo Alto, California, she had never felt the need to seek out her biological parents. Her adoptive parents, who had passed away within months of each other a few years ago, had been her world. Their passing had left a void in her life, but their love and support had been instrumental in her becoming Dr. Janet Doerr, a graduate of Stanford University.

Despite their advanced age, they had loved her as their own. Often mistaken for her grandparents, strangers often ask her father if she was his granddaughter whenever they visited the Stanford Mall, to which he would simply smile and nod, avoiding the question. Their pride in her achievements was recognizable, and she was equally proud of them for their influence and connections, which had been instrumental in getting her into Stanford.

As her mouse cursor hovered over the Shutdown icon, a wave of satisfaction washed over her. The day's work had been challenging yet rewarding.

She rose from her chair, grabbed her belongings, and departed the building. The moment she stepped out into the blistering heat of Naples, Florida, she was hit by a wave of humid air. It was HOT, a stark reminder of her new life in Florida. Her prestigious position as a medical examiner at the Naples Forensics Laboratory had not only given her a sense of purpose but also the means to indulge in luxuries like her brand-new 2000 Toyota Avalon—a stark contrast to the vintage 1966 Ford Fairlane her father had left her.

As she navigated down the bustling Tamiami Trail North Street, she pulled into the familiar parking lot of her favorite Publix grocery store. She chose a spot at the far end of the lot, a small sacrifice to pay to protect her new car from potential dings and scratches.

As she approached the entrance, her eyes were drawn to a handsome stranger engrossed in the public notice board. *Hello!* A spark of intrigue ignited within her. It had been a while since she had been approached by a man who piqued her interest—so, why not seize the moment and make the first move?

"Hello. Hi. Um, I noticed you're looking at places for rent. I have a beautiful little cottage nearby I'm renting. Would you be interested in looking at it?"

Boom. She'd done it. She'd stepped out of her comfort zone and taken the initiative. At thirty-one-years old, she was fed up being single. Now, the ball was in his court. Would he engage in the game or simply let it pass by?

"Ah, yes. I like very much to see it."

Oooh la la. A rush of excitement coursed through her. Not only was he tall, dark, and handsome, but his exotic accent ignited a deep, primal desire within her.

"I'm on my way there now. You're welcome to follow me." She held her breath, hoping the man would agree.

"I am sorry. I am not with car. If it is good with you, may I have ride?"

A flicker of doubt crossed her mind. No car? Was he just another freeloader? She had to tread carefully.

She was financially stable, thanks to her job as a city-employed medical examiner. And with the real estate market in Naples booming recently, her house's value had increased significantly. Money wasn't an issue. Her problem was falling for silver-tongued, smooth-talking men who ended up living off her, inevitably turning into couch potatoes glued to her large-screen TV, especially during football season.

She had made the first move. But this man, he seemed different somehow. *What if he's a deadbeat. . . . Oooh, he is incredibly attractive. Maybe he just landed from overseas and hasn't had the opportunity to buy a car yet?*

"Alright. I can give you a ride," she said.

"Please. I tell you. I am not here too long. I am here for one month and a half maybe. Is this good to you?"

"That's fine. My car is over there. I'm Janet, by the way." She extended her hand.

"I am very nice to meet you. I am . . ." Mario hesitated, grappling with his new identity. "I am Mario." He couldn't bring himself to lie. He wanted to start his new life in America on a positive note, even if it meant defying the Templars' orders.

Mario. Italian? she thought to herself. He was incredibly handsome and polite. He wouldn't be here long, so if he turned out to be a freeloader, she could easily get rid of him.

* * *

One of the Vatican's most intriguing assets is its extensive network of informants scattered across the globe via the leadership of local Catholic churches. If the Vatican desires to uncover information about a person of interest, they simply inquire with the local priest, gaining access to even the most private confessions. The loyalty of the priests to the Vatican is unwavering and absolute.

Father Burns, a devout priest, was seated at the Catholic Charities table outside the Publix supermarket surrounded by volunteers from his church. When he wasn't engaging in conversations about charitable donations for global causes, the elderly priest took pleasure in observing the people around him. Not too far off from his left, a strikingly handsome man was engrossed in reading the advertisements on the community information board.

Perhaps a parishioner, Father Burns mused. *He's quite the catch. . . . Ah, it seems I'm not the only one who thinks so.*

The priest chuckled to himself as he watched a young woman make a swift U-turn, reminiscent of a teenager fleeing one of his Sunday sermons. The sight of budding romance always warmed his heart.

"Hello. Hi. Um, I noticed you're looking at places for rent. I have a beautiful little cottage nearby I'm renting. Would you be interested in looking at it?" Father Burns overheard the young woman's proposition to the handsome stranger.

"Ah, yes. I like very much to see it," came the man's reply, laced with a foreign accent.

An accent. Not a local. Why does he seem so familiar? Father Burns pondered, his gaze fixed on the stranger, trying to place him. Lost in thought, he caught the last of the conversation.

". . . I'm Janet, by the way."

"I am very nice to meet you. I am . . . I am Mario."

Realization hit Father Burns like a lightning bolt. *He's the young priest featured on the cover of* L'Osservatore Romano*! Won't monsignor love to hear we have a "celebrity" from the Vatican in our midst.*

Chapter 86

May 9, 2000
Tuesday, 5:45 p.m.
Naples, Florida

Janet guided Mario through the charming one-bedroom cottage nestled behind her main house. It boasted its own private entrance, a winding cement path connecting the main house to the cozy hideaway.

"Here's the kitchen. It's been recently renovated with all-new appliances. Are you a fan of cooking?" she asked, hoping to pique his interest.

"I cook a little. My friend better cook. How you say . . . *cullnering* person?" he asked, his accent making the word sound exotic.

"Culinary. Yes, that's right," she corrected gently, her eyes scanning the room, thinking of what else she could highlight to persuade him to rent the place. It wasn't about the money—she didn't need it—it was more about . . . well, she wanted a man in her life. Not just any man, but a real man. One who embodied traditional values, chivalry, and would treat a woman with respect like her father had. This was something she felt was missing in her life. Sure, she had male colleagues at the medical examiner's office and through her connections with law enforcement, but their interactions were strictly professional. Perhaps they were intimidated by her.

As she passed by Mario, she caught a whiff of his Italian cologne and wanted to swoon. "This is the bathroom," she said, flicking on the light to illuminate the small room. "And this is the bedroom. It's modestly furnished, just the essentials, but you're welcome to bring in more of your own things if you'd like."

"I no have much," Mario admitted, appreciating the simplicity of the accommodations. This would do for his temporary stay in Naples.

"Do you like it?" she asked, her heart pounding in anticipation.

"Sì. What do you want from me?" he asked.

His question caught her off guard. "What do I want from you?" Janet blushed, wondering if he could read her thoughts.

"How much money I give?" he clarified.

"Money? Oh! Right. Rent." Janet blushed again at her misunderstanding. "Yes. It's seven hundred a month plus a five-hundred-dollar deposit."

Mario reached into his fanny pack—a gift from Roberto—and pulled out a money clip. He turned away from Janet to count out twelve one-hundred-dollar bills. Once he confirmed the amount, he put the money clip back in his fanny pack then handed her the stack of money.

"Oh, wow, okay. Hold onto that for now. Let's go inside my house to fill out the paperwork. I'll give you a receipt for payment." Janet led the way back to the main house. "We can fill out the paperwork over some iced tea. How does that sound?"

"Grazie."

Grazie. I love this guy, Janet thought, her heart fluttering with excitement.

Chapter 87

All her adult life, Janet Doerr had worked out religiously, dedicating herself to a rigorous fitness regimen designed to sculpt her body to perfection. She'd transformed her third bedroom into a personal gym equipped with the latest NordicTrack treadmill and a Stairmaster, her secret weapons in her battle against gravity and time. A collection of two-, three-, and five-pound dumbbells lined the wall, ready to be thrust about in her quest to keep her arms firm and toned. She wasn't aiming for a bodybuilder's physique, but rather a toned, feminine form that exuded strength and grace. After all, the men of Naples seemed to appreciate a woman who could hold her own yet retained a feminine allure. And for those situations where physical strength wasn't enough, there was always the can of Mace tucked away in her purse.

The wall of her gym was adorned with a large blow-up poster of Halle Barry as Jinx from the James Bond movie *Die Another Day*. She served as Janet's silent cheerleader, pushing her to reach her fitness goals. She relished the times men and women alike would draw a comparison between her and the sultry Bond girl.

"You remind me of that sexy woman in the orange bikini from the James Bond movie. What was it called?" Janet would respond innocently as if she had never heard this compliment before, "Oh, you mean *Die Another Day*?" "Oh yeah. That one. Have you heard you look like her?" Janet liked being compared to Halle Barry. The character she played was badass, a force to be reckoned with. Janet aspired to embody that same strength and confidence in her everyday life.

As the NordicTrack shifted gears, her thoughts drifted to the Italian stranger residing in her cottage. "Don't. . . . go. . . . there. . . . Janet!" She quickly shook off that naughtiness and focused on the grueling uphill run. *What is it about him that intrigues me so?* She pondered this as she pushed through the eight-mile-per-hour ten-percent-incline segment.

The workout flew by, perhaps because her thoughts kept wandering back to Mario. Had she found this new motivation to tone up because of this exotic stranger? She knew the allure of the opposite sex often provided her an adrenaline rush that made even the most challenging tasks achievable. Lately, her energy levels had been dwindling due to a lack of excitement in her life, but this handsome stranger had clearly sparked a renewed vigor within her.

"Aaaaaaah!" she screamed as the timer counted down the last seconds. *4. . . . 3. . . . 2. . . . 1. . . . Beep. Beep. Beep.* "Yes!" She pumped her fists in the air as the treadmill slowed to a halt.

Grabbing her towel, she wiped the sweat off her face and stepped off the NordicTrack with a sense of accomplishment. Her legs felt sturdy, her body vibrant.

Must be all the adrenaline, she chuckled to herself. *Or perhaps it's estrogen,* she mused, laughing at the thoughts that came to mind.

Her exhilaration following the vigorous workout was a welcome relief after a long day at work. Not that her job was a serious source of stress, but maintaining a regular fitness routine was her secret weapon against the work-related tension that crept in over the long-term. Emerging from her home gym, she made her way down the hallway to the bathroom and splashed her face with icy water. The chill was invigorating.

As she glanced out of her second-story bathroom window, she spotted Mario inside the cottage hunched over the dining table, engrossed in his notebook. A substantial wad of cash lay next to his backpack on the table. She narrowed her eyes at it, feeling curious. Rather than deter her, this unexpected sight only heightened her interest in the handsome Italian.

Five minutes later, Janet found herself at the door to the cottage, ostensibly to check on her new short-term tenant. Although her intentions were more calculated than a simple check-in. She didn't want to come across as intrusive, or bothersome, or . . . desperate.

Why was she behaving so oddly around Mario? What emotions was this attractive foreigner stirring within her?

Shaking her head, she decided to abandon her plan at the last moment, turning away from the cottage door. As she did so, the door swung open, revealing Mario on the verge of leaving.

"Aaah!" they both exclaimed, startled by the unexpected rendezvous.

"You scared me," Janet admitted, her cheeks flushing with embarrassment.

"Scusi," Mario apologized, genuinely shaken. After the series of traumatic incidents he'd experienced months ago, the last thing he expected was to find Janet—or anyone else for that matter—at his front door.

"Whew," Janet exhaled, catching her breath. "I was just coming over to check if everything was okay with the cottage."

"Si. Bella. Uh, yes, good. Would you like to come in for . . ." Mario gestured towards the kitchen. "Err, water, no gas."

"The gas isn't working?" Janet's face fell, embarrassed that the stove wasn't functioning. "I'll get it fixed, I'm sorry."

"No, no. Scusi. I mean water, like from sink, with no . . ." He paused, searching for the right word. "No fizzy?"

Mario was struggling to find the term for noncarbonated water. He found it peculiar that in the United States people paid almost a dollar a bottle for something you could get from your tap. Rome boasted some of the finest drinking water in the world, and was fascinated that people would pay so much in the stores for a simple luxury that was readily available.

"Oh. Got it. Water. Yes, please."

As they stepped inside the cottage, Janet noticed that nothing had really changed from when she had shown Mario the rental the day before.

"Please, have a seat."

"Thank you." She settled herself before looking around the room. "Can I ask you something?"

"Of course," Mario responded, his demeanor shifting into a comfortable mode. As a priest, he had often been the recipient of confessions, a trusted ear for those seeking solace. He found it intriguing that even in his civilian attire, people seemed drawn to him, ready to unburden their secrets. Janet, however, was unaware of his past vocation.

"What do you do?" Janet asked, her curiosity piqued by the wad of money she had seen through the window. Was he involved in the mafia? He seemed too awkward for that.

"I recently am fired from work," he confessed, zipping his backpack closed. "I hope this will not be problem. I have plenty money to pay rent. Promise."

"No, no. It's not a problem. I didn't mean to pry," she quickly reassured him, feeling her awkwardness creeping in again. "You just seem . . . interesting. I want to know more about you."

Mario was at a loss for how to explain his complex situation. His life was in turmoil, and he was not adept at deception—Roberto had reminded him of that fact often enough. Perhaps that was why he'd become a priest—he was incapable of lying and therefore people were drawn to him, eager to share their deepest secrets.

Roberto's past wisdom came to Mario like a sage speaking from the beyond. *She doesn't want to know about you. She wants to tell you about herself. Trust me. She's into you, Mario.*

After a moment of awkward silence, Janet broke the tension. "I'm making snapper for dinner tomorrow night. Would you like to join me?"

Mario felt a surge of validation—Roberto had been right! She was interested in him. "Yes, I would like that. Grazie."

"Great. Dinner will be ready at eight o'clock. You don't need to bring anything. I'll take care of it all."

"Grazie." Mario smiled, a warm feeling spreading through him. Janet's interest in him stirred up emotions he'd never experienced before. As a priest, he had taken a vow of celibacy for life, but the Vatican's attempt on his life had changed everything.

Feeling this desire for another person made him realize why Roberto had always made such a big fuss about it. Mario had never felt this way before. It felt . . . nice.

Chapter 88

May 10, 2000
Wednesday, 6:35 p.m.
Naples, Florida

Mario found himself nestled in the bustling heart of Kinko's, a copy center sporting an abundance of technology amidst the otherwise quaint town of Naples. Huddled at a computer station, his fingers danced over the keys, navigating to the search engine Roberto had sworn by. His search on dogpile.com was precise, just a name and a location: "Trevor Muldoon, Naples, Florida."

Trevor Muldoon, the acclaimed author, will be our honored guest for the AOL Chatroom interview series on the evening of Monday, May 15th, 2000 at 7 p.m. EST.

The interview promises an intimate discussion where Mr. Muldoon will announce his latest World War II thriller. It is set to hit the shelves on June 6th.

The event will also feature a Q&A session with Mr. Muldoon fielding questions from the virtual audience. We encourage you to submit your questions early.

Mark your calendars. You don't want to miss this exciting event.

A flash of opportunity ignited in Mario's mind. The AOL Chatroom interview series was the perfect venue to reach out to Trevor. The Muldoons, ensconced in their gated community, were apparently notoriously difficult to access. Their community was a fortress, home to Naples' wealthy elite who paid a premium to keep uninvited visitors at bay.

This online event, this virtual meeting could be Mario's golden ticket. It was likely his best chance to persuade Trevor Muldoon to extend him an invitation to his residence for a private discussion.

Chapter 89

Mario knocked on the back door of Janet's house. Standing there and waiting, he heard the rhythmic pulse of Mr. Mister's "Broken Wings" seeping through the door into the night air.

So take,
these broken wings,
and learn to fly again,
learn to live so free.
When we hear,
the voices sing,
the book of love will open up,
and let us in. . . .

"Mario, come in," Janet beckoned, her voice a warm invitation as she opened the door to her dinner guest. "I was just about to slide the fish into the oven," she said as she retreated into the kitchen. The mangrove snapper, a local delicacy, had been caught fresh in the Gulf of Mexico by the skilled hands of local fishermen. It would take a mere five minutes in her Breville toaster oven to transform it into a mouthwatering main course.

"Grazie. The smell is delicious." Mario trailed after Janet into the kitchen. He found himself captivated by her graceful movements as she expertly prepared their meal. Her back to him as she worked the stove, he truly noticed her toned physique for the first time. She was a stunning woman who seemed to harbor a certain fondness for him. Roberto's wise counsel from beyond echoed in his mind. *Dude, she likes you.*

"Would you mind uncorking the wine?" She glanced over her shoulder to find Mario appreciating her figure; his eyes were obviously fixed on her firm posterior.

"Sì, ah, mi scusi," Mario stuttered, caught off guard. He reached for the Napa Valley Pinot Grigio resting on the island and deftly uncorked the bottle. He had opened countless bottles of red wine during Sunday services, but this was his first encounter with white wine.

He filled two glasses with the crisp white wine then navigated around the counter to offer one to Janet. As he neared her, he was enveloped by the scent of roses and a hint of Lancôme Miracle Eau de Parfum. The fragrance was unfamiliar to him, but intoxicating nonetheless. Roberto would have recognized the effort Janet had put into their evening and predicted a promising end to the night—Mario, however, remained blissfully unaware of these subtle cues.

On her way home from work, Janet had made a special detour to Sephora after gathering the dinner ingredients at Publix. She was determined to leave a lasting impression on the intriguing Italian who had unexpectedly entered her life. The local men had lost their appeal; she craved someone more exotic. She was trying to make this as obvious as possible to her Italian guest.

"I forgot to ask yesterday, do you like fish?"

"Sì. I go Ostia for fresh fish sometimes." Mario spoke of the coastal city near Rome, his voice carrying the rhythm of the sea. "I know fish with bees fresh. Fish with flies old."

Janet stirred the rice pilaf in the frying pan, her attention captivated by Mario's explanation. His accent was like a melody, a symphony she could lose herself in for hours.

"Sometimes, fisherman try selling old fish to tourist not know difference."

"Well luckily, I believe these are fresh." Janet glanced at Mario and smiled. He was standing so close to her. "Publix sources their fish from local fishermen."

"It appear fresh." Mario leaned in, peering through the glass of the toaster oven. "What is seasoning?"

"I use a simple recipe with just three ingredients—salt, Cajun spices, and parsley flakes. I also add red potatoes, yellow peppers, cherry tomatoes, lime, green onions. The oil gives it a crispy exterior and a juicy interior," Janet said, noting this man was having a similar effect on her.

Mario, oblivious to her hints, felt a strange sensation. To be sure, he didn't mind the attention from Janet. She was indeed beautiful. Moving to the other side of the island, he perched on a barstool, staying out of Janet's way as she continued her culinary magic. He had learned from Roberto to stay clear unless he was assisting as a sous chef.

"Maybe I set table?"

"That would be wonderful. The silverware is in that drawer."

"Piatti?"

"I'm sorry?"

"Mi scusi. . . ." Mario searched for the English word, "Plates?"

"Oh, oh. Don't worry about them. I'll prepare the plates and bring them to the table." Janet giggled at Mario's adorable Italian question. His presence was a breath of fresh air, a joy she had been craving for a long time.

Mario was delighted to witness her laughter. He felt a warmth around this woman that he couldn't recall ever feeling before. It was a pleasant sensation. He had seen this in the teenage boys who attended church on Sundays. They would transform into goofy, love-struck adolescents around the girls they fancied. During Mass, their attention would be on the girls seated elsewhere, their ears oblivious to the sermon. Mario would observe these silent exchanges throughout the church—a boy stealing a glance at a girl, the girl giggling quietly when she caught the boy's gaze, both quickly looking away, hoping the other hadn't noticed. It was a dance of young love.

As a devout priest, Mario had always suppressed the stirrings of desire, honoring his vows of celibacy. He was no stranger to the frailties of the flesh, a temptation that led many a priest astray. He knew that succumbing to these feelings would result in his expulsion from the priesthood, a fate he couldn't bear. The Catholic Church was his life. Yet, when the Church severed its ties with him, it was as if a dam had burst within him, releasing a torrent of suppressed emotions. As he set the dining room table, his thoughts were consumed by Janet.

The distant *ding* of the toaster oven rang through the house. Janet's voice floated from the kitchen. "The fish is ready."

Drawn by her voice, he returned to the kitchen and stood behind the island, his eyes riveted on Janet as she plated the food with the finesse of a Michelin-starred chef. He felt a sense of gratitude wash over him. Roberto had often treated him to delectable meals, but having a woman cook for him was a different experience altogether. It was a unique bond, a connection that transcended friendship, and Mario found himself relishing it.

Janet turned her head, catching his appreciative gaze. A smile tugged at her lips; it was becoming apparent the handsome Italian reciprocated her feelings. Setting the spoon down, she picked up the plates and turned to head to the dining room. "Dinner is served."

Mario's smile widened as he watched Janet, her pride in the meal she'd prepared evident. He collected the wine glasses and followed her into the dining room. Setting down the plates, she moved to a small curio in the corner to retrieve some candlesticks and a lighter. She placed the candles on the table and lit them; their flickering light cast an intimate glow over the room.

"Bella," Mario praised, his eyes taking in the meticulously arranged dinner.

With a gentlemanly grace, he moved behind the woman and pulled out her chair. Janet was taken aback by his chivalry, a trait seemingly lost among American men. She cherished this old-fashioned attention from Mario, a refreshing change from what she usually encountered.

Her father, a man of an older generation, had taught her to value manners and respect. It seemed men her age had skipped learning these crucial lessons. Mario, however, appeared to understand the importance of treating women with respect.

"Thank you," she murmured, settling into the chair he'd pulled out for her.

He took his own seat, lifting his wine glass in a toast towards Janet. "Bellissima." Their glasses clinked together, and they each took a sip, officially commencing the meal. Janet's smile widened, her heart fluttering at Mario's Italian praise for her culinary efforts.

His first bite of the succulent snapper was met with a sigh of pleasure. "Delizioso," he murmured, his eyes closing as he savored the exquisite flavors.

"Thank you."

A silence fell over them as they relished the expertly prepared meal, each bite a testament to Janet's culinary prowess. She began to feel a twinge of unease at the prolonged silence. She yearned to know more about this man, for him to fill the silence with his stories. Just as she was about to probe, Mario broke the silence.

"What do you do?" he asked, wine glass in hand, his curiosity piqued about his enchanting hostess.

"I'm an M.E." Seeing Mario's puzzled expression, she quickly clarified, "Medical examiner. I'm a medical examiner at the Naples Forensics Laboratory not too far from here."

"You enjoy being medical examiner?"

"It's been a lifelong fascination. I've always been drawn to biology and life sciences since I was a child. What about you?"

"I no like dead things," Mario confessed, his mind drifting back to the grim dissections of frogs, worms, and crawdads in his Catholic middle school biology classes.

Janet's laughter rang out, a delightful contrast to Mario's grimace as he recounted his aversion to the subject that had ignited her passion. Their meal progressed, punctuated by the clink of cutlery and the hum of engaging conversation. Janet painted a vivid picture of her childhood in Palo Alto, California, and the warmth and affection she received from her adoptive German parents.

"You were adopted?"

"Yes. Why do you ask?"

"I was raised in orphanage," Mario revealed, a hint of a smile playing on his lips upon discovering their shared experience, albeit different in detail. "But never adopted."

"I'm sorry," Janet whispered, her voice soft with empathy. She could barely stand imagining the absence of parental love he must have endured.

"Is okay," Mario reassured her, his mind drifting back to the cherished memories he'd shared with Roberto at the orphanage. Adoption or no adoption, those times held a special place in his heart.

He was thoroughly enjoying the evening—the company of this enchanting woman made every moment memorable. As he drained his first glass of wine, he rose to fetch the wine bottle from the kitchen. Upon his return, he refilled both their glasses, depleting the bottle.

"This"—Mario gestured with his fork laden with snapper—"delizioso."

Janet's cheeks flushed at the compliment, Mario's Italian accent adding an irresistible allure to his words. She sipped more wine and found her nerves were gradually melting away in the warmth of her dinner companion's presence.

Noticing their glasses were nearly empty again, she retrieved a second bottle of Sauvignon Blanc from her wine fridge. Growing up in the Bay Area so close to wine country, she'd developed a fondness for Napa wines.

"Could you open this?" she asked, handing Mario the wine and corkscrew.

He obliged, uncorking the bottle and filling their glasses with the crisp white wine. As they finished their meal and progressed to their fourth glass of wine, a warm, relaxed atmosphere enveloped them. Mario collected the plates and carried them into the kitchen, his considerate gesture not going unnoticed by Janet.

"Would you like to move to the living room and continue our conversation?"

"Sì. I would like that," Mario agreed, the alcohol loosening his inhibitions and fueling his desire to prolong this enchanting evening with Janet.

"What do you do for a living?" Janet asked, her gaze fixed on Mario as they settled onto the plush couch.

Mario hesitated, his mind racing. He couldn't claim to be a priest anymore; that chapter of his life had ended. For the first time in years, he was adrift, unsure of his path.

"I'm between jobs," he finally admitted.

"I didn't mean to pry," Janet quickly apologized, her eyes softening. "I'm just intrigued by you. You're different from the men I've met here in Naples. You're courteous, chivalrous . . ." She smiled, recalling his gentlemanly gestures. "And your accent is absolutely enchanting."

"Grazie," Mario responded, his heart pounding. He was navigating uncharted waters, and he wished he had Roberto's wise counsel to guide him.

In a bold move, Janet leaned in to press her lips against his. Mario was taken aback, but the wine had worked its magic, and he found himself reciprocating the kiss.

Their lips danced together in a passionate ballet for a few intense minutes. Then Janet, emboldened by their shared passion, ventured, "Would you like to continue this in my room?"

"Sì," Mario responded, his voice husky with desire. He was ready to surrender to the intoxicating allure of the moment.

With a coy smile, she took his hand, leading him down the dimly lit hallway towards her bedroom.

Chapter 90

May 12, 2000
Friday, 6:47 a.m.
Naples, Florida

Mario awoke, ensnared in the luxurious expanse of Janet's king-size bed. Was he still dreaming? His hand roamed his bare midsection, confirming the absence of any clothing. Daring to delve beneath the covers, his fingers mapped the terrain of Janet's equally bare form, his touch lingering on her hips. His head pounded, his mind a foggy maze as he tried to piece together the events of the previous night. The memory of their intimate encounter slowly seeped back into his consciousness.

"Good morning," Janet whispered, her voice laced with a smile as she felt Mario's hand tenderly tracing her midsection.

"Good morning," he echoed, his hand retracting swiftly. An uncomfortable silence hung in the air. This was foreign territory he felt unprepared to navigate. He was a stranger in this intimate landscape.

Janet, sensing his discomfort, sought to dispel the tension. "I really like you. Last night . . . it was special."

Mario's smile was hesitant as he absorbed her words. The intimacy of the previous night . . . it had certainly been a new experience, a radical departure from his usual solitary existence. He had never been in a relationship, let alone shared such intimacy. This was Roberto's domain. Yet, he had crossed that boundary, surrendered to the allure of this captivating woman. "I think you are bella. Beautiful."

" . . . But?" Janet's voice was laced with apprehension as she studied Mario, bracing herself for the inevitable rejection.

"But?" Mario echoed, taken aback.

"But I'm not your type, or you're not looking for a serious relationship, or . . ." Janet's voice trailed off, her mind replaying the litany of excuses she'd heard in the past when a man wasn't interested.

"No, no. No 'but'," he hastily corrected, his words tumbling out in a rush. "I have . . . something to do."

She fell silent, her mind racing, trying to decipher his words. She feared she'd made a grave mistake in surrendering to this exotic stranger.

"I share with you?" he asked, a newfound trust in Janet blossoming after their intimate encounter.

"Absolutely. Please do."

"I am trouble. No, *in* trouble. Dangerous people in Rome."

Janet's mind raced, conjuring wild images of Mario being pursued through the exotic streets of Rome, bullets slicing the air around him. Little did she know how close to the truth her imagination was.

"I came to America be safe. Hide from bad people want me dead," Mario confessed, his voice laced with a bitter envy for those who lived without such threats.

Janet remained silent, allowing him the space to unravel his story.

"I look for person hiding too."

"Who is this person?" Janet asked, a pang of jealousy gnawing at her. An old flame? A past indiscretion?

"Trevor Muldoon."

"The renowned author? What, he's in hiding too? You can't be serious."

Mario caught the skepticism flickering in Janet's eyes. He himself was still grappling with the reality of the tumultuous events that had turned his life upside down. Mere months ago, he'd been happily engrossed in scanning documents at the Vatican Secret Archives, a job he cherished. His best friend was alive, sharing in his triumphs. Now, he was under the protection of the Templars in the United States, his best friend brutally snatched away by the very institution he had pledged his life to. He was in hiding and feared for his life. It all felt too surreal.

"Scusi. I say too much," he said, abruptly clamming up. He chose to follow Roberto's methods; he only wished to savor this moment with Janet, pushing aside thoughts of the Vatican and the Muldoons.

"Are you in danger?"

"I say too much."

She propped herself up, clutching the sheets over her bare breasts. Her curiosity was piqued, her heart pounding with the thrill of the unknown. How could this kind, enigmatic Italian man be such a danger that people wanted him dead? She was captivated, oblivious to the potential peril she was inviting into her life. She urged Mario to continue his tale.

He studied Janet, torn between his desire to protect her and his need to share his burden. He had seen the deadly consequences of his involvement before. But he was under the protection of the Templars, hidden away from the Church. How could they possibly find him?

"I found pope journal. He wrote bad things of World War II. Pope was *dominante* Hitler."

"Dominante?"

"Scusi. Controllo?"

"Controlling?"

"Sì. Controlling. Pope controlling Hitler in war."

Janet's eyes widened in shock. "I've always heard it was *Hitler* who controlled the pope. You're saying it was the other way around?"

"Sì. Pope control Hitler to become Führer."

"All of this was in a journal you found?"

"Sì."

"And where is this journal now?"

"Rome."

"And how is Trevor Muldoon involved in all this?"

Mario hesitated, contemplating his next words. He couldn't prove that Trevor was indeed Pope Pius XII's son. That's why he needed to meet him and Anna, to confirm if the pope had indeed fathered a child with Anna in 1941. "I say too much."

Janet's eyes were locked onto Mario as she struggled to comprehend the bizarre tale he'd spun. Her gaze flicked to the digital clock on the nightstand. The glowing numbers read 7:18 a.m. "I need to get ready for work," she announced, untangling herself from the bed and vanishing into the bathroom. The door snapped shut behind her.

Mario was left alone, the sound of the shower starting up starkly reinforcing his sense of solitude. He stared at the closed bathroom door, a sense of unease creeping in. This was uncharted territory for him.

Rising from the bed, he located his scattered clothes and dressed in silence. What was the protocol after a night of passion? He yearned for Roberto's wise counsel, but the silence from beyond was deafening. Uncertain, he approached the bathroom door, the sound of cascading water seeping through. Tentatively, he cracked it open. "I leave now."

"Wait. Can you stay until I'm finished?" Janet called from within.

"No, scusi. I go."

"Okay." Janet's disappointment was noticeable, her hopes of a tender farewell kiss dashed.

Chapter 91

May 15, 2000
Monday, 7:00 p.m.
Naples, Florida

Mario had been evading Janet all weekend, unsure of how to face her after their intimate encounter. The best coping strategy he could come up with was to keep his mind occupied with his task at hand: reaching out to Trevor Muldoon. He spent the majority of his time at the town's library, immersing himself in research about Trevor and crafting compelling questions that he hoped would capture the author's attention.

Mario had devised a plan to instant message Trevor during the AOL Chatroom interview. It was a risky move, one that could potentially alarm the man, but Mario was willing to gamble for a chance to meet with the renowned author.

AOL Host: Good evening, cybernauts! I'm your host, Jesse James, back with another electrifying episode of our AOL Chatroom interview series. Tonight, we're thrilled to be in the virtual company of the renowned author Trevor Muldoon. Welcome aboard, Trevor.

Trevor Muldoon: Thanks for having me, Jesse. It's a pleasure to be here.

AOL Host: We've got a chatroom bursting at the seams with over a thousand eager fans, all itching to pick your brain about your latest literary masterpiece. Why don't you give us a sneak peek of your book, and then we'll dive into the sea of questions from our chatroom audience.

Trevor Muldoon: Absolutely. This book is the next thrilling chapter in the saga of Secret Agent DiMaggio, who's on a mission to thwart the Nazis' sinister plan to harness the power of the underworld. Deep within the bowels of Himmler's Castle in Germany, the Nazis are conducting unholy rituals to summon Satan himself. If they succeed in controlling him, they'll have the world at their mercy. It's up to DiMaggio to prevent Himmler and Hitler from unleashing hellfire.

AOL Host: That's spine-chilling! We're all on tenterhooks for your book's release on June 6th. Now, let's dive into the questions. WWIIGirl, you're up first.

WWIIGirl: Why did you decide to kill off DiMaggio's love interest in the last book?

Trevor Muldoon: I know it was a controversial move. Even my agent warned me against it. But without giving too much away, let's just say that love might be in the air for Agent DiMaggio in future books.

AOL Host: Intriguing! That's how you keep your readers coming back for more. We can't wait to meet this potential new love interest. Now, SecretAgentM, what's your burning question?

SecretAgentM: How do you come up with the names for your characters?

Trevor Muldoon: Excellent question. I'm a huge baseball fan, and I needed an Italian name for my protagonist. For some reason, Joe DiMaggio, the legendary New York Yankees player, popped into my head. Given Joe's World War II injuries limited him to only 13 seasons in the Major Leagues, it seemed like the perfect fit for my main character.

AOL Host: What a fascinating tidbit about Joe DiMaggio. Are you a Yankees fan, or do you root for the Tampa Bay Rays?

Trevor Muldoon: The Yankees are a team you either love or loathe. I respect their achievements, but my heart belongs to the Rays here in West Florida.

AOL Host: Spoken like a true believer. No wonder you're a local celebrity. Let's move on to our next question. Nowisee1941, what's on your mind?

In the bustling queue of questions in the AOL Chatroom, Mario got his opportunity. He had carefully crafted his name to catch Trevor's eye; now he just had to pose the perfect question to ignite Trevor's interest.

NowISee1941: Did your father's legacy play a role in shaping your writing?

Trevor Muldoon paused, fingers hovering over the keyboard. His knowledge of his father was limited to the tales his mother had shared. Hannah "Anna" Muldoon had painted his father as a war hero of the Second World War. Her influence had indeed left an indelible mark on his writing through the subject matter of these stories. But Trevor knew better than to publicly disclose his father's influence in any interview or public forum—his mother had taught him well.

NowISee1941 had presented a loaded question. Did he know? Had he somehow stumbled upon their closely guarded family secret?

Trevor Muldoon: Indeed, his legacy did shape my writing. May I ask who this is?

AOL Host: Intriguing question. Moving on. Our next question comes from FlyBoy45.

Trevor quickly located NowISee1941 in the chatroom directory. Clicking on the IM, he initiated a private conversation, eager to uncover the identity of this mysterious participant.

Trevor Muldoon to NowISee1941: How do you know about my father?

NowISee1941 to Trevor Muldoon: Can we speak over the phone? I have information you will want to hear about him.

Trevor Muldoon to NowISee1941: Here's my number. Call me tomorrow.

Mario jotted down Trevor's phone number, a triumphant grin spreading across his face. He'd done it. Now he could meet with Trevor Muldoon directly and ask if he knew Pope Pius XII was his real father. Even better if his mother were present.

AOL Host: Mr. Muldoon, are you still with us? FlyBoy45 had a question about Agent DiMaggio's prowess in piloting the P-51 Mustang fighter plane during the war.

Jolted back to the AOL Chatroom discussion by the host's prompt flashing on his monitor, Trevor refocused his attention on his eager online fans.

Trevor Muldoon: Yes, sorry, Agent DiMaggio learned to fly . . .

Chapter 92

May 16, 2000
Tuesday, 11:05 a.m.
Naples, Florida

Mario dialed the number Trevor Muldoon had given him during their AOL Chatroom exchange.

Trevor: Good morning. Trevor Muldoon speaking.

Mario: Good morning. I am Mario Marino. We Instant Message during AOL interview.

Trevor: Ah, Mr. Marino, is it? I've been expecting your call. You hinted at having some information about my father.

Mario: Sì. May I come over?

Trevor: You're asking a lot of me, Mr. Marino. I don't even know you. You only just told me your name. You'll need to convince me that the information you claim to possess is credible before I'll agree to a meeting.

Mario: Ask your mother about Treblinka.

Trevor: How . . . how could you possibly know about that?

Mario: I know information on your father. May I come over?

Trevor: Alright. Here's my address. When you arrive at the front gate, ask them to call me for access. Be here at 6 p.m. sharp.

Mario: Grazie, Mr. Muldoon.

Mario slammed the phone down, his pulse thundering in his ears like a wild drum. His fist shot into the air. "Yes!"

He was inching closer to sharing the shocking revelation that Trevor Muldoon was the secret progeny of none other than Pope Pius XII. The question that gnawed at him was whether Trevor's mother would be there to corroborate this truth about her son. Mario wanted both of them in the same room so he could see their reactions raw and unfiltered. Only then could he be certain it was the right choice to persuade them to join his cause—to rip off the veil of deceit shrouding the Vatican and expose its festering corruption that had seeped into every corner of the world.

Chapter 93

May 16, 2000
Tuesday, 5:15 p.m.
Naples, Florida

Mario anxiously paced the room, glancing at the clock every few seconds. It was already a quarter past five, and Janet was still not home from work. He needed to reach Trevor's gated community within the next forty-five minutes, meaning he was depending on borrowing Janet's car. More than that, he needed to address the elephant in the room—the events of last Thursday night. He and Janet hadn't spoken or seen each other since that fateful morning, and he suspected the impending conversation was going to be a minefield of awkwardness. As he heard her car pulling into the garage, he steeled himself and walked over to her home's back door.

Janet drove into her garage, her mind clouded with thoughts of Mario. More than anything, she felt regret; she'd been berating herself for falling for yet another man who seemed to only want a one-night stand. She sighed, resigning herself to the fact that perhaps all men were the same. As she walked into her kitchen, Publix grocery bag in hand, she nearly jumped out of her skin at the sight of Mario standing at the window next to her back door.

She opened the door, her voice icy. "What do you want?"

"Janet, I-I sorry," Mario stammered.

Janet's gaze was frosty. She felt skeptical of his apology.

"It first time. I confused what to do."

"Your first one-night stand?" Janet retorted, bracing herself for a slick explanation.

"No, scuzi. My first time . . . *ever.*"

Janet's eyebrows shot up in surprise. "You were a virgin?"

"Sì. Virgin."

Suddenly, the pieces fell into place. His awkwardness that night wasn't due to the excessive alcohol, but rather the nervousness of a man experiencing intimacy for the first time.

"I come in?" he asked, his voice soft yet filled with anticipation.

"Of course, come in," she replied, her voice suddenly warm as she opened the door wider to let him in.

They found themselves seated at the breakfast table in the kitchen, the air between them thick with unspoken words. Mario reached across the table, his hands gently enveloping hers. "I'm sorry I no tell you, Janet. I like you much too."

"Why didn't you come over and talk to me? I thought you didn't care for me," Janet's voice broke, tears welling up in her eyes. The silence over the weekend had been unbearable, especially knowing he was just a stone's throw away.

"I didn't know. I meet you, but have something to do."

"Trevor Muldoon," she murmured, pulling one hand away to wipe at her tears.

"Sì. I go to Trevor."

"When?"

Mario glanced at his watch; the time read 5:28 p.m. "Thirty minuti." He hesitated, then asked, "I take your auto?"

Janet studied Mario, wondering if his claim of innocence was genuine or just a ploy to use her car. But he seemed sincere. "Do you truly care for me?"

"Sì. I like much."

"Promise?"

"Promettere." Seeing the puzzled look on Janet's face, he did his best to pronounce the unfamiliar English word: "Promise." He smiled and gazed at her, cherishing the intimate moment. He wished their relationship could be free of turmoil—it would be so nice if not for the pope's journal, the Vatican's assassins, and the Templar protection program—but he had a mission to complete before he could fully commit to this wonderful woman.

Janet returned Mario's smile, her heart warmed by his sincerity. She pulled out her car keys and handed them to him. "Thank you for your honesty. Can we continue this conversation when you return?"

"Sì. After, I come back. . . . Promise." He leaned over the table and planted a brief but meaningful kiss on Janet's lips before heading for the garage. He checked his watch—it was 5:32 p.m.

Chapter 94

May 16, 2000
Tuesday, 6:01 p.m.
Naples, Florida

"Thank you your time, Mr. Muldoon," Mario said at the grand entrance to the Muldoon family's seaside estate.

"Step inside," Trevor beckoned, his voice laced with anticipation, the door yawning wide to swallow them whole. "What you've hinted at, Mr. Marino, I've never shared with the public. I'm very interested in hearing what you have to tell me. Please, follow me." They traversed a hallway that soon led them to the heart of Trevor's sanctuary—his office, a cavernous room that served as his creative haven.

Upon entering, one's gaze was immediately drawn to the colossal bookshelves, a monolith of knowledge stretching from floor to ceiling. They were a testament to Trevor's obsession with the World Wars, a dark-wood shrine brimming with relics from a time of turmoil. His collection was a veritable pantheon of history, a blend of Time-Life series, fiction, documentaries, interviews, notes, journals, picture books, film reels, and even VHS tapes. Every fragment of history Trevor could lay his hands on had been added to this ever-expanding memorial to the past.

In the heart of the room, three regal leather chairs stood, their backs high and their brass-nail trim exuding an air of antiquity. Trevor gestured for Mario to take a seat. The leather groaned under their weight as they sank into the chairs' welcoming embrace.

"May I offer you a beverage, sir?" a voice echoed from the doorway. Mario swiveled enough to catch a glimpse of a tuxedoed man standing at attention before turning to face Trevor again.

"Oh, you're new." Trevor's voice held a note of surprise. "What happened to Hobson?"

"Mr. Hobson is currently indisposed, sir. I am his temporary replacement," the butler replied without emotion.

"Very well. Two iced teas, if you please."

The butler inclined his head in approval.

"Thank you, sir . . . and your name is?" Trevor asked.

"Alistar, sir." The butler's gaze locked on the back of Mario's head. "Your iced teas will be served shortly."

"I never meet person with butler," Mario admitted, his eyes wide with the novelty. His experiences with Roberto were the closest he'd come to such affluence. His old friend had done well for himself, but never indulged in such extravagance.

"What can I say? My novels have been rather successful. Have you read any?" Trevor's curiosity piqued. Was his guest a fan?

"Sì. I finished one. Two days," Mario replied, eager to show his host he'd made an effort before their meeting.

"You mentioned you have information about my father?" Trevor's voice held a note of skepticism. How could this stranger know secrets about his father that weren't already public knowledge?

"Sì. I have news."

"That seems unlikely, considering you don't appear a day over thirty."

"Long story."

Trevor lapsed into thoughtful silence, his curiosity warring with his suspicion as he waited for the young man to elaborate.

"I am priest. Um. *Was* priest. I digitize Vatican Secret Archives."

"Really." Trevor's interest was instantly ignited. He had always been fascinated by the Vatican Secret Archives but had never been granted research access due to his reputation for penning fictional World War II thrillers. The Vatican only permitted certain scholars into the Secret Archives. Hearing Mario's claim, he was all ears.

Mario saw Trevor's eyes spark at the mention of the Archives. "I scan books. I stumble upon package, wrapped in brown paper and sealed wax."

Mario could hear Roberto's voice from beyond. *Too many details, buddy. Get to the point.* Sage advice, naturally—it was clear he was losing Trevor's interest amidst the details.

"I discovered secret journal."

Trevor leaned in, his eyes filled with intrigue. "What kind of secret journal are we talking about?"

In the shadowy hallway outside the office, Alistar eavesdropped. This was the intelligence he had been ruthlessly pursuing following his accomplice Mateo's interrogation of Roberto. Mario was unwittingly spilling the very secrets Alistar had been hunting for.

"Secret journal by . . ." Mario faltered, questioning whether Trevor would believe his outrageous claim. He inhaled deeply. "Pope Pius XII."

"Really? You unearthed *a pope's diary* in the Secret Archives?" Trevor leaned back in his chair, his excitement deflating.

Alistar, holding a tray of iced teas, paused outside the door. *He found the journal.*

He entered the room. "Your iced teas, sirs," he announced, placing the tray on the table nearest the door. He exited swiftly, ensuring Mario didn't catch a glimpse of his face.

"Thank you, Alistar." Trevor turned back to Mario. "I understand every pope's journal is in the Secret Archives. What makes this one so extraordinary?"

Mario was rattled by Trevor's lack of interest in Pope Pius XII's personal journal. After the whirlwind of events he'd endured in recent months, he was disheartened by the indifference the renowned fiction writer was showing, especially given the possibility this pope was his father. Mario felt like a desperate salesman trying to pitch to an uninterested buyer. Why was this so challenging? "You're familiar with Pope Pius XII?"

"Yes, of course." Trevor was taken aback by the blunt question. "He was a controversial pope during World War II. So what?"

"Not controversial," Mario's voice rose, his conviction unwavering.

Trevor, noticing his guest's growing agitation, was beginning to question his decision to invite him over. "Enlighten me."

"Pope Pius XII controlling Hitler and Nazis."

"Is that so?" Trevor's patience was wearing thin as he realized he was about to be subjected to a tale involving some elaborate conspiracy theory.

"Pope bribe Hitler with Jew artwork for Führermuseum," Mario blurted out, his excitement undisguised as he veered off the main point of his mission.

That did it. As a Jew himself, Mario had unwittingly struck a nerve. Trevor's family tree had been brutally pruned by the Nazis, leaving only him and his mother. Horrific tales of extermination camps, narrated by his mother, had fueled his World War II novels, catapulting him to fame and fortune.

"Alistar, is it? This iced tea is divine," came a woman's voice, complimenting the butler who was lingering outside the office door.

"Thank you, madam."

An elegant septuagenarian entered Trevor's office. "I apologize, son, I wasn't aware you had company over. I can return later." She began her retreat.

"Mother, please stay. I believe you should hear what this young man has to say."

Mario's nerves jangled as he found himself in the same room as the woman he'd read about in the Templar library. "It's you!" he blurted out, unable to contain himself.

"I beg your pardon?"

"Scusi, it's just . . ." Mario fumbled for words. "I read lots about you."

"Do I know you?"

"No. I read journal in Templar basement. Your journal."

Anna's face paled. She moved to the other chair and sat down. The Templar protection program had assured her her anonymity—now, with this stranger in their midst, their safety was in jeopardy.

"Where did you find this information?"

"Basement. Beneath Trinity Bank."

Bingo! Alistar had hit the jackpot. The Templars' location was a crucial piece of intelligence long sought by the Black Nobility. They and their proxy, the Vatican, had always been stymied in their attempts to locate the Templars' base in Rome.

Alistar needed to alert his team so they could finally deal with the Templars for good and obtain Solomon's treasure.

Mario watched as Anna's face drained of color. He realized he'd overstepped her boundaries. Unfortunately, his adrenaline-fueled enthusiasm often caused him to spill secrets before his brain could think better of it. This habit had landed him in retreats of silence ordered by his superiors more times than he cared to remember. He recognized this was one of those regrettable instances.

An oppressive silence filled the room. Mario, feeling the sting of his faux pas, rose from his seat. "Scusi. I say too much. I go now."

"I think that would be best," Trevor agreed, rising to escort the strange Italian out of his home. The mansion door slammed shut behind Mario with a force that mirrored the intensity of his own self-reproach.

"Mario, you idiot!" he berated himself in Italian, regretting his lack of preparation for this crucial meeting. He'd bungled his handling of sensitive information around Trevor and Anna Muldoon. The fact remained that it was imperative Trevor know the truth about his father—that was Mario's trump card, capable of securing the Muldoons' cooperation in exposing the truth about the Vatican.

Mario couldn't undertake this mission alone. He resolved to try again in a few days, hopefully once more face-to-face. Sliding into Janet's 2000 Toyota Avalon, he navigated the winding driveway towards the main entrance of the gated community. Turning onto Tamiami Trail North, he headed back to Janet's house.

* * *

"What was he talking about, mother?" Trevor asked, his confusion evident.

"Trevor, please sit. There's something I need to tell you."

Trevor took a seat opposite his mother, his eyes searching hers, trying to decipher the secrets hidden within their depths.

"I've never shared this with you, or anyone," Anna began, her voice barely above a whisper. She looked down at her hands folded in her lap. "I escaped from the Treblinka Extermination Camp when I was sixteen years old."

Trevor's eyes widened in shock. His mother had never spoken of her past, and he had never pressed her. The memories were too painful.

"I made it all the way to the pope's summer residence to plead for your grandparents' release from Treblinka." Anna closed her eyes, bracing herself for the next part of the story. She had always told Trevor that his father was a war hero. That narrative was about to change. "I discovered that Pope Pius XII was just a man, like any other." She took a deep breath, her eyes still closed. "He . . . took advantage of me. And I fell pregnant."

Trevor's mouth fell open in shock. "My father was Pope Pius XII?"

Anna looked up at her son, her eyes filled with regret. "Yes, but my being pregnant with you is what saved our lives."

She had wanted to keep this secret from her son for as long as possible, preferably taking it to the grave. She'd dreaded the day would come he'd find out. And that day was today, when a stranger had walked into their home and exposed Anna's past.

Outside the office door, Alistar listened in. Great. Yet another mess he would have to clean up. The revelation that the pope had spawned this bastard son was a secret that could not be made public.

Trevor rose and walked to the window. He looked out at the surf as he grappled inwardly with the shocking truth about his father. His entire life he'd been fed tales of a war hero father, stories that served as the foundation for his bestselling novels. The heroic narratives, the vivid images of bravery and valor— all were a fabrication. His father was the pope?

As he turned to confront his mother, he noticed the new butler standing ominously behind her chair. "Alistar, what's happening?" he demanded.

"Sit down, Trevor," Alistar commanded, his voice cold as he brandished a silenced gun and aimed it at Trevor.

Anna Muldoon's body slumped lifelessly in her chair.

With the gun trained on him, Trevor moved cautiously around his desk and sank into the leather chair opposite his mother. "What did you do to her?" he whispered. There was no response.

Alistar moved to a table near the door to retrieve a syringe from his open briefcase. He filled it with a precise amount of fluid from a small vial. Approaching Trevor, the Vatican assassin seized his head and plunged the syringe into his neck. Trevor's screams filled the room as a searing pain shot up his left arm, heading straight for his heart. Within seconds, the renowned author slumped forward in his chair, lifeless.

One by one, Alistar pushed the bodies onto the floor, arranging them to appear as if they had suffered simultaneous heart attacks. The coroner would have no reason to suspect foul play.

Retrieving his cell phone, Alistar dialed the number for his team, who were nearby, awaiting instructions. His voice was cold and detached as he said, "Collect Dr. Janet Doerr immediately."

He ended the call and quickly typed out a message on the encrypted Vatican line:

```
Templar base at Trinity Bank
```

He hit Send.

Chapter 95

May 16, 2000
Tuesday, 6:48 p.m.
Naples, Florida

Oblivious to the lurking danger, Mario knocked on the garage door connected to Janet's house. He was met with an eerie, unsettling silence. He rapped on the door again, louder this time, hoping she had merely missed his initial knock. He tried the knob and found it was unlocked. With a whirlwind of thoughts swirling in his mind, he pushed the door open and called out, "Janet? Are you here?" More silence. He fumbled for his cell phone to scan it for any missed messages from her. Nothing.

Suddenly, his phone buzzed. A text message from an unknown number flashed on the screen:

> If you want to see your girlfriend
> again, hand over the journal.

A wave of fear crashed over him as he processed the menacing text. His hand trembled as he dialed the unknown number. With a quivering voice, he questioned, "Who is this?"

"The butler," responding in their native Roman tongue.

A jolt of icy terror shot down Mario's spine as the horrifying truth dawned on him—the Vatican's lethal assassins had already found him. His thoughtless actions had unwittingly ensnared Janet in this deadly game of cat and mouse.

The air crackled with tension as Mario tried to form words. He failed.

"Mario, your assistance in locating Anna and her illegitimate offspring was invaluable. I understand you hoped to recruit them to your schemes. Unfortunately, they've had a . . . change of heart."

Alistar's icy, methodical actions confirmed Mario's darkest fears. His relentless pursuit had led this assassin straight to his sole confidant in his mission to expose the Vatican's sinister deeds. Remembering the Vatican left behind no trace of evidence, Mario interpreted the assassin's cryptic statement— he had skillfully staged Anna and Trevor's deaths to look like heart attacks, the signature method of execution for the Vatican's killers.

"Where's Janet?"

"Deliver the journal and your girlfriend will be returned. Any false moves and she'll meet the same fate as the Muldoons."

Mario was certain the assassin wouldn't release Janet willingly, regardless of what he did. The Vatican couldn't afford any loose ends. Alistar would ensure the journal was safely returned to the Archives, while Mario and Janet would be permanently silenced.

"I don't have the journal. It's stashed at my friend's place in Rome."

"You're lying. We scoured every inch of that mansion."

"I can meet you there tomorrow at noon. It will take me until then to fly to Rome so I can give you the journal." Mario was a terrible liar. This diversion was a desperate attempt to sidestep the lie and buy some time to come up with a plan. Roberto had taught him this tactic. He could only pray the assassin would take the bait.

"If you fail to appear, your girlfriend will meet her end, Father Mario Marino."

The merciless killer whispering his name sent a new surge of bone-chilling fear pulsating through Mario's veins. He had never faced such raw, unfiltered evil head-on. It reminded him of an exorcism, though he'd never borne witness to one in person. He had only heard second-hand accounts from veteran priests about the nightmarish rage that erupted during such ceremonies, brought on by demonic spirits writhing within the possessed. Right now, Mario was convinced his situation was even worse— the assassin's cold-blooded disregard for life was nothing short of a living nightmare.

He stared at his phone, plotting his next course of action. The journal was at the epicenter of this malevolent turmoil that had upended his life since he'd discovered it. He had to surrender it. Who were the pivotal players in this deadly chess game? The Vatican and the Templars. He would have to draw both parties into this perilous match to have a chance at securing Janet's survival.

Removing the card Dominic had entrusted him with from his wallet, he dialed the number on its face.

"Dominic, it's Mario. I am so sorry for disturbing you at this late hour, but I'm in desperate need of help. I have a situation and require your immediate assistance."

Dominic's voice, groggy with sleep in greeting, instantly hardened, his senses on high alert. "What do you need?" he demanded, his tone sharp and focused.

"I wasn't entirely truthful when I was with you," Mario confessed, his voice heavy with guilt, "but I do in fact possess the journal of Pope Pius XII."

A chilling silence fell over the line as Dominic absorbed the ramifications of Mario's confession.

Sensing that this wasn't enough to fully engage the Templar, Mario added, "It contains detailed accounts by Pacelli on how he manipulated Hitler during World War II in his attempt to gain control of Solomon's treasure."

"What do you want me to do?"

"I need to get to Rome and hand the journal over to you for safekeeping. Can you arrange for a private jet to fly me to Rome immediately?"

"I'll have it prepped"—Dominic glanced at his clock, calculating the time he could have the jet ready—"in Memphis at 10 p.m. your time."

"No, wait, I'm currently in Naples, Florida. Can you reroute it to Naples?"

The line went silent for a moment. "Why are you in Florida?"

"That's a convoluted tale. Can you just get the jet here?"

"You can explain your presence in Florida when you arrive here."

"Thank you, Dominic. I truly appreciate it. So, still 10 p.m., but in Naples, Florida?"

Dominic glanced at the clock again. "Make it 8:00 p.m. Fortunately for you, it's already at the airport in Naples right now."

"Thank you." Mario rubbed his right thigh, feeling the microSD card sewn into his flesh. This was his insurance policy. Handing over the original journal to the Vatican assassin was the ransom he'd pay to ensure Janet's safe return.

After hanging up, he retreated to his cottage to pack his essentials before making his way to the airport.

Chapter 96

May 17, 2000
Wednesday, 10:32 a.m.
Rome, Italy

Five men in black suits passed through the entrance to the Trinity Bank of Italy. Like a well-oiled machine, they fanned out, each taking a customer under their wing and guiding them towards the exit. Their voices were hushed whispers, their words chosen carefully to avoid inciting panic. They were the Vatican's elite, their mission: clear the bank under the guise of a potential gas leak.

As the final customer vacated the premises, a pair of the Vatican's finest remained at the entrance, their stance a silent warning to any who dared approach. The sign on the door flipped to Closed. Another two operatives took up strategic positions on opposite walls of the bank. Their right hands remained concealed within their suits, fingers curled around silenced 9mm handguns, ready to quell any form of resistance.

"Your presence is required at the Vatican," Vittorio, the lead assassin declared, his eyes locked on the bank manager that was making his way to the center of the bank. The manager, a Templar known as Francois, had known what was about to transpire from the moment the men entered. He appreciated the courtesy the assassins had shown, ensuring the bank was devoid of innocent bystanders before violence ensued.

"And why is that?" Francois responded, maintaining a veneer of professionalism amidst the escalating tension in the air.

"An unresolved matter regarding our account here."

"I'm certain we can address any concerns you might—"

"Enough with the charade," Vittorio snarled, cutting him off.

"How did you track us down?"

"Your 'altar boy' was spotted outside a grocery store in Florida. You underestimated our global surveillance. Did you really believe a priest could remain hidden in Florida?"

"Have you come to exterminate us?" Francois asked, his voice unwavering.

"No. As I stated, the Vatican requests your presence. The pope merely desires a private conversation with your leader."

"Ah. He's currently unavailable, but I'll be sure to pass along the message."

Growing impatient, the assassin cut to the chase. "The Vatican seeks what is rightfully ours."

"And what might that be?"

The assassin grew visibly agitated. "You know damn well, Francois. We are the rightful heirs to Solomon's treasure."

Francois remained silent, refusing to acknowledge Vittorio's claim. Solomon's treasure could never fall into the Vatican's hands. His gaze shifted to the assassins at the door, his mind racing, knowing this confrontation was far from over.

"By the way, excellent hiding place. I must say, we never thought of this." Vittorio gestured expansively, his arms sweeping across the resplendence of the bank's interior. "Genius. Hidden in plain sight, right under our nose."

"Your words honor us," Francois responded, placing his right hand on his stomach as he dipped his head in a respectful nod to his formidable adversary. "Do extend my regards to His Holiness," he added, straightening up while his hand surreptitiously sought the remote hanging from his neck. "However, we have more urgent matters to attend to." Locating the remote under his shirt, he pressed the button, triggering the self-destruct sequence.

The Templars had meticulously designed and constructed the building for this exact moment, anticipating the day the Vatican might uncover their covert operation. They had danced dangerously close to the flame for decades, always evading detection. But now, the jig was up.

The remote activated electronic locks on the front doors—heavy steel barriers slid into place, sealing everyone inside. Gas lines embedded in the walls ignited, setting the white-oak walls ablaze.

"Checkmate," Francois smirked at the Vatican assassin.

Without skipping a beat, Vittorio drew his handgun and shot Francois in the forehead. The Templar's body crumpled to the floor, blood pooling around his head on the polished cement. "Eliminate the rest and let's get out of here."

The assassin on the left side of the bank swiftly shot the two Templars near the teller counter. Meanwhile, the two assassins at the entrance grappled futilely with the impenetrable steel doors.

In the basement, pipes affixed to the ceiling sprayed liquid gas over the entire Templar basement quarters, offices, and archives. The entire underground below the bank erupted in a fiery inferno. The twenty Templar staff, trained for this moment, each bit down on a cyanide capsule, opting for a swift death over the raging flames. The temperature quickly soared to over a thousand degrees, reducing the archives to ash.

Back in the bank lobby, instead of water, the sprinkler system doused the room with gasoline. The Vatican hit squad scrambled to avoid the flammable rain. As the flames roiled, the men screamed in agony, frantically trying to extinguish the fire consuming their flesh. Vittorio, seeing his team was suffering, mercifully shot each man. His own body now a living torch, he pressed the gun to his heart and pulled the trigger.

Trinity Bank had become a fiery tomb. In less than thirty minutes, the destruction would be complete. The booby-trapped building, rigged for total annihilation, collapsed in on itself, obliterating all traces of the Templar outpost. Any subsequent investigation by local authorities would conclude that the building had been destroyed by an accidental gas leak.

Chapter 97

May 17, 2000
Wednesday, 10:52 a.m.
Private Airfield
Rome, Italy

Mario's eyes were fixated on the row of hangars as the Gulfstream G650ER maneuvered its way towards them. He could make out Dominic's silhouette standing with an air of readiness beside a sleek black limousine, the vehicle primed to transport them to Rome's bustling train station. A knot of anxiety twisted in the pit of his stomach, gnawing at his resolve. With Janet's life hanging in the balance, he'd made the critical decision to orchestrate a face-off between the Vatican assassins and the Templars. If they were hell-bent on pursuing this blood feud, he would play the role of matchmaker, setting the stage for their deadly rendezvous. Amidst the pandemonium, he hoped to find a fleeting opportunity to rescue Janet.

Noticing his cell phone reception was back, he dialed Alistar's number.

"Where are you?" came Alistar's dead voice, his tone carrying the slightest trace of impatience. He was seated in the back seat of a Mercedes sedan parked inconspicuously outside Roberto's residence, awaiting Mario's arrival. The driver, glancing in the mirror at Alistar, eavesdropped on the conversation. Janet was bound and gagged in the backseat, the assassin looming over her.

"You were right. I lied," Mario confessed, praying his admission wouldn't trigger Janet's execution. "The journal you want is at the Rome train station."

"Are you fucking with me, Father?"

"No, I swear. It's the truth. The locker is near the bathrooms. Locker number 629. I'll be there at noon, I swear."

"If not, your girlfriend dies."

"I'll be there. I promise."

The Gulfstream came to a halt in front of the limousine parked in front of the Templar's private hangar. Mario stood at the door, waiting for the aircraft's staircase to extend. As he descended the steps of the luxury jet, Dominic approached him. "What's going on, Mario?"

"I met someone in the U.S. and I just want to be *done* with the Vatican."

"Why didn't you confide in me earlier?"

"I wasn't sure if I could trust you, given everything I've been through. Try to see it from my perspective."

"We risked our lives to save yours. Even lost one of our own. How can you question our trust?"

"I realize that now. That's why I want to entrust the journal to you. I know you'll do what is right."

"You said it's at the train station?"

"Yes. Can we go there now so I can give it to you?" Mario was acutely aware the clock was ticking. He had forty-five minutes to reach the train station, or else Janet would be killed. If they could get there ahead of the assassins, they might have a chance at outmaneuvering them. He was no strategist—all he could do was improvise a plan with one goal in mind: save Janet's life.

"Get in. I want to hear more about this journal."

As they journeyed towards the Rome train station, Mario began to tell the Templar about the secrets he'd unearthed inside Pope Pius XII's private journal. Dominic, his attention riveted, listened intently as Mario painted a vivid picture of Eugenio Pacelli's ascension to the papacy, all the while puppeteering Hitler and the Nazis from behind the scenes. While Dominic was no stranger to much of this information, the existence of physical evidence—confirmation in the form of an actual journal penned by Eugenio Pacelli, Pope Pius XII himself—cast a damning shadow over the Vatican and its public image. It was the ultimate leverage, perhaps capable of ending this centuries-long shadow war once and for all.

Upon arriving at the train station, Mario's eyes darted about, scanning for any telltale black suits worn by Vatican assassins. As he stepped out of the limousine, Dominic followed suit. Their bodyguard swiftly exited the front seat of the vehicle to guard Dominic's flank. A black Lincoln Town Car tailing the limousine disgorged two more Templars, who fell into step with the others. This was standard protocol when Dominic made public appearances—a three-man protection team always at his side.

As the trio of bodyguards plus Dominic escorted Mario into the bustling building, a surge of confidence washed over him. He was certain the combined might of four trained Templars could overpower even the deadly Vatican assassins.

As they navigated through the throng of people inside the busy train station, Mario made his way towards the bank of lockers situated near the train-platform doors. Amidst the sea of faces, his eyes locked onto Janet's—he saw her gaze darting around anxiously amidst the crowd. Her back was to the locker containing the journal. He turned towards Dominic, his voice barely above a whisper. "I see a Vatican assassin waiting for us."

Dominic, without missing a beat, signaled for two Templars to encircle the locker and establish a secure perimeter. "Mario, retrieve the journal. We'll cover you."

As Mario approached the locker, he found Alistar standing guard, flanked by an assassin gripping Janet's forearm tightly.

"I'm surprised you showed up," Alistar taunted, his gaze sweeping over Mario with blatant contempt. "I half-expected you to remain the same spineless boy you were back at the orphanage, willing to throw your beloved under the bus to save your own skin."

Mario struggled to suppress his astonishment at the sudden revelation of his childhood tormentor. How could a place as esteemed as their orphanage churn out such a malevolent assassin as Alistar? He disregarded the stinging remark about their shared history, focusing instead on his mission to liberate Janet and himself. He was no longer the vulnerable child that Alistar had once tormented on the playground of Santa Maria Orphanage. "Are you interested in the journal or not?" he retorted, his voice trembling.

With a dismissive wave of his hand, Alistar gestured towards the locker. The other assassin, his hand clamped around Janet's arm, moved her out of the way with a bone-chilling force, his grip unyielding.

"Ow. You're hurting me."

Mario's eyes darted towards Janet, a swift, silent exchange that held a silent promise of rescue. His heart pounded in his chest, adrenaline coursing through his veins like a raging torrent, pushing him to the brink of his physical limits. He knew he had to rely on his cunning and quick thinking to outsmart these seasoned killers. It was a dangerous game of survival he was playing, a deadly dance where one misstep could mean the end. Either they would escape this lethal trap together, or they would both perish in his insane attempt to defy these professional assassins.

Turning towards the locker, Mario's fingers delicately manipulated the dial, each turn swishing in the tense silence until the pointer finally settled on the last number. With a swift upwards tug, the locker door swung open, revealing the journal cleverly hidden within the disemboweled Bible. Mario removed the disguised journal, the Pandora's box that had upended his life since its discovery.

Without warning, Alistar's hand darted out, snatching the book from Mario's grasp with the precision of a striking snake. The journal, not anchored to a spine, slipped from the Bible cover and tumbled to the cold, hard ground.

"Pick it up," Alistar commanded, his voice cold as ice.

As Mario bent down to retrieve the fallen journal, he found his eyes was opportunely level to Alistar's privates. A surge of adrenaline, potent and electrifying, coursed through every muscle in his body. Seizing the moment, he gripped the book in a viselike hold and swung it with all the force he could muster, striking Alistar's groin. The assassin doubled over, his face contorted in agony from the unexpected brutal blow. Using the momentary chaos to his advantage, Mario shoved Alistar backwards into the other assassin, knocking him off balance, causing him to lose his grip on Janet. Without wasting a second, Mario seized her hand and pulled her towards the train station platform.

"GO!" Dominic's voice thundered through the bustling train station.

The two Templars at the far end sprang into action, guns drawn and ready. Hearing Dominic's shout, the assassin that had been holding Janet swiftly pulled out his silenced weapon and fired. The first bullet found its mark in the forehead of the first charging Templar. The second went astray, hitting an innocent bystander in the back of the head, inciting screams of terror that rippled through the crowd.

The second Templar, narrowly avoiding the stray bullet, retaliated with deadly precision, killing the offending assassin with a single shot. His lifeless body crumpled to the ground, landing at the feet of a bent-over, wincing Alistar.

Pandemonium broke out—the crowd was scattering in all directions. Dominic's bodyguard, undeterred by what was happening, forged a path for Dominic, shoving the panicked crowd aside to close distance on Alistar.

Wincing in agony as he propped himself up against the locker, Alistar locked his sights on the second Templar, who was barreling towards him. With a swift, practiced motion, he yanked his silenced 9mm from its holster, steadied his aim, and squeezed the trigger. The bullet whistled through the air, finding a home in the Templar's chest, killing him instantly.

But the Vatican assassin didn't have eyes in the back of his head.

Dominic, with his imposing bodyguard working the crowd, drew close to Alistar, stopping just a few feet behind the assassin. "Checkmate," he declared with grim satisfaction. Yet the assassin didn't react.

Instead, Alistar's gaze slowly drifted upwards, drawn magnetically to a TV monitor mounted on the wall, its flickering display drawing his attention. The monitor was broadcasting the local news, its sound muted, but the images it displayed were deafening in their horror. The once majestic Trinity Bank was now nothing more than a smoldering crater, a grotesque testament to the destructive power of his associates. The horrifying images filled the large screen, painting a grim picture of devastation and chaos. A sinister smirk slowly spread across his face.

Dominic's eyes followed Alistar's line of sight and landed on the chilling scene displayed on the monitor. He read the caption scrolling across the bottom of the screen, a cold dread settling in his stomach: *The Trinity Bank of Italy in Rome has been obliterated by an apparent gas leak that reduced the entire structure to rubble within minutes. We are awaiting confirmation on casualties. . . .*

Alistar, his right arm draped across his midsection, aimed his silenced gun behind him and pulled the trigger in rapid succession. The bullets tore through Dominic and his bodyguard, the hollow points leaving gaping, bloody wounds. Both Templars collapsing to the ground, their lifeblood pooling on the train station floor.

Alistar, his gun now empty, holstered his weapon and straightened up, wincing at the throbbing pain in his groin. He limped away from the carnage, making his way toward the train platform. As a nearby train sounded its slow departure, he continued to hobble along until he was out of the train station, leaving behind the havoc he'd wrought.

Chapter 98

May 17, 2000
Wednesday, 12:09 p.m.
Rome, Italy

Mario yanked Janet away from the escalating chaos. Weaving through the panicked crowd, they made their way onto the train platform and boarded the closest train. They practically hurtled into the first two empty seats they could find. Glancing out the window while keeping his head low, Mario saw no signs of pursuit amidst the chaos. The platform was a scene of pandemonium—a sea of terrified faces, people huddling behind walls or trash bins out of fear another hail of bullets would come.

"We are safe," Mario reassured Janet, his eyes unable to look away from the scene outside the window. It appeared they had truly evaded their pursuers. Their breaths ran ragged, lungs burning from the adrenaline-fueled sprint to the train.

"Who were those people?" Janet breathed heavily, her voice shaky.

Mario glanced down at her bound hands. He quickly removed his coat to conceal the ropes and avoid drawing unwanted attention. "Mi scusi. Sorry. Sorry. I no want you involved. Vatican assassin found me. He take you."

"The Vatican has assassins?" Janet asked, her eyes wide with fear and disbelief.

"Sì. I told you. Bad people," Mario replied, his voice heavy with regret.

She listened intently as Mario continued to explain the dangerous world he was unwillingly a part of.

"Vatican assassin is bad person," he reiterated.

"Yeah, I got that," Janet replied, her voice laced with newfound respect for the peril they had just evaded.

Mario's eyes continued to dart across the chaotic scene, struggling to believe they were out of danger. The crowd was a tumultuous sea of bodies, each person a wave crashing against the next in a desperate, frenzied scramble onto the safety of the platform.

Every single soul, gripped by a primal fear, sought refuge from the escalating chaos that had taken over the main terminal. They sought shelter behind anything they could find - garbage cans that reeked of decay, cold, hard benches that offered little comfort, outdated phone booths that echoed with the frantic calls of yesteryears, and even the smallest alcoves that offered a sliver of protection.

Mario's gaze swept across the scene, his heart pounding in his chest like a desperate SOS signal being tapped out in Morse code. The rhythm was frantic, a relentless drumming that echoed the terror coursing through his veins. Yet, amidst the pandemonium, he saw no sign of the deadly assassins or the Templars. Their absence, rather than providing relief, only served to heighten the sense of impending doom looming in the air like a thick, suffocating fog that threatened to choke the very life out of him.

His gaze was drawn to a TV monitor mounted on the wall broadcasting images of Trinity Bank, now a smoldering ruin. Realization hit him like a punch to the gut—the Vatican assassins had obliterated the Templar satellite operation. The sight of the bank's destruction was a stark reminder that he was now utterly alone. The sanctuary he and Janet could have sought refuge in was no more.

Janet's eyes followed his gaze to the TV monitor. "What's that about? Another terrorist attack?"

"They hide me," Mario confessed, his mind filled with images of the workers who had cared for him during his time there. His heart ached with the knowledge they were all likely dead.

The train jolted into motion, a welcome sign they were moments away from escaping the chaos in the station. In a matter of seconds, they would be whisked away to safety. "Come, let's find better seat." He gently guided Janet down the aisle, his hand firm on her arm.

They found solace in an empty cabin near the front of the train. Its automatic door closed behind them with a reassuring thud. He carefully removed the jacket that had been concealing her bound hands and, kneeling before her, began the delicate task of loosening the ropes. Janet watched, her eyes wide, as he worked to free her. She studied him, sensing a kindness that seemed out of place in their current predicament. How had he become entangled in such a dangerous web?

"What happens now?" she asked, her voice barely above a whisper.

He paused in his task to look up at her. "We disappear," he said, his voice heavy with the weight of their new reality. His next word hung in the air like a specter. "Forever."

Janet's gaze locked onto his upon hearing the finality of that word.

"Vatican never stop looking. We know much. How do I explain?" Mario's voice was filled with a mix of frustration and resignation.

Janet glanced up at the cabin's digital display; their destination glowed bright on the panel. "It looks like we're headed to Milan. We've got time. Start at the beginning."

For the next hour, Mario delved into the intricate tale of Eugenio Pacelli's journal, detailing how the man and his backers the Black Nobility puppeteered Hitler into his infamous role as the Führer of the Third Reich and the Nazi Party. He recounted the chilling story of the Vatican assassins who orchestrated the death of Pope Pius XI, paving the way for Pacelli to ascend as Pope Pius XII. He laid bare the harrowing details of his own pursuit by a Vatican assassin in Rome two months ago, his uncanny replacement by doppelgänger, and him taking refuge in the Templar bank.

"That was the bank we saw ablaze on the news," Janet interjected, the image from the local news broadcast seared into her memory.

"Sì. I read at bank Trevor Muldoon is pope son," Mario confirmed.

"Wait. The pope had a son?" Janet asked, incredulous.

"Pacelli is Pope Pius XII. Pope have sex with Trevor mother."

"So, the Vatican is hell-bent on eliminating anyone who could potentially expose their dark secrets. Is that the gist of it?" Janet asked, piecing together the puzzle.

"Sì. Now you too," Mario said with a heavy heart.

"Over my dead body! They're not getting away with this," Janet declared defiantly, her mind already a whirlwind of strategies to counterstrike against the Vatican. The idea of a life spent in perpetual hiding was far from enticing, even if she shared it with a captivating Italian man like Mario.

He observed Janet, her eyes glazed with determination, her mind deep in thought crafting a plan to retaliate against the

Vatican. The thought of turning against the institution that had been his sanctuary his entire life had never crossed his mind. How did one betray the hand that once fed him?

"It's a pity you don't have that journal. Then we could prove to the world the pope controlled Hitler," Janet pondered aloud.

"I do."

"You do what?"

"I have journal."

"Where?"

"Right here," Mario revealed, extracting the journal from within his jacket and resting it on the worn-out bench seat next to Janet.

Her eyes widened in surprise. "We are going to tell the world about this shit. They'll never know what hit 'em. Bastards!"

"No!"

"What do you mean, 'no'?"

"No. They kill us. They kill you," Mario confessed, his voice shaking as he dropped his head into his hands, the weight of defeat crushing his shoulders. "They kill Roberto. Kill Hannah. Trevor. Templars. Everyone."

Janet's gaze bore into him, her mind a tempest of bewilderment. They had an obligation to expose the Vatican and its intricate web of deceit. How could Mario say no?

"I return it."

"What?" Janet's eyes went even wider with astonishment.

"I no lose you." Tears cascaded down Mario's cheeks and splashed onto the cold, hard floor. The enormity of his loss engulfed Mario. He crumpled into her lap crying uncontrollably, his sobs echoing through the empty cabin.

She tenderly rested her hand on his head, offering a soothing touch. A surge of empathy washed over her for the torment this man had suffered. She was reluctant to pressure him, but a life of constant evasion and living in the shadows was not the future she had envisioned for herself.

"I return book. Be done."

Janet pondered their future, a life of ceaseless flight from Vatican assassins. After a long, heavy silence, she finally mustered the strength to say, "Okay."

Mario remained nestled in her lap, his tears flowing freely as he thought of all the death and destruction that had plagued his life. His recklessness had ensnared this woman in a perilous situation. How was he going to protect her? What would their life look like from now on? Where would they go?

A memory of Roberto's contingency plan surfaced, one last whisper from his dearly departed friend. Mario blinked and nodded his head.

"We go to Switzerland."

"Why?"

He lifted his tear-streaked face to meet Janet's eyes. "My friend leave money."

"How much?"

"Ten million."

"Are you serious? Let's go get it, then." Her eyes sparkled with excitement at this unexpected turn of events.

Chapter 99

Mario found himself perched in his seat at the antique writing desk nestled in the corner of their clandestine hotel room. They had registered under an assumed identity paying cash, a necessary precaution to elude the ever-watchful eyes of the Vatican. The room, dimly lit by a single lamp, cast long shadows that danced along the walls, mirroring the turmoil in Mario's heart.

Involving Janet in his life of perpetual evasion from the Vatican was a decision haunting him every waking moment. Now, he found himself on the edge of a desperate plea—a plea to the pope himself, begging for liberation from the relentless shadow of death that ceaselessly pursued them. He yearned for a life untethered from the Vatican and its intricate labyrinth of deceit.

In a moment of profound humility and desperation, Mario reached for the ornate pen that lay dormant on the desk, ready to inscribe the deepest fears and hopes etched in his heart. The cool metal, a stark contrast to his feverish hand, offered a strange sense of reassurance as he began to craft the meticulously worded letter. It was a plea for their lives, a desperate cry for freedom:

21 May 2000

Your Holiness, Pope John Paul II,
I hope this letter finds you in good health and high spirits.
I am writing to you about a matter of utmost urgency. It is
important enough to require your immediate attention.

With a heavy heart, I must confess to a transgression I
committed during my recent honored position in the Vatican
Secret Archives. I am deeply ashamed to admit that I succumbed
to a moment of weakness and removed a journal not belonging
to me. The journal, a beautiful artifact, had been hidden in the
Archives, and I was captivated by its historical significance and
beauty. However, I now realize the gravity of my actions and
the disrespect I have shown towards you and the sanctity of the
Vatican Secret Archives.

I understand my actions have not only violated the law
but also the moral and ethical principles I hold dear. I am deeply
remorseful for my actions and the potential harm they may have
caused.

Over the past several weeks, I have been subjected to a
series of unfortunate incidents involving individuals who, I
am led to believe, are associated with Vatican Secret Security.
These individuals have caused physical harm to multiple people
I hold dear to my heart, including my best friend. This has
caused me much distress, affecting my personal well-being. I
understand there may have been some misunderstanding or
miscommunication leading up to this situation.

Acting in good faith, I have enclosed the journal from Pope Pius XII. In return, I kindly request you instruct your associates to cease their actions against myself and Dr. Janet Doerr immediately. I am sure that, as a respected and responsible entity, you would not endorse nor condone such actions that cause harm and distress to others.

If my request is not honored, I am more than willing to discuss these matters with the media. As you might have inferred from this letter, I firmly believe that dialogue with influential individuals is key to mediating conflicts and misunderstandings.

I look forward to your prompt response. I am hopeful my letter will resolve this issue amicably and without further escalation.

Thank you for your understanding and cooperation.
I pray for Your Holiness's health and peace.

Respectfully yours,
Mario Marino

Chapter 100

May 24, 2000
Wednesday, 7:43 a.m.
Switzerland

"Mario!" Janet burst into their clandestine hotel room, her hand waving a newspaper like a victorious flag. "You're free!" She unfurled the newspaper, revealing the headline that might as well have screamed "freedom" beneath a picture of Mario.

L'OSSERVATORE ROMANO

GIORNALE QUOTIDIANO POLITICO RELIGIOSO

Unicuique suum Non praevalebunt

PRIEST
EXONERATED

As Mario's eyes meticulously navigated through the lines of the article, a smile gradually spread across his face, his eyes glistening with unshed tears. "We are free," he murmured, the words rolling off his tongue like a sweet symphony of liberation.

In a flurry of joy, Janet clambered onto him, her arms wrapping around him in a fervent embrace, her lips seeking his in a passionate kiss. They were finally *free*. Free to live the remainder of their lives devoid of the perpetual threat the Vatican assassins represented.

A subtle twinge in Mario's right thigh served as a reminder of the microSD card Janet had meticulously extracted just three days prior. It was their insurance policy. At some point during their years of dinner conversations, Roberto had taught Mario the intricate art of orchestrating a mass digital information release to the media—and Mario had paid attention.

He'd harnessed this knowledge to construct a fail-safe for him and Janet. If the Vatican ever dared to dispatch their assassins on them, reneging on their "deal", the media would be instantaneously inundated with damning evidence. Any unfortunate mishap that befell either of them would trigger an email to major media outlets across the world—all the incriminating evidence Mario had collected would be released into the wild. The world would be forced to confront the grim truth about Pope Pius XII, the Vatican, and their malevolent role behind the darkest chapters of World War II.

Chapter 101

EPILOGUE

May 29, 2000
Monday, 10:02 a.m.
Rome, Italy

"Why don't I clarify the reason behind your presence here?" Pope John Paul II began addressing the young priest with a serene smile. "I'm guessing you're brimming with questions. Allow me to shed light on why you were handpicked."

Father Luigi Gasparri remained silent, his attention riveted on the most revered figure on the planet.

"Within these hallowed walls, we possess what is known as the Vatican Secret Archives, a repository of history. This treasure trove houses countless books and fragile documents of deep historical import. Our goal is to modernize these in line with the current era."

Father Gasparri listened with rapt attention.

"To put it plainly, we wish to digitize these volumes, transferring them onto computerized storage. The Vatican II Council convened recently and expressed concern over the potential loss of these invaluable documents sometime in the distant future should they remain only in their original format.

A mishap could result in the irrevocable loss of this delicate information that's currently preserved in paper form. In fact, we recently experienced a close call where one of these crucial volumes was nearly lost to us. Fortunately, it was recovered." The pope was relieved that Father Mario Marino had seen reason and returned Pope Pius XII's journal. "Our hope is that you could assist us in our monumental task of digitizing these volumes, safeguarding them into perpetuity." Pope John Paul II paused, allowing the young priest to digest this information. "Father Gasparri, would you be able to undertake this endeavor?"

Father Gasparri's heart swelled with pride and joy. Having been raised and nurtured in the Santa Maria Orphanage, it was almost predestined he would be the next candidate working within the Vatican Secret Archives. "It would be my privilege to undertake this task for you, Your Holiness."

"I am forever grateful, as is the Vatican II Council," the pope expressed, his head bowed in reverence towards this latest recruit to the Secret Archives project. "I find myself with some spare moments. Would you be available for a personal tour of the Sistine Chapel?"

"That would be wonderful, Your Holiness."

The pope, with an air of regality, glided across the marble floor towards the door, the young priest trailing in his wake. As they exited the esteemed antechamber, they crossed paths with a towering figure, a man whose chiseled features were as distinct as his attire—an all-black ensemble consisting of a two-piece suit, shirt, and tie. The young priest felt a shiver run down his spine as he locked eyes with the man, whose gaze was as cold and hard as obsidian.

Alistar maintained his icy expression, staring at the Vatican's newest addition as the pope led him towards the Sistine Chapel. *I'll be watching you closely. Your predecessor slipped through my fingers, but that won't happen again.* His groin still throbbed with the memory of Father Marino's unexpected attack. That yellow-bellied rat may have landed a low blow, but the journal was back where it belonged.

The assassin straightened up, a sense of satisfaction washing over him. Every last document belonging to the Vatican was safely tucked away in the Vatican Secret Archives. Pope Pius XII's journal was secure. It would remain forever unknown to the world.

THE END

Acknowledgements

In the fascinating journey of over three decades of research that led to the creation and publication of The Vatican Dictator, I have been blessed with the support and patience of countless individuals. SelfPublishing.com, my guiding star in this voyage, has been instrumental in shaping the physical and digital presence of my book. From the captivating cover design to the meticulous formatting for Amazon Kindle, they have been my steadfast companions. A special note of gratitude to Ramy Vance, whose expertise and guidance breathed life into Part 2 of my novel, making it a thrilling read.

To Steve McFaul, whose lens captured the perfect image for my back cover, I extend my deepest appreciation.

Shavonne Clarke of Motif Edits, your magic wand of editing and line revisions has elevated my novel to unprecedented heights. Your encouraging words and insightful feedback have been a beacon of light in my writing journey. I am eternally grateful for your unwavering support.

The rich tapestry of history that forms the backdrop of The Vatican Dictator has been woven together from countless novels, books, encyclopedias, journals, and Google searches. Each one has added a thread to the intricate plot, making the narrative all the more thrilling.

To my dear family and friends, who have patiently endured my endless chatter about the novel, I owe a debt of gratitude. Your patience and interest have been a source of motivation. I am thrilled to announce that The Vatican Dictator is finally published, and you can now experience the story as it was meant to be told.

Last but certainly not least, my deepest thanks to my wife, Melanie. Your patience, feedback, and suggestions have been invaluable. You have been my sounding board, my critic, and my cheerleader. Without your unwavering support and encouragement, this novel would still be a mere figment of my imagination. Thank you for helping me bring it to life.

Line edits and proofreading by
Motif Edits - www.motifedits.com

About the Author

Alan Bayer is the creative mind behind the transformative self-help book, "Who Am I?" Alan's unique strength, Ideation, has led him on a fascinating journey of discovery, unearthing unexpected connections between seemingly unrelated phenomena. This journey, spanning over thirty years of research, has culminated in the creation of his revolutionary debut novel, "The Vatican Dictator".

Alan resides in the vibrant city of San Antonio, Texas, alongside his cherished wife. When they're not exploring new destinations, they find joy in the art of cooking, using fresh produce from their own flourishing garden to create delicious meals together.